THE STRUCTURES OF VIRTUE AND VICE

Selected Titles from the Moral Traditions Series
David Cloutier, Andrea Vicini, SJ, and Darlene Weaver, Editors

The Vice of Luxury: Economic Excess in a Consumer Age
David Cloutier

Diverse Voices in Modern US Moral Theology
Charles E. Curran

Consumer Ethics in a Global Economy: How Buying Here Causes Injustice There
Daniel K. Finn

Kinship across Borders: A Christian Ethic of Immigration
Kristin E. Heyer

Radical Sufficiency: Work, Livelihood, and a US Catholic Economic Ethic
Christine Firer Hinze

Keeping Faith with Human Rights
Linda Hogan

Humanity in Crisis: Ethical and Religious Response to Refugees
David Hollenbach, SJ

The Fullness of Free Time: Leisure and Recreation in the Moral Life
Conor M. Kelly

Reimagining Human Rights: Religion and the Common Good
William O'Neill, SJ

Hope for Common Ground: Mediating the Personal and the Political in a Divided Church
Julie Hanlon Rubio

Love and Christian Ethics: Tradition, Theory, and Society
Frederick V. Simmons, Editor

All God's Animals: A Catholic Theological Framework for Animal Ethics
Christopher Steck, SJ

THE STRUCTURES OF VIRTUE AND VICE

DANIEL J. DALY

GEORGETOWN UNIVERSITY PRESS / WASHINGTON, DC

© 2021 Georgetown University Press. All rights reserved. No part of this book may be reproduced or utilized in any form or by any means, electronic or mechanical, including photocopying and recording, or by any information storage and retrieval system, without permission in writing from the publisher.

The publisher is not responsible for third-party websites or their content. URL links were active at time of publication.

Library of Congress Cataloging-in-Publication Data

Names: Daly, Daniel J. (Professor of moral theology), author.
Title: The structures of virtue and vice / Daniel J. Daly.
Other titles: Moral traditions series.
Description: Washington : Georgetown University Press, 2021. | Series: Moral traditions | Includes bibliographical references and index.
Identifiers: LCCN 2020010115 | ISBN 9781647120382 (hardcover) | ISBN 9781647120399 (paperback) | ISBN 9781647120405 (ebook)
Subjects: LCSH: Christian ethics—Catholic authors. | Virtue. | Vice. | Social ethics. | Social structure—Moral and ethical aspects.
Classification: LCC BJ1249 .D34 2021 | DDC 241/.3—dc23
LC record available at https://lccn.loc.gov/2020010115

22 21   9 8 7 6 5 4 3 2 First printing

Cover design by Jeremy John Parker

To Kate

CONTENTS

Acknowledgments ix

Introduction 1

PART I. DIAGNOSIS

1 Catholic Ethics in the Twenty-First Century 11

2 The Structure-Agency Problem in Catholic Ethics 33

PART II. RESOURCES

3 The Critical Realist Solution to the Structure-Agency Problem 63

4 The Growing Ends of Catholic Theological and Ethical Traditions in the Age of Pope Francis 97

PART III. SYNTHESIS AND APPLICATION

5 A Theocentric, Personalist Virtue Ethics 123

6 Structures of Virtue and Vice 161

7 The Output Power of the Structures of Virtue and Vice 195

Bibliography 221

Index 237

About the Author 245

ACKNOWLEDGMENTS

I have many people to thank. For the past twenty years, James Keenan has been my mentor, my colleague, and my friend. He has provided unfailing encouragement and guidance during this project. He is the exemplar of a teacher/scholar/mentor. Jim's influence on my thinking is present on every page. Daniel Finn introduced me to critical realist social theory and has helped me understand it. I am profoundly grateful for his generosity. In addition to serving as the Moral Traditions Series editor, David Cloutier provided essential critiques of an early draft. Also, the four anonymous reviewers made this a markedly better book. I am grateful to so many members of the Catholic Theological Society of America and the Society of Christian Ethics for their helpful questions and suggestions on this topic throughout the past ten-plus years. It has been a pleasure to work with Glenn Saltzman, the book's managing editor, as well as with two directors of Georgetown University Press, Hope LeGro and Al Bertrand. The copyediting work of Alfred Imhoff has greatly improved the book's prose.

This book underscores the necessity of virtuous institutions in building up the common good. I have benefited greatly from the support that I received at Saint Anselm College, including a sabbatical; the Jeanne D. Smith Research Incentive Fund Grant; and a Summer Writing Grant. Support from Boston College's School of Theology and Ministry helped me complete the book. In particular, Christian Lingner provided essential assistance as the book neared completion. Thanks, as well, to the students of Saint Anselm College and Boston College, who helped me develop my ideas and pushed me to communicate them more clearly.

Although the writing of this book relied on the direct academic support and assistance of the people and institutions listed above, it would not have been possible without the love and companionship of many not involved in the research and writing processes. I have been blessed to have many friends and family members who have sustained me in ways they will never know. I am grateful for my lifelong friends, especially Chris and Mike, for their laughter and companionship.

Daniel and Paula Daly have been loving and supporting parents throughout my life. They are the most selfless people I know. Their entire adult lives have been dedicated to the care and support of their children and grandchildren. My wife's parents, Richard and Rosemary McBride, have been incredibly generous to our family. This book would not have been completed if not for their many hours of watching our children so that I could write. I am blessed with wonderful siblings, siblings-in-law, nephews, and a niece: Chrissy, Mike, Timothy, Bridget, Joel, Tammy, Mark, Janet, Samuel, Oscar, Katelyn, Damian, Henry, and Theodore. My brother Mark has been a constant friend.

As the book grew, so too did my family. Brendan and Daniel have been the greatest blessings that my wife, Kate, and I have received. God is a gift-giver—God is good. Finally, words cannot express my love and gratitude for my wife, Kate. I simply could not have done this without her unfailing love.

To Kate, I dedicate this book.

INTRODUCTION

Why is it so difficult to be virtuous and so easy to be vicious? Why is it that most of us lack temperance, ecological virtue, and solidarity with the poor? The Catholic theological tradition has rightly identified original sin as that fallen state of human existence which inclines us to choose against what is good and right. In addition to this ontological reality, we can identify social factors (themselves by-products of original sin) that causally influence our freely willed actions. Experience suggests that social structures and cultural realities often impede virtue while facilitating vice. However, Catholic ethics has been less than precise regarding the inner workings of the relationship of these social realities and moral agency.

This book emerges from the realization that Catholic ethics does many things well—but analyzing sociostructural problems is not one of them. The concept "structures of sin" has served its purpose over the past fifty years in conceptualizing the fact that structures, in an analogous manner, can be morally categorized. It remains, however, a limited concept. This book is an attempt to forge a new ethical approach to issues of social structures—an approach that reimagines, from the ground up, how Catholic ethics might best analyze how social structures both shape the character of persons and influence the well-being of individuals and communities.

The moment one confronts a sociostructural problem—say, global warming—one quickly encounters two areas of Catholic ethics that require development. The first area is the nature of a social structure. What does it mean to say that global warming is a sociostructural problem, as so many have claimed? Is it woven into physical structures, is it in the minds of individual agents, or does it bubble up from the isolated actions of individuals? Often ethicists employ the term "structure" in an ambiguous and equivocal manner. This is the case because in Catholic ethics, "concepts are frequently pressed into service . . . without even the most cursory attempt to establish what their real referents are."[1] This quotation is from Dave Elder-Vass, regarding conceptual deficits in the social sciences. It is equally valid in aspects of Catholic ethics. Nowhere is lack of precision more evident than in the use of the concept of a "social structure." Like the common good and human dignity, it falls into the category of "often used, rarely defined." Daniel Finn has noted that "Catholic social thought has no coherent account of what a structure is."[2] This lack of specificity is problematic for an ethics that regularly identifies and condemns structures of sin and unjust structures.[3]

This first problem leads to another, what social theorists call the "structure-agency problem."[4] The structure-agency problem exists because it is difficult to describe what a social structure is, how structures influence human agency, and how agency influences social structures. Again, consider global warming. To what degree has it been caused by individual agents making decisions that warm the globe, and to what degree has it been caused by social structures that smooth the paths to a lifestyle that entails high carbon consumption? Further, who created the structures? Individuals? Corporations? The governments of the Global North? Moreover, do those structures then shape what people do, and who people become?

Social theorists have grappled with such questions for decades, and many schools of thought abound, each offering its own solution to the questions and "problem" identified above. The solution ultimately will be found in an accurate account of the relationship between social structures and human agency. Of course, a solution to the structure-agency problem is only as true as the account of social structure that explains the "structure" end of the relationship. Catholic ethics, then, requires solutions to both issues—regarding what a structure is and how structures and human agency relate—if the field is to address moral reality today. In the absence of such solutions, Catholic ethics remains open to the charge that it is more inspirational than analytical. Put differently, too often Catholic social thought is "not an exercise in social analysis, but a sermon."[5]

Mindful of these problems, this book concerns itself primarily with structure and only secondarily with culture. Why? Theological ethicists write often and well about culture. Take, for instance, H. Richard Niebuhr's classic *Christ and Culture*. In the first chapter of the text, Niebuhr defines culture. There, he writes that "culture is the 'artificial, secondary environment,' which man superimposes on the natural. It comprises language, habits, ideas, beliefs, customs, social organization, inherited artifacts, technical processes, and values."[6] He dedicates the next six pages to further explaining his definition. This kind of developed account is nearly absent in theological work on social structures.[7] The first goal of this book endeavors to remedy this situation.

However, this is a book of Catholic theological ethics, which turns to social theory in order to understand how to live a Christian life today. The solution to the structure-agency problem must be integrated into an ethical framework if it is to guide action. Thus, in addition to finding a solution to the structure-agency problem, "it is necessary to choose one form of ethics" in order to make sense out of the Christian moral life.⁶ Ethicists have typically leaned on manualist era principles to make sense of the Christian moral life concerning social structures. The principles of double effect and cooperation, for example, have been used to make normative claims about structural evils and injustices. These concepts have their value and deserve a place in the conversation regarding the morality of social structures. However, as chapter 1 argues, they have their limits.

Like many other contemporary Christian ethicists, I contend that virtue ethics offers the best account of the moral life. Chapter 5 argues this point. That chapter also argues that contemporary Catholic virtue ethics has deficiencies that need to be redressed. After a period of retrieval and growth, aspects of virtue ethics have plateaued due to a reliance on a small canon of scholars and a dated theological anthropology. The maturation of the field, I argue, will emerge from two movements. First, it needs to more fully integrate the "growing ends of the tradition" into virtue theory. That is, virtue theory needs to be more explicitly theocentric and personalist. Specifically, Catholic virtue theory needs a theocentric and personalist architecture. Second, Catholic virtue theory needs to draw more deeply on contemporary work in philosophical virtue theory. That body of literature recently has produced helpful descriptions of virtue and virtue formation. The result of such an integration is the second goal of the book: a synthesis of the best of the Thomistic tradition with a contemporary theological anthropology and an enhanced philosophy of virtue.

These two proximate goals—an understanding of the relation of social structure and moral agency, and an updated Catholic virtue theory—are at the service of the book's ultimate goal: the development of concepts capable of ethically categorizing and scrutinizing social structures. Specifically, I develop concepts that explain how structures shape moral development and agency, as well as how structures causally contribute to or impede the well-being of people and groups.

There is an obvious critique of what follows. Some will find it too ambitious. I not only argue that Christian ethics should turn to social theory in order to understand structures and the structure-agency problem; I also proceed to develop a theory of virtue that is based on a personalist theological anthropology. Either one of these tasks could be the focus of a monograph on Christian ethics. I have decided to take up both here because (1) the lack of sophistication regarding social structures has prevented the discipline from producing accurate claims regarding sociostructural issues and (2) virtue ethics requires a revised virtue theory if it is to reflect how theologians view the person today. Both these issues are pressing. Thus, I decided against merely analyzing the relationship of structures and agency through the lens of traditional Thomistic virtue theory.

This is decidedly a work in Catholic theological ethics. Although it is not limited to Catholic theological sources, the theological sections of the text draw principally on the works of Thomas Aquinas, magisterial writings, and the work of late-twentieth- and early-twenty-first-century Catholic ethicists. A word is in order regarding what I mean by "Catholic ethics." Catholic ethics, as a whole, is that tradition that has emerged from within the interplay of the lived moral practice of the faith, which has been scrutinized, understood, and challenged in the work of theologians and has been codified in magisterial teaching. Each of these arenas is engaged with and influenced by the others. For this reason it is meaningful to write of Catholic ethics as a whole—as a conversation among the laity, theologians, and the Magisterium within the universal Catholic community.

This book follows the insight of liberation theology that contends that theological ethics and magisterial teaching can be enriched by greater encounter with, attention to, and reflection on the lives of the poor. As Alexandre Martins puts it, a true preferential option for the poor changes the practice of theology. This option begins with "an existential commitment that leads us to live in solidarity with [the poor]" and leads to "a *new way* to do theology, that is, *from below*" (emphasis in the original).[9] The point of departure of this book is the experience of structural injustice that afflicts the global poor in the twenty-first century. The book then attempts to understand, judge, and offer provisional solutions to the sociostructural issues that devastate the lives of the poor.

In addition to Catholic ethics, both social theory and philosophical ethics figure prominently in what follows. In order to address the structure-agency problem, which has plagued Catholic ethics, I turn to critical realist social theory. Critical realism offers an account of social structure that profits both Catholic social thought and Catholic virtue theory. The book also demonstrates to social theorists that their theorizing benefits the work of ethicists and those interested in questions of moral development and social justice.

There are two notable exclusions from the scope of the project. I have chosen to draw on only critical realist social theory and not on other modes of social analysis, such as ethnography or critical race theory. I have done this for two reasons. The first is for the sake of clarity. The primary readership for the book is ethicists and theologians. These are scholars who typically lack academic preparation in social theory. By limiting the scope to critical realist social theory, I hope to impart to the reader a clear portrait of how this theory contributes to contemporary theological ethics. Second, as far as I can tell, neither ethnography nor critical race theory offers a developed account of what constitutes a social structure. As I have already suggested, contemporary theological ethics requires such an account. However, this is not to claim that critical realism is the only insightful sociological approach. Critical realism is not sufficient, but it is necessary. Certainly, what follows could be enhanced through an encounter with both ethnography and critical race theory.

In addition, the reader should know that the cases presented in chapters 5, 6, and 7 are illustrative of the core concepts and are not themselves the focus of these chapters. Although the structural ethical analysis that I develop is useful in applied ethics, the current project does not attempt to exhaustively scrutinize the moral problems of sweatshop labor and global warming. Such work will need to wait until a later date.

PROGRESSION OF CHAPTERS

The book is made up of three parts. Part I is diagnostic. Chapter 1 finds that the contemporary theoethical resources and approaches for evaluating structural evils are deficient. Specifically, manualist era principles are inadequate for evaluating structural issues. This is due, in part, to the fact that these manualist principles, such as double effect and cooperation, reflect a "liability approach" to ethics. That is, agents incur moral guilt when their intentional action causes harm to another person or group. Although a liability approach suggests that purchasing sweatshop-made clothing is not morally wrong, our moral intuitions indicate that such an act is unjust. Thus, chapter 1 closes by calling Christian ethics to fulfill its task of being able to make accurate claims about how to live the Gospel in this highly structured age. In order to do so, ethicists will need to discover a new moral nomenclature.

Chapter 2 diagnoses still another problem in contemporary theoethical approaches to structural issues: the lack of understanding of what a structure is and how structures and moral agency are related. Thus, a sociologically acceptable notion of social structure and a solution to the structure-agency problem are needed.

With these lacunae exposed, part II marshals the constructive resources needed to patch the tradition. Chapter 3 addresses an issue presented in chapter 2. Namely, it provides a sociologically sophisticated account of social structure as well as an account of how structures emerge and how social structures shape persons. The chapter argues that critical realist social theory solves these problems for Catholic ethics. Chapter 4 identifies three key developments in post–Vatican II theology and ethics that should be the growing ends of the theoethical tradition: theocentrism, personalism, and virtue ethics. This chapter shows that the tradition has moved beyond manualist era concepts, and it provides ethicists with an updated and fuller account of the moral life than given in the earlier concepts.

Synthesis and applications are the goals of part III. Chapter 5 draws on the insights of chapter 4 by developing a virtue theory that is architecturally theocentric and personalist. In doing so, the chapter moves away from the tradition of powers-based accounts of virtue and toward a relational account. Chapter 6 continues the synthesis by defining, and then demonstrating, the explanatory capacity of the structures of virtue and vice. There, the concepts of the structures of virtue and vice emerge from the relation of the above-mentioned critical realist account of social structure and the theocentric, personalist account of virtue.

Because critical realism maintains that social structures can enable or constrain moral agency and action, moral character is likewise enabled or constrained in and through an agent's participation in social structures. In addition, the chapter argues that the enablements and constraints within social structures causally contribute to, or undermine, human and ecological well-being.

The applicative aspect of part III is contained in chapter 7, which begins by arguing that the structures of virtue and vice are a conceptual improvement over previous modes of sociostructural ethical analysis. The chapter demonstrates the value of moving away from a liability approach of assigning guilt and toward a character approach that assesses the quality of an agent's relationality with others. The chapter then employs the structures of virtue and vice to render normative claims regarding examples presented in the previous six chapters.

NOTES

1. Elder-Vass, *Causal Power*, 64.
2. Finn, "What Is a Sinful Social Structure?"
3. See, e.g., Second Vatican Council, *Gaudium et spes*, 25, 32, 44, 73, 75; Latin American Bishops, *Church*, I: 2; Romero, *Voice*, 68, 143, 183; Latin American Bishops, *Evangelization*; Boff and Boff, *Introducing Liberation Theology*, 25, 28; Segundo, "Human Rights," 66; John Paul II, *Reconcilatio et paenetentia*, paragraph 16; John Paul II, *Sollicitudo rei socialis*, paragraph 36; and Francis, *Evangelii gaudium*, 188, 202.
4. Elder-Vass, *Causal Power*, 1.

5. Goulet, "Search," 130.
6. Niebuhr, *Christ*, 32.
7. The first monograph to develop a substantive account of what constitutes a social structure is Finn's, *Consumer Ethics*.
8. Spohn, *Go and Do Likewise*, 27.
9. Mattins, *Cry*, 67.

PART I

Diagnosis

CHAPTER 1

Catholic Ethics in the Twenty-First Century

"The ones who walk away from Omelas" are the presumed paragons of virtue in Ursula K. Le Guin's allegory of the same title.[1] Omelas is a utopia whose residents have achieved a life of temporal well-being and happiness. Omelans live a life of comfort, devoid of disease and violence, with political freedom, superb scholarship, beautiful music, lavish festivals, and perfect weather. However, all this depends on a single "child's abominable misery." Locked in a cell beneath a house, a child sits naked, in excrement, denied human contact and affection. The child begs to be released from the cell but receives only an occasional kick and a bowl of cornmeal. To release the child, or even comfort the child, would destroy this utopia.

As adolescents, the residents of Omelas must come to understand this grand social bargain. Most residents feel helpless to change the situation, and they continue on with their lives. And then there are the ones who walk away from Omelas. Their eyes now opened to the structural injustice in their community, and their consciences stirred, they refuse to benefit from the suffering of another person. They walk away, and they sacrifice living in utopia.

Walking away from structural injustice is, indeed, morally tempting. Those who live in the Global North live in an Omelas of sorts. The comfort and material well-being of Global Northerners are achieved at the expense of the well-being of Global Southerners. Like Omelas, some walk away from this social arrangement. Neo-utopian communities enable members to live off the grid, with an alternative economy that subverts factory farming and the sweatshop industry. Such people, like the ones who walk away from Omelas, are prophetic through their noncooperation in social injustice. Those who walk away are inspired by "the notion that none of us, actually, have to be complicit to political, social and economic forces with which we don't agree."[2]

This book challenges the notion that walking away is the most virtuous response to structural evil. Walking away from Omelas does not change the fact that the child is still locked in the basement. Walking away from contemporary society does not change the fact that garment workers still will be exploited and that the globe still will warm dangerously. Crucially, walking away is not likely to be the solution that the child, or the garment worker, would recommend. Notions of complicity and cooperation seem inadequate to guide the ethical reasoning that is required for these situations. Perhaps we should be asking different questions than those concerning our complicity and cooperation in structural evil.

THE COLLAPSE AT RANA PLAZA

On the morning of April 24, 2013, the Rana Plaza building collapsed on the outskirts of Dhaka. The collapse was not the result of an earthquake and was not entirely unforeseen. A day before the collapse, large cracks emerged in the structure, forcing workers to flee the building. That day, an engineer determined that the structure was unsafe. The office workers, who worked on the first floors of the building, agreed with the engineer and refused to work. There were, however, garment workers also scheduled to work in the top levels of the structure. The building's owner, Sohel Rana, had converted the top floors into garment factories, which made clothes for retailers such as the Children's Place. To power the factories, he installed several large generators on those floors so that the garment work could continue even when regular blackouts hit the city. Although garment workers were hesitant to begin their shifts on the 24th, Rana and the owners of the various garment factories in the building urged and then ordered workers to enter the building. Shortly thereafter, the generators were started, which, as usual, caused the structure to shake. This time the shaking caused the building to buckle and collapse, killing 1,127 people.

This preventable tragedy calls into question not only identifiable human actions but also the impersonal structures that facilitated it. The collapse at Rana Plaza did not result from a series of unfortunate, isolated events. It resulted from regularized processes—processes from which those in the Global North derive significant economic benefit. Who or what was to blame for this terrible loss of life? Was Sohel Rana uniquely responsible? After all, he decided to retrofit his building without regard for the well-being of his workers. He decided to order the seamstresses into a structurally compromised building. Did the Children's Place bear moral responsibility for this event? The Children's Place appears to have been a causal factor in the building's collapse by incentivizing and rewarding Rana for producing a consistent stream of inexpensive garments. Finally, were consumers to blame? These labor practices enabled consumers to purchase the inexpensive clothing that they urged retailers to produce.

To answer these questions, we need to identify the best ethical lens for the task. Ethicists continue to turn to manualist era principles, such as double effect and cooperation, to assign moral guilt for structural evils. However, as I show in this chapter, such principles are incapable of doing the heavyweight work these situations require.

MANUALIST PRINCIPLES, HUMAN RIGHTS, AND STRUCTURAL EVIL

Albino Barrera's *Market Complicity and Christian Ethics* is an excellent example of how ethicists continue to lean on manualist principles to analyze structural harm.[3] Before I critique his use of these principles, a few comments in praise of the book are in order. His text is an excellent presentation of the complex economic realities that confront consumers in the twenty-first century. I chose this text because it is well researched and argued, and because it draws deeply on the Catholic moral tradition.

As a trained economist and theologian, Barrera brings two important knowledge bases to bear on issues involving the actions of the corporations and consumers of the Global North. Specifically, he explains and evaluates the largely unintended but devastating effects of their accumulated actions on the poor of the Global South. Throughout the text, he introduces contemporary cases and economic situations for which there are no easy answers. These cases are key contributions of the text because they help explain the economic realities that have given rise to critical socioeconomic issues in the age of globalization.

In his book, Barrera analyzes the exploitation of garment workers in Saipan, which is one of the Mariana Islands in the South Pacific and a commonwealth of the United States.[4] Saipan has a lower minimum wage than the United States, but its commonwealth status enables factories to put a "Made in the USA" tag on clothing produced there. Barrera shows that throughout the island, the garment industry has run sweatshops that violate international labor standards due to unsafe working conditions, unpaid overtime, and work weeks of seventy to eighty hours. The island has supplied clothing for major US brands such as Gap, Abercrombie & Fitch, and Target.

Barrera teases apart the varying degrees of causal roles of factory owners, retail outlets, apparel brands, and consumers. This aspect of his analysis is quite helpful. However, his moral analysis suffers when he utilizes the principle of double effect (PDE) to analyze the actions of retail chains, brand owners, and consumers.

Barrera argues that the PDE has three conditions: "The act considered independently of its evil effect is not in itself wrong; the agent intends the good and does not intend the evil either as an end or as a means; and the agent has proportionately grave reasons for acting, addressing his relevant obligations, comparing the consequences, and, considering the necessity of the evil, exercising due care to eliminate or mitigate it."[5] In the Saipan example, he argues that retailers and brands have violated all three conditions of the PDE:[6]

> Inhumane working conditions that violate human rights are morally unacceptable acts to begin with, regardless of the intention or circumstances surrounding the case (first condition of the PDE). Moreover, one cannot achieve the good of the laudable intention (stretching the consuming public's real income) by employing morally unacceptable means (exploiting workers) (second condition of the PDE). Furthermore, even if we were to accept, for the sake of argument, that the maltreatment of workers was merely an unintended consequence, the harm inflicted on the Saipan workers simply outweighed whatever benefits may have been produced for the American public (third condition of PDE).[7]

Throughout the text, Barrera presses the PDE into service to adjudicate moral quandaries such as these. In fact, he opens chapter 1 of his book by presenting the principle. Clearly, the PDE is ensconced within the canon of Catholic moral theology and has aided in the analyses of countless moral quandaries. However, Barrera's use of the PDE is problematic for four reasons.

First, the precondition of the PDE is that it applies only to cases where a single action produces two inseparable effects: one good and intended, the other bad and unintended. This precondition of the PDE requires that the good effect can *be produced only* if the bad effect is also produced and foreseen by the agent. In this way, the Catholic tradition has used the PDE, and its four conditions, to sort through the ethics of nondirect abortions and unintended civilian deaths in war.

Given this precondition, the PDE should not be used with regard to sweatshop labor. Brands and retailers can achieve the "good effects," which I argue are principally concerned with profitability and only secondarily concerned with "stretching the consuming public's real income," without producing or encouraging the production of sweatshop-made garments. Thus, the good effects can be realized without necessarily producing the bad effect. Sweatshop conditions exist not out of necessity but, rather, to support the excessive compensation packages and investor returns that brands and retailers have decided take precedence over working conditions. Compare this with the case where the death of an unborn child is *praeter intentionem* for the saving the life of a woman with uterine cancer; the only way to save the life of the mother is to perform a hysterectomy, which also necessarily, unavoidably, and foreseeably causes the death of the child. If the mother's cancer could be cured and the child's life spared, the woman and physician would be morally obligated to choose the medical treatment that produced that outcome. But in the case of a pregnant woman with a cancerous uterus, there is currently no procedure that produces both good effects. Notice that unlike the death of the unborn child, neither brands nor retailers have a moral need for sweatshop labor to exist. Because the good effects can be realized without producing the bad effect of sweatshop labor, the PDE does not apply to this issue.

Second, sweatshop conditions are not merely unintended effects of an otherwise virtuous decision; the conditions themselves are the products of intentional action. The brands and retailers about which Barrera writes indirectly exert pressure on subcontractors to use sweatshop labor. As noted above, Sohel Rana was incentivized and rewarded by the Children's Place and others to produce clothing as inexpensively as possible.

Third, Barrera assumes that a proportional analysis shows that the harm to workers "simply outweighed whatever benefits may have been produced for the American public." Many economists would disagree with such a claim and instead would argue the opposite point: sweatshops produce goods for corporations, consumers, and for workers.[8] I maintain that there is no plausible way of comparing good and bad effects in this case. Proportionality is notoriously difficult to ascertain, even when only two people are involved. One cannot establish proportionality with so many millions implicated in sweatshop labor. How would one begin to quantify and then weigh the benefits for end-line consumers against the harm suffered by garment workers and their families? Any attempt to do so would be mere conjecture. The same is not true in the case of the pregnant woman with uterine cancer. There, the effects can be reasonably determined and then compared.

Fourth, sweatshop labor has thousands of good and bad effects, and there is no meaningful way to identify the causal connections between them. Recall that the third condition of the PDE is that the bad effect cannot cause the good effect. This condition morally requires that causality move only from the good to the bad, not from the bad to the good. The adage that "one should not do evil that good may come from it" applies here. This third condition is helpful when adjudicating the ethics of the pregnant woman with a cancerous uterus. In this case, the death of the unborn child does not produce the good effect of removing the cancerous organ from the mother's body. The PDE is helpful because the action is a known agent's easily identifiable, one-time action, whose effects and their causality are both apparent. Conversely, the case of sweatshop labor presents the ethicist with a multitude of actions, which are being executed by a variety of kinds of actors, all of which are connected in a global web of relations and structures.

Ironically, Barrera agrees, in part, with a critique of the PDE. After noting that "some believe that the principle of double effect should not be used in economic ethics,"[9] he writes that "these criticisms have a point. Nevertheless, in the absence of an alternative method, the principle of double effect is by far one of the most useful conceptual tools we have in sorting through moral dilemmas in economic life. We just have to use the principle with appropriate caution and safeguards."[10] He closes his first chapter with yet another critique of manualist principles, particularly the PDE. He lists four reasons why "these principles are still insufficient for our study." His third point is that "for this study, we have to deal with socioeconomic accumulative harms. Neither of these principles provides a straightforward method for disentangling interlocking market harm and benefits and unraveling interdependent economic agencies."[11] His solution is to complement the principles with "moral standards, premises, and methods drawn from both within and beyond Christian ethics."

The Principle of Cooperation

Other ethicists, such as Julie Hanlon Rubio and Gerald Beyer, have employed the principle of cooperation (PC) to address labor injustices. Rubio, more than any other contemporary ethicist, has utilized the PC in analyzing issues in social ethics.[12]

Rubio has defined the PC as "help afforded another—to carry out his purpose in sinning."[13] The tradition clearly holds that formal cooperation, or willingly assisting another to commit an evil action, is always wrong. However, material cooperation, "in which one performs a good or indifferent action and foresees but does not intend that it will assist an evildoer, could sometimes be justified."[14] Rubio's account of the PC shows that the cooperator must be a causal factor in the evil action. This point was emphasized in the US Conference of Catholic of Bishops' 2018 revision of *The Ethical and Religious Directives for Catholic Health Care Services*. There, the bishops note that

> the cooperation is material if the one cooperating neither shares the wrongdoer's intention in performing the immoral act nor cooperates by directly participating in the act as a means to some other end, but rather contributes to the immoral activity in a way that is causally related but not essential to the immoral act itself. While some instances of material cooperation are morally wrong, others are morally justified. There are many factors to consider when assessing whether or not material cooperation is justified, including: whether the cooperator's act is morally good or neutral in itself, how significant is its causal contribution to the wrongdoer's act, how serious is the immoral act of the wrongdoer, and how important are the goods to be preserved or the harms to be avoided by cooperating.[15]

For Rubio and the bishops, the principle of material cooperation attempts to determine if and to what extent the cooperating agent actually played a causal role in the execution of the evil action. Questions of causality are crucially important when such causality reasonably can be determined, as in the case where a nurse provides preoperative care for a woman scheduled for a direct surgical abortion.

Rubio has turned to the PC for guidance regarding the moral responsibility of the consumer for systemic labor abuses in the garment industry. In *Hope for a Common Ground: Mediating the Personal and the Political in a Divided Church*, Rubio offers key diagnoses regarding social sin in moral theology. First, she notes that the normative claims of Catholic social teaching have often "lacked teeth" because of their inability to identify personal responsibility for social evils.[16] Second, she acknowledges that many people of good conscience feel morally responsible, to a degree, for the social evils in which they participate. Put differently, Rubio rightly notes that many moral agents recognize that social evil has personal moral consequences. Finally, Rubio argues that in a globalized situation, "We can no longer limit our discussion of justice to direct relationships with shopkeepers, neighbors, and employers."[17] Here, Rubio argues for an ethics of relationality that goes beyond the traditional ethics of interaction—a point that I develop in chapter 5.

Rubio then argues that the PC could aid Catholic social teaching in cutting teeth but that it "was less than fully developed" regarding social sin.[18] As a corrective, she blends the PC with a notion of social sin: "Social sin can be broadly defined as social forms of opposition to the Kingdom of God, and our participation in this opposition can involve personal sin."[19] The fusion of PC and social sin enables Rubio to argue that personal cooperation in social evils is, in fact, a cause of such evils. Individual agents, then, are morally responsible for some but not all of their cooperation in social sin.[20]

In Rubio's use of the PC for situations of social sin, such as purchasing sweatshop-made clothing, she acknowledges the inconsequential nature of singular actions to directly cause social evils. Clearly, an American father's purchase of sweat-made sweatpants is not necessary for labor abuses to transpire in Bangladesh.[21] However, like Barrera, who has suggested that there are "socioeconomic, accumulative" types of harm, Rubio has endorsed an aggregated notion of social sin and evil. She has argued that individual actions "added together" can produce substantial social results.[22] Further, she draws on Cathleen Kaveny's notion of "aggregated agency," noting that one's own personal actions, "'added to those of others,' shape reality, even if they intend to harm no one, and even if their one vote, phone call, or purchase will not change the system."[23]

Although Rubio's work, like Barrera's, engages a number of pressing issues, it also invites ethicists to consider two substantive questions. First, is individual agency aggregated? If agency is truly aggregated, then it follows that each consumer's actions causally exacerbate, in some small way, the overall social evil suffered by poor garment workers. However, such a claim must be critically appraised, given that it offers a sociological portrait of social evil. In chapter 3 I contest the notion that structural evil, such as sweatshop labor, is aggregated. Second, if it is the case that a person who has bought clothing at the Children's Place does not causally exacerbate sweatshop abuses in the manner suggested by Rubio, one must ask if the PC is the proper ethical category under which to analyze such social evils. As Rubio notes, the PC involves helping or being a causal factor in an evil action. Does the consumer "help" the Children's Place abuse garment workers? And if so, how?

On this question, I agree with Kaveny that consumers do not cooperate in sweatshop labor but do benefit from it.[24] In an essay that introduced the concept of appropriation, Kaveny argues that "appropriators make no causal contribution to the evil action whose fruit or by-products they appropriate; generally speaking (but not always), at the time they confront the decision about whether to act, the evil act has already been done."[25] Unlike cooperation, in which the cooperator assists the principal agent in his or her wrongdoing, the appropriator simply benefits from, but does not assist, the evil action. When a father buys a pair of sweat-made sweatpants, his action is distant geographically, temporally, and causally from the labor abuses inflicted on the worker in Bangladesh.[26] Importantly, his purchase occurs after the evil act (labor abuse) has transpired. It is impossible to aid an act that has already occurred. One could argue, instead, that the purchase of sweat-made clothing aids *future* labor abuses by providing the profit needed for corporations to continue to exploit garment workers. But though more plausible, this position is untenable. The father's purchase of a sweat-made garment does not aid any identifiable evil action. No one person is enabled to abuse workers through the father's purchase. Compare this with the example of the taxi driver who knowingly and willingly brings a john to a brothel. Here, the taxi driver aids in the commission of an evil action that one can easily name and identify. Instead, the father's action is embedded in a larger social structure through which the father benefits and the garment worker suffers. In short, the PC does not provide guidance in the ethics of buying sweatshop-made garments, because it pertains only to an agent's aiding in discrete evil actions and not participating in and benefiting from structural evil.

Gerald Beyer's essay, "Advocating Worker Justice: A Catholic Ethicist's 'Toolkit,'" analyzes cases of worker injustice at Catholic universities by using, among other concepts, the principle of cooperation. Beyer draws on an earlier work of Rubio in order to claim that "although the traditional Catholic concept of cooperation in evil did not deal with actions in the economic, social, and political spheres, it can provide a language for describing the moral complicity of individuals in structures of sin."[27] While recognizing critiques of the PC, Beyer, like Rubio, maintains that "cooperation in evil nonetheless remains a useful tool for thinking about complicity in social sin."[28]

Beyer then uses the PC to analyze the scandalous treatment of adjunct faculty at Catholic universities. He rightly notes that "tenure-track faculty members fail to practice solidarity with their adjunct faculty colleagues" and that "full-time faculty benefit from the evil actions committed by others at the university."[29] Although Beyer argues that such benefit is scandalous, and thus in violation of the PC, in a footnote he gestures toward Kaveny's distinction between appropriation of evil and cooperation with evil, and he suggests that such faculty are complicit in and are appropriating the evil done to adjuncts.[30]

Beyer's move toward the appropriation of evil is an improvement over the PC. Tenure-track faculty members do not aid in the creation of adjunct lines by administrators, but they do benefit from the existence of adjunct faculty. There is no causal connection between a tenure-track professor's ability to do research and the labor abuses that adjuncts suffer. Instead, a highly complex web of relationships between many social agents produces both benefits for some and burdens for others.

Importantly, the work of Barrera, Rubio, and Beyer can further attune theological ethicists to problems involving sinful social structures and personal moral agency. In doing so, they break the barriers between the traditional categories of social ethics and personal ethics in three ways. First, each focuses on the inner workings of structural injustice, whether they be accumulative or predicated on a benefit/burden dialectic. Second, though all three draw on manualist concepts in order to guide their normative claims, each explicitly recognizes the limits of these principles in situations of social evil. Third, given the limits they recognize in the PDE and PC, each attempts to augment or support these principles with other social scientific and theological concepts.

In the end, Barrera, Rubio, and Beyer argue that the PDE and PC offer the best available resources with which to evaluate pressing social ethical/personal moral concerns. As Barrera writes, there is an absence of alternative methods with which to scrutinize structural types of harm. This is precisely the problem. In the absence of alternative methods, ethicists must choose among less than appropriate tools. This problem can be traced back to what counts as a moral issue for the manualists.

Manualist principles emerged in a moral universe that attempted to discern moral culpability and sin. For instance, the famous Anglophone moralist Thomas Slater began his book *Cases of Conscience* by asking, "What is required for a human act and for sin to be imputable?"[31] He responded, "We are not responsible for those actions over which we have no control. We are responsible for those which we freely produce."[32] Here, moral responsibility pertains only to those actions that are freely willed. The *Catechism of the Catholic Church* also reflects such an approach. The *Catechism* holds that "freedom makes a man responsible for his acts to the extent that they are voluntary."[33] Voluntary actions are those executed with reason and free will. Because "every act directly willed is imputable to its author," these acts are the basis for moral praise or blame.[34]

The *Catechism* also recognizes some of the complexities that arise from within directly willed actions, such as the unintended effects caused by intentional action. An effect can be tolerated without being willed by its agent—for example, a mother's exhaustion from tending to her sick child. A bad effect is not imputable if it was not willed either as an end or a means of an action—for example, dying as a result of aiding someone in danger. For a bad effect to be imputable, it must be foreseeable and the agent must have the possibility of avoiding it, as in the case of manslaughter caused by a drunken driver.[35]

Let us apply this logic to the purchase of sweat-made clothing. Is sweatshop labor a foreseeable bad effect of one's purchase of inexpensive clothing? That is, does purchasing sweat-made clothing cause labor abuses? Well, not in the conventional sense of moral causality. As Rubio has suggested, a counterfactual account suggests that purchasing sweat-made clothing does not cause labor abuses. One can ask, Would the injustices still exist if I did not buy the sweat-made garment? The answer is yes. Further, will sweatshops still exist if I do not purchase sweat-made clothing? Again, yes. So is buying sweat-made clothing imputable? Is the consumer morally responsible for the abuses that garment workers suffer? If she is, it is certainly not in the way that a person is morally responsible for manslaughter in the case of drunken driving.

Note that in each of the *Catechism*'s examples, the causal chain is short and direct. The bad effect (manslaughter) is closely causally related to the action (drunk driving). In buying from the Children's Place, one cannot reasonably draw a causal connection from my purchase to labor abuses. Although I have control over my purchases, I do not have control over the conditions under which the clothing was made or, more important, the clothing options from which I can and must choose. There is no meaningful causal responsibility here, at least not in the ways that the Catholic moral tradition has discussed such responsibility.

Liability, Responsibility, and Culpability

The work of the political scientist Iris Marion Young helps to bring the issue into focus.[36] Young argues that conventional models of act analysis maintain that only direct relationships can yield moral responsibility. That is, an agent is morally responsible only if she directly harms another person. This approach resonates with a legal model in which a specified agent directly harms a specified person. Young calls this the liability model of responsibility.

In a similar way, Kenneth Himes distinguishes between the concepts of responsibility, liability, and culpability when discussing social sin.[37] Responsibility is a causal term for Himes. A responsible agent actually causes harm to a certain degree. Children or those with psychological illnesses can be responsible for an action but are often not considered morally culpable for wrongs suffered. Further, Himes distinguishes responsibility from liability. One can be liable for harm even if one is not responsible for it. For instance, a business owner can be liable for her employee's actions. In such instances, the owner plays no causal role in the harmful actions but can still be required to suffer a penalty because of the actions. Finally, Himes argues that culpability requires causal responsibility and free moral agency. The culpable person is morally blameworthy, not just causally blameworthy.

There is a logic to imputing moral responsibility for only those actions one controls and chooses. Again, this model remains reasonable in a more localized context for personal action. We need to ask if such an approach to ethics is the *only* one to which Catholic ethicists ought to have recourse today. As suggested above, the traditional accounts of responsibility, liability, and culpability are difficult if not impossible to determine for an agent's participation in sociostructural moral problems, such as buying sweat-made clothing. What do "freely produce" and "directly willed" mean today, when one lives in an era of global social structures? What does "directly willed" mean when one chooses among garments made in sweatshops? People in the Global North derive enormous benefit from structures that they do not directly will, over which they have no direct control, and from which the poor of the Global South and the climate suffer.

An approach to ethics that includes the determination of causality and culpability appears to have significant difficulties in dealing with sociostructural harms. As I have demonstrated, such an approach struggles to pass moral judgment on buying sweat-made garments. The limited and tentative conclusions offered by manualist principles offend the moral intuitions of many people of goodwill, who genuinely find something morally wrong about buying sweat-made clothing. The question is, Where is the moral evil in the garment industry? Further, how ought one analyze the industry to understand how one's moral agency relates to these structural evils? To answer these questions, ethicists need to move beyond manualist principles and a manualist mind-set.

Human Rights and Social Evils

Earlier in this chapter, I showed how the PDE would not be appropriate for a case like this; but what about human rights theory? Human rights theory analyzes moral issues through the lenses of human rights, such as those contained in the Universal Declaration of Human Rights. As such, rights theory focuses on the moral claims that persons can make to be given access to certain goods (positive rights) or to be unmolested (negative rights).

However, as liberationists in the 1970s argued, human rights theory is centrally focused on individuals and fails to attend to the structures that facilitate or undermine the rights of individuals.[38] Juan Luis Segundo has argued that, with few exceptions, "no court, national or international, will entertain a complaint of hunger" because often there is not a single identifiable person responsible for the malnutrition of large groups of people.[39] Segundo has little use for a human rights approach because it fails to understand that human rights violations are often structurally caused.

Further, liberationists rail against the presuppositions of human rights theory. In an article on the conflictual relationship of liberationists and human rights, Mark Enger has written that "human rights language does not provide the conceptual tools with which one could even understand oppression in institutional, rather than individual, terms. The very structure of a violation that can be isolated and acted upon presumes the existence of a basically orderly politic-economic system in which such an event would be an aberration."[40]

The case of worker abuse in sweatshops is nonaberrant. Instead, the harm suffered by garment workers is caused by a global web of fixed relations. Thus, in focusing on the identifiable actions of individuals and groups, human rights theory traditionally has neglected to attend to the structures that facilitate or undermine the rights of individuals. Like Segundo, Enger's point is that rights violations are caused, to a high degree, by structures and institutions. The political and economic order consistently violates the rights of the poor. Far from being anomalous, rights violations are regularized.

Human rights theory fails in these situations because it follows the culpability model of act analysis: a person or group is morally guilty only if it can be demonstrated that they directly and intentionally were causal factors in the evil action and its harm. Typically, it is difficult, if not impossible, to claim that local and national governments, agribusiness, and the global elite directly and intentionally cause the malnutrition of an identifiable child. And so the human lament continues, children die, and no party is held morally and politically responsible for human rights abuses because impersonal structures appear to be at fault.

The point is this: Manualist principles and human rights theory neglect social structures. Because these modes depend on a culpability approach to moral reflection, they fail to account for complex webs that give rise to human suffering. Another approach is needed.

THE TASK OF CHRISTIAN ETHICS

The inability to make moral sense of structural harm is a significant problem for Christian ethics. Bernard Haring has rightly asserted that the task of Christian ethics is to discover moral truth. James Keenan has further specified Haring's claim and has argued that the long-range purpose of moral theology is to "find for the Church the way to live the upright life of Christian discipleship."[41] Drawing on Haring and Keenan, I argue that the task of

Christian ethics is to investigate and make normative claims about how to live the Gospel of Jesus Christ in each age. Christian ethics must, then, begin with a twofold encounter: with contemporary reality and with Jesus Christ and his community of disciples. The former is the point of departure in the Second Vatican Council's signature document on living the Christian life today, *Gaudium et spes*—which begins with the realities and the circumstances of the world, not doctrine.

To this end, ethicists must develop concepts capable of accounting for and passing normative judgments on new moral realities. This is to say that Christian ethics should have a high degree of both explanatory capacity and output power. Explanatory capacity is the ability of a moral theory or concept to help ethicists understand, explain, and morally judge human action.[42] A theory possesses high explanatory capacity if it presents a coherent picture of human agency, the moral act, and moral character (and its development). Further, such a theory should have an account of how genetics, psychology, social structures, and culture causally influence these moral realities. Output power is a theory's ability to produce new normative judgments. A theory has high output power if it can provide moral guidance in a number of different areas of moral concern, for instance, from the ethics of raising children to economic ethics. This is the breadth of a theory's output power. High output power is also present in theories that produce novel normative insights. According to the bioethicists Tom Beauchamp and James Childress, "a theory has output power when it produces judgments that were not in the original database of considered moral judgments on which the theory was constructed."[43] At times, the Christian tradition has risen to meet its task, and it has developed theories with high explanatory capacity and output power; at other times, it has failed to do so.

Casuistry: A Response to New Moral Realities

In their important book *The Abuse of Casuistry*, Albert Jonsen and Stephen Toulmin have argued that casuistry, or the case method of doing ethics, developed in the sixteenth century because of rapid changes in the world.[44] Theologians, kings, judges, and the laity were constantly encountering new cases and situations that required adjudication. The wars of religion in Europe, the development of the nation-state, the exploration of the New World, and the explosion of overseas trading and commerce gave rise to new social situations: "New circumstances pressed the casuists into new doctrines. From the 13th to the 18th centuries the economy of Europe changed from subsistence farming to an extensive mercantile and commercial market, ... so new circumstances pressed the casuists, as the economists of their time, to set new doctrines.... They sought, in the midst of the economic pressures, to bring to light the morally relevant circumstances that would permit meaningful moral discriminations."[45]

Heads of state regularly relied on theological ethicists for guidance in these complex matters. The esteemed theologian Francisco de Vitoria wrote his *Relectio de Indis et de Jure Belli* in 1539 at the request of Emperor Charles V, who was in the process of colonizing South America. On this matter, the emperor also consulted with the great advocate for the native peoples, Bartolomé de Las Casas. King James I commissioned Francisco Suárez to write *Defensio fidei Catholicae adversus Anglicanae sectae errores*, which was a case study on the morality of Catholics submitting to Anglican rulers.

In this rapidly changing world, the great medieval synthesis of faith and reason in the *Summa theologiae* of Thomas Aquinas could provide only provisional guidance.[46] In short, the established methods lacked explanatory capacity and output power. New cases required novel methods of deliberation. Casuistry emerged as an ethical methodology that could guide rational reflection on these unique situations. Casuistry did not rely on old and outdated rules and principles that did not account for the new realities of the sixteenth century. When Vitoria, Las Casas, and Suárez found their inherited moral resources stretched thin, each turned to casuistry as a way to bring accepted moral practices, in the form of paradigm cases, to bear on new situations and cases.[47] Jonsen and Toulmin note that the period of high casuistry employed taxonomic reasoning in comparing similar cases. The taxonomic method was sensitive to circumstances, used analogies, and relied on prudential reasoning. The case in question, *Q*, would be matched with a settled, paradigm case, *P*. *P* would be chosen if it was the same kind of moral case as *Q*. That is, *P* would be a morally similar situation and have morally similar circumstances to *Q*. Because *P* already had a moral solution, theorists could use that solution to solve *Q*.

The casuists developed new doctrines through their codification of a new methodology, casuistry. Over time, a normative consensus emerged on certain questions as well as regarding certain principles that emerged through the adjudication of cases. For example, theologians developed the PDE and the PC by articulating the points of agreement that existed among a variety of related cases. The PDE emerged when moralists named and codified four conditions that typically guided the analysis of tragic dilemmas. Keenan has stressed the fact that the PDE was not deduced from other moral values or principles but rather emerged from the concrete reflections and articulations of moralists who had resolved hundreds of cases. Moralists took a broad view of the cases they had adjudicated and, Keenan suggested, inductively discovered common precepts, such as the PDE. Furthermore, the PDE was contextualized by its origins and usefulness within casuistry. It was never intended to serve as a stand-alone principle that justified actions if they passed the four conditions contained therein.[48]

The case method stands as an example of a time when theological ethicists fulfilled their shared task to make normative claims about how to live the Gospel in their own age. In order to accomplish this task, they needed to develop a complex ethical method that enabled a keen moral analysis of the new world order.

Manualism: Detached from the Moral World

Eventually, the casuist's principles, such as the PDE, became unmoored from the cases that gave them life. Jonsen and Toulmin have argued that the 1687 publication of Isaac Newton's *Philosophiae Naturalis Principia Mathematica* reinforced the direction that all serious academic disciplines, including theological ethics, should take. True sciences were able to compose a set of abstract, theoretical concepts and principles and present them in an axiomatic system.[49] As a result, by the end of the seventeenth century, "case books" were focused on the articulation and deductive application of principles to cases. The taxonomic comparison of cases that characterized the period of high casuistry was lost, and a geometric model emerged. The geometric model, or "low casuistry," was a deductive application of a principle to a case, and was largely ahistorical and dismissive of circumstances.[50] The moral manuals, which dominated Catholic ethics from the eighteenth century to Vatican II, employed low casuistry in their adjudication of actions. The manuals left behind the suppleness of high casuistry, with its ability to address new moral issues, and instead focused on the articulation and deductive application of moral precepts.

After the Council of Trent, the moral manuals emerged as the textbooks of Catholic morality. Moral pathology was their principal focus. Two examples illustrate this. First, Thomas Slater penned the most prominent English-language manual of the early twentieth century. His narrow vision of moral theology was explicitly articulated when he wrote that "in moral theology we abstain as a rule from treating of what concerns perfection; it is our task to distinguish between what is sinful and what is not, for the use of the confessor in the sacred tribunal of Penance."[51] Here, ethics does not aid in knowing and loving God; rather, it merely allows for the recognition of sin. Second, Heribert Jone's prominent manual contained only a single sentence on the morality of the hydrogen bomb. By contrast, it contained an extensive list of cities and the exact minute that constituted local midnight, because local midnight differed due to a city's distance from the start of the time zone. Jone determined that true midnight is 11:44 p.m. in Boston, 11:46 p.m. in Providence, and 12:20 a.m. in Pittsburgh.[52] Fasting, according to Jone, should begin and end then. Jone's book was published until 1962. The focus on personal sinfulness and the confession of sins informed Catholic ethics from the mid-sixteenth century to roughly the mid-1960s.

The coda of this narrative occurred when theologians such as Haring recognized that the moral manuals were unable to address the critical issues of the age.[53] The manuals not only ignored atomic weaponry but also failed to address friendship with God and neighbor, social obligations to the global poor, and an understanding of sex that went beyond procreation. In short, the manuals lacked explanatory capacity and output power. They could neither produce a moral account of the problems that threatened human existence and well-being nor could they produce true normative claims regarding what should be done regarding these problems.[54]

Two points merit attention from this brief historical study. First, the casuists developed new methods of reflection and new concepts to more accurately account for their changing moral universe. They jettisoned the methods and concepts that lacked explanatory capacity and output power and discovered new modes of ethical analysis. In this way, the sixteenth century should serve as a model for our contemporary period. Each period has seen rapid changes, new political and economic relationships, a new level of engagement between global actors, and new moral dilemmas. Second, the failure of manualism was its inability to develop in light of a changing world. As the examples from Slater and Jone demonstrate, the manuals became obsolete and irrelevant because they could not provide guidance on the important issues of the times.

The "Normative Abyss"

Thus far, I have suggested that questions of structural harm, such as the collapse at Rana Plaza and global warming, are relatively new and stretch the limits of the conceptual systems that ethicists, both secular and theological, have at their disposal. Christian ethicists struggle to produce strong normative claims about how to live the Gospel in this age due to imprecisions in their accounts of personal and social realities. Specifically, ethicists lack a clear understanding of what a structure is and how structures and moral agency relate. Although I have merely suggested this point, chapter 3 provides an argument for it.

A second problem emerges from the first. Because ethicists struggle to understand structural realities, they also struggle to discern which moral frameworks should be used to analyze such realities. For example, imagine rendering a moral judgment regarding abortion in a case where the mother's life was endangered by her pregnancy in the absence of any knowledge of fetal development. Would one have any clue about which conceptual resources ought to be employed in such an adjudication? Christian ethics in the twenty-first century is inadequate to its task because it lacks explanatory capacity—specifically, the ability to explain and account for the influence of social structures in human agency and action.

These issues are caused, in part, by globalization. Globalization creates what Richard Falk has called "the normative abyss."[55] Traditional concepts presuppose proximate relationships in which one agent directly affects another. As I argue in chapter 3, the twenty-first century is an age when persons share a relation with many people they will never meet. Therefore, we must adapt and develop concepts and methods to facilitate a new moral analysis. The global age's normative abyss confronts the contemporary world with, in Falk's term, a Grotian moment. The emergence of a new world order with the rise of the nation-state in the mid-seventeenth century forced the polymath Hugo Grotius to rethink the norms of ethics, politics, and law. Ours is a Grotian moment because "this is a time of potential transformation from one type of world order to another, that the prospects for change are of qualitative significance that calls for a possible reformulation of world order, and that the authoritative interpretation of these circumstances has yet to be made from a juridical perspective in a manner comparable to what Hugo Grotius contributed to our grasp of international law and society in the early modern period."[56]

As a matter of principle, Thomas Aquinas would have agreed with Falk. Aquinas argued that ethics is done well when it accounts for all relevant realities of a given moral situation.[57] As circumstances change, Aquinas maintained, so too should the acts of virtuous persons. The task of the ethicist, then, is to discern what those realities are and how they affect how one ought to live the Christian life. Globalized social structures are morally relevant realities that must be accounted for in twenty-first-century Catholic ethics. The circumstances within which we act are more highly structured than ever before. And, as I argue later in this book, structures are a special form of circumstances. They are the "surrounding conditions" of human agency. And yet few theological ethicists ever define "social structure."

DISCERNING THE GROWING END OF THE TRADITION

On the eve of the Second Vatican Council, John Courtney Murray wrote that the Church must discern the "growing end of the theological tradition."[58] To do this, it must avoid "fixism," the fallacy that maintains that the Church's theology ought to stop at a certain stage, and "archaism," the fallacy that older theological articulations are purer.[59] Theology must develop for reasons internal to theology itself, namely, because its subject of study, God, can never be finally comprehended. But it also must develop for reasons external to theology. Theologians continue to learn more about reality and encounter new and changing realities as history transpires. New realities prod theologians to discover new concepts and methods with which to understand and morally respond to the world as it is.

This chapter has shown the need for the moral tradition to grow in two ways. First, it needs to produce an ethical framework capable of addressing moral reality as it is, not as it was. As I have shown, manualist principles are insufficient for dealing with structural evils. Just as Vatican II deemed it insufficient to put new wine into the old wineskin that was manualism, it is likewise insufficient to simply articulate isolated virtues and norms for the global age. Principles, notions of responsibility, and what counts as a virtue and a vice should be rethought. Catholics need a more accurate account of good moral character that transcends simple moral culpability or liability. Using Beyer's metaphor, Catholic ethics needs an expanded tool kit. What is required is a comprehensive ethical framework that accounts for *this* moral world.

As I argue in chapter 2, this is not only a meta-ethical problem. The problem is also descriptive. Contemporary ethicists have an inaccurate picture of moral reality. Specifically, they have failed to acknowledge that the structure-agency problem requires a sociological solution. The relationship between structures and agency is a problem because of its complexity. A solution to the problem requires a definition of what structures are, what human agency is, and how structures both shape and are shaped by human agency. In sum, what is needed is an instrument capable of executing a structural ethical analysis. The purpose of this book is to produce just such an instrument.

Thus, in order to develop new concepts, we will first need to better understand the field in which human action takes place; we will need a solution to the structure-agency problem. Although it is difficult to conceptualize the complex workings of social structures, in the words of Charles Taylor, we need a "best account" of these moral realities. Taylor argues that we need concepts for complex realities that elude easy understanding.[60] And though such an account will be amended and ultimately supplanted by an even better account in the future, a best current account facilitates deliberation among persons and groups. To produce the best account of social reality, we must draw on contemporary social theory. The social sciences have revealed how our discrete actions are part of larger webs of actions and how they help to create and reinforce social and economic structures. In turning to the social sciences, Catholic ethicists may come to more fully understand how to live the Gospel of Jesus Christ in this new age.

NOTES

1. Le Guin, "Ones Who Walk Away."
2. Mariani, "New Generation."
3. Barrera, *Market Complicity*.
4. Ross, *Slaves to Fashion*, 139–40.
5. Barrera, *Market Complicity*, 15.
6. The PDE has been understood traditionally to contain four necessary principles. In his *Medico-Moral Problems*, Gerald Kelly presented the four conditions as "1. The action, considered by itself and independently of its effects, must not be evil . . . 2. The evil effect must not be the means of producing the good effect. . . . 3. The evil effect is sincerely not intended, but merely tolerated. . . . 4. There must be a proportionate reason for performing the action, in spite of its evil consequences." See pp. 12–16.
7. Barrera, *Market Complicity*, 130.
8. Some scholars justify and defend the existence of sweatshops. See Powell, *Out of Poverty*.
9. Barrera, *Market Complicity*, 17, citing Gowri, "When Responsibility Can't Do It."
10. Barrera, *Market Complicity*, 18.
11. Barrera, 27–28.
12. See Rubio, "Moral Cooperation"; Rubio, *Hope*; and Rubio, "Cooperation."
13. Rubio, *Hope*, 49. The principle of cooperation is among the most complex concepts in Catholic theological ethics. Henry Davis provided a traditional account of the principle of cooperation in his moral manual, *Moral and Pastoral Theology*, chap. 8. There, Davis noted that material cooperation is distinguished between immediate and mediate. Immediate material cooperation involves "co-operating in the sinful act of the other" and is typically wrong according to Davis. Mediate material cooperation is an act that is secondary and subservient to the main act of another and may be morally permissible. Mediate material cooperation is further distinguished into proximate and remote varieties. Proximate mediate material cooperation occurs "if the help given is very intimately connected with the act of another," while remote material cooperation "is not closely connected with the other's act." In general, acts that are less intimately connected to the action of the principal agent are more likely to be morally justifiable. In the determination of the morality of cooperation, Davis urges the reader to consider both duress and the reason for which the cooperator is cooperating. See also Austriaco, *Biomedicine*, 263–69; and Ashley, DeBlois, and O'Rourke, *Health Care Ethics*, 55–57.
14. Rubio, "Cooperation," 102.

15. US Conference of Catholic Bishops, *Ethical and Religious Directives*, part six, "Introduction." The conference's 2018 version of *The Ethical and Religious Directives* added a section on cooperation and serves as an important contemporary articulation of the principle. While Rubio's and Beyer's work predates this definition, it may be helpful for the reader to understand how theologians articulate the principle today. Notice that the principle of material cooperation attempts to determine if and to what extent the cooperating agent played a causal role in the execution of the evil action. Questions of causality are crucially important when such causality reasonably can be determined, as in the case where a nurse cares for a woman after a surgical abortion. Though Rubio's and Beyer's work predates the bishops' articulation of cooperation, they gesture to the fact that the principle is not ideally suited for questions regarding moral agency within structurally vicious situations.
16. Rubio, *Hope*, 42.
17. Rubio, 45.
18. Rubio, 32.
19. Rubio, 37.
20. Rubio offered a remarkably nuanced analysis in this regard. Throughout *Hope for Common Ground*, she acknowledged the limited capacities of an individual person to avoid cooperation in evil. She also recognized that "because I am only one finite human being, I cannot be responsible for everything all at once" (p. 47).
21. Throughout this book, I refer to clothing produced under sweatshop conditions as "sweat-made."
22. Rubio, *Hope*, 46.
23. Rubio, 46.
24. Kaveny argued that social moral problems such as sweatshop labor required a new moral category, which she termed the "appropriation of evil." See Kaveny, "Appropriation."
25. Kaveny, 289.
26. The PC considers the cooperator's proximity to the primary agent's evil action. The principle makes a distinction between proximate and remote material cooperation. In note 10 of her article "Appropriation of Evil," Kaveny notes that material cooperation invites the agent to attend to "a three-dimensional graph incorporating the axes of temporal proximity, geographical proximity, and causal proximity. All else being equal, the more proximate an act of cooperation is to the illicit activity of the principal agent, the harder it is to justify."
27. Beyer, "Advocating Worker Justice," 234. There, Beyer draws on Rubio, "Moral Cooperation."
28. Beyer, "Advocating Worker Justice."
29. Beyer, 245.
30. Kaveny, "Appropriation of Evil."
31. Slater, *Cases*, 16. Slater also notes that "moral theology does not cover the whole field of Christian conduct. Its object is not to place high ideals of virtue before people and train them in Christian perfection. Its task is much more restricted and humble. It lays down rules for determining what is right and what is wrong according to the teachings of the Christian faith. Its primary object is to teach the priest how to distinguish what is sinful from what is lawful, so that he may fruitfully administer the sacrament of Penance and perform the other duties of his sacred ministry" (p. 36). Slater has something of an intellectual conversion in the 1920s, when he responded to Arthur Vermeersch's new course in moral theology. Following Vermeersch, Slater insisted that Catholic morality was "laid down by Jesus Christ in the Sermon on the Mount; it is the standard of Christian perfection according to which Jesus Himself lived. [Vermeersch] regards Moral Theology

as the science not only of right and wrong, but as the science of Christian perfection and beatitude.... In the next place [ethicists] must give a more honorable place to the treatment of the principles of Christian perfection"; quoted from Kelly and Ford, *Contemporary Moral Theology*, 62.
32. Slater, *Cases*, 16.
33. *Catechism*, 1734.
34. *Catechism*, 1736.
35. *Catechism*, 1737.
36. See Young, "Responsibility."
37. Himes, "Social Sin," 188–90.
38. The eventual appropriation of human rights language of some liberationists was the result of political, not conceptual, development. In human rights language, they found a useful tool. Nongovernmental organizations in Latin America, many of which had done excellent work to promote the liberation of Latin Americans, spoke and wrote of human rights. See Enger, "Toward the Rights," 350–51.
39. Segundo, "Human Rights." See also Enger, "Toward the Rights," 345; and Regan, *Theology*, chap. 4.
40. Enger, "Toward the Rights," 365.
41. Keenan, *History*, 5.
42. The following texts define and employ the concept of explanatory capacity (or power): Miller and Knobel, "Some Foundational Questions," 19–40; Bhaskar, *Possibility*, 225, 238; and Donati, "Morality," 65. For an account of both explanatory capacity and output power, see Beauchamp and Childress, *Principles*, 353–54.
43. Beauchamp and Childress, *Principles*.
44. This paragraph relies on Jonsen and Toulmin, *Abuse*, chap. 7.
45. Jonsen and Toulmin, 193–94.
46. Keenan, "Moral Discernment." On p. 673, Keenan writes that "as the world expanded, local cultures and practices demanded newer directives, and tradition, failing to provide sufficient insight, was losing its influence." For his discussion of casuistry, see pp. 673–76.
47. Keenan, 144.
48. Keenan.
49. Jonsen and Toulmin, *Abuse*, 275–76.
50. Jonsen and Toulmin, 26–28; Keenan, *History*, 159.
51. Slater, *Cases*, 119.
52. Jone, *Moral Theology*, 357.
53. Keenan, *History*, 30.
54. Christine Gudorf recognized the deficient explanatory capacity of the manuals during the twentieth century, when she wrote that structures were left out of manualist moral theology because they could not go to confession. See Gudorf, "Admonishing Sinners," 8.
55. Falk, *Global Village*, 31.
56. Falk, 4.
57. Aquinas, *Summa theologiae*, I-II, 18.
58. Murray, "Problem," 561.
59. Murray, 561.
60. Taylor, *Sources*, 7.

CHAPTER 2

The Structure-Agency Problem in Catholic Ethics

Chapter 1 diagnosed a problem in Christian ethics: the inadequacy of the field's moral frameworks to address structural evils. Double effect, cooperation, and other manualist principles are unhelpful when various types of harm are woven into structures. The chapter suggested that the lack of an adequate moral framework was tied to another problem: the tradition's inability to understand morally relevant realities. Specifically, Christian ethics has failed to acknowledge that the "structure-agency problem" is in need of a solution. This chapter develops what the previous chapter merely suggested, and proves that contemporary Catholic ethics is in need of a better account of the relation of social structures and human agency if it is to offer strong normative claims regarding social structures and how persons should act when implicated within social structures. The chapter also looks to the culture-agency problem in Catholic theology and ethics and likewise makes the case that the discipline will profit from a more rigorous notion of culture and how culture, agency, and structures relate.

The chapter explores the development of Catholic thought on social structures. It first recounts the incisive analysis of the social structures produced in early Latin American liberation theology. Here, the contributions of Gustavo Gutiérrez and the General Conference of the Latin American Bishops are analyzed. The chapter also takes up the Magisterium's appropriation and modification of the innovations of the liberationists by looking at the papal writings of John Paul II, Benedict, and Francis. It then turns to the work of Catholic theologians on the topic. After establishing the state of the question, it concludes by arguing that Catholic theological ethics needs a better account of social structures if its social ethics is to be relevant in today's highly structured world.

THE SEEDS OF THE "STRUCTURES OF SIN"

Leo XIII's *Rerum novarum* not only inaugurated the papal tradition of social encyclicals; it also turned the institutional Church's attention to social structures.[1] In this encyclical, Leo XIII insists that though society's purpose is to make people virtuous, industrialization, coupled with the breakdown of the guild system, led to the poverty of the masses and "a general moral deterioration."[2] He proposes that a return to Christian institutions and social practices could remedy the social situation.[3] And he maintains that moral character and social institutions are intertwined. Just economic institutions, he reasons, would help to form virtuous persons.

The connection between moral character and social institutions mostly went undeveloped in moral theology until Vatican II. Margaret Pfeil has noted that some of the council fathers explicitly reject the use of the concept of "social sin" in the Constitution on the Sacred Liturgy, *Sacrosanctum concilium*.[4] The council addresses the moral influence of society in several places.[5] *Lumen gentium* calls the laity to "remedy the institutions and conditions of the world when the latter are an inducement to sin, that these may favor rather than hinder the practice of virtue."[6]

The transformative moment in the Church's teaching occurred at Vatican II, with the promulgation of *Gaudium et spes*. This document made two lasting contributions to Catholic ethics. First, it contains a systematic expression of the fundamental categories of Catholic ethics. Human dignity, love, the common good, social justice, and solidarity with the poor are presented as the central values and virtues of Catholic life.[7] Thus, *Gaudium et spes* corrects the narrow focus on avoidance of sin that had persisted from the Council of Trent onward. It calls the faithful to build a just society. Second, the document calls for a reading of the signs of the times in light of the Gospel; the Church was charged with taking an account of the social situation in the world and responding accordingly.[8] This catapults the Church into a more profound engagement with the problems facing the world. The document places a particular focus on issues within the political and economic spheres. The council argues that both areas find their purpose and goal in the common good.[9] The state, for instance, exists for the sake of contributing to the common good, the good that is realized by individual persons when all others have ready access to the goods needed for a dignified and flourishing existence.[10] Thus, though the document maintains its focus on the moral acts and character of individual persons, it also shows an awareness that social, political, and economic structures have the ability to thwart a person's goodwill and direct her to act in ways that undermine human dignity and the common good. The council fathers write that "when the structure of affairs is flawed by the consequences of sin, man, already born with a bent toward evil, finds there new inducements to sin, which cannot be overcome without strenuous efforts and the assistance of grace."[11] Here, the council fathers note that society has the potential to both strengthen authentically human qualities and enable persons to sin.[12] The council maintains that the social order profoundly influences moral agents, for better and for ill.[13] Society, therefore, should create conditions conducive to the practice of virtue and the simultaneous formation of the common good. Vatican II advanced the Catholic Church's focus on the moral importance of society and its influence on the moral character of the person.

LIBERATION THEOLOGY AND NAMING THE PROBLEM

Although the Church's social encyclicals and Second Vatican Council documents provided the seeds for a theory connecting social structures and human character and action, Latin American liberation theologians expounded on it. The 1968 Medellín Conference of the Latin American bishops was the landmark event in the institutional genesis of liberation theology. First, the bishops looked at their social situation and "found humanity suffering."[14] Second, they drew on *Gaudium et spes* and argued that much of the suffering on their continent constituted a "sinful situation" that was the result of "unjust structures."[15] The Medellín document includes the first magisterial articulation of the concept of structural and institutional sin. Personal sin, they argue, is crystallized in unjust social structures. The bishops explicitly name these impersonal social structures as sinful.[16] In the second paragraph of the conference's final document, the bishops underscore the structural nature of many sins in the Latin American context: "To all of this must be added the lack of solidarity which, on the individual and social levels, leads to the committing of serious sins, evident in the unjust structures which characterize the Latin American situation."[17] The solution to the situation of sin present in Latin America involved both conversion and structural change. The bishops understand conversion and structural reform as interwoven: "The uniqueness of the Christian message does not so much consist in the affirmation of the necessity for structural change, as it does in the insistence on the conversion of men which will in turn bring about this change. We will not have a new continent without new and reformed structures, but, above all, there will be no new continent without new men, who know how to be truly free and responsible according to the light of the Gospel."[18]

For the bishops, neither conversion nor structural change is sufficient. Although both conversion and structural reform are affirmed, the bishops prioritize conversion. They maintain that personal conversion is the point of departure for moral transformation. Personal conversion subsequently produces structural change.

Justicia in mundo, the document that emerged from the 1971 Synod of Bishops, provided further reflection on structural evils. There, the bishops write of social structures that create systematic barriers to charity.[19] These structures can be overcome through an education in justice, in which the Christian is enabled to both critique her society and militate against its manipulative aspects.[20] The bishops argue that the liturgy and the sacraments are the primary practices whereby the faithful are educated in justice. The sacraments of Baptism, Penance, and the Eucharist are named as practices that form just persons and their communities.

Thinkers such as Gustavo Gutiérrez, Clodovis and Leonardo Boff, and Juan Luis Segundo have developed these ideas into systematic theories that name structural sin as the cause of poverty. Gutiérrez's groundbreaking work on liberation theology, *A Theology of Liberation*, also published in 1971, draws on Medellín and further develops the social nature of sin. In language that closely resembles that of the synod, Gutiérrez argues that the entire political and economic system of Latin America is sinful because it is characterized by the breach of friendship between persons, and God and neighbor.[21] Although he focuses on the institutional aspect of structural sin, he also underscores that human agency produced these structures: "An unjust situation does not happen by chance; it is not something branded by a fatal destiny: there is human responsibility behind it."[22] Gutiérrez's analysis of the Latin American situation led him to find fault both in human agents and the structures and institutions they created and sustained.

Gutiérrez and others make a further contribution. Gutiérrez emphasizes that "the social sciences . . . are extremely important for theological reflection in Latin America."[23] Enrique Dussel notes that early liberation theology constituted the first time that the critical social sciences were used in Christian theology.[24] The turn to the social sciences, according to Dussel, is not to understand abstract concepts such as "structure" or "institution" but to understand the mechanisms, such as liberal capitalism and the paradigm for development that caused so much hunger, misery, and premature death in Latin America. It was a concrete social analysis, to address the continent's current social problems.

The Boff brothers, employing the Marxist concepts that would lead to their curial censure, write of the "dialectical explanation of poverty."[25] Here, poverty is the "inevitable by-product of an economic system that either exploits or excludes the great majority of people from the production process."[26] The rich then get richer, while the poverty of the poor worsens.

Segundo turns the focus from individuals who enact structural injustice to the structures themselves: "But when human rights are violated because the game rules governing relations among peoples, races, and social class demand it, even the most recent social encyclicals agree that the denunciation ought not to be aimed so much at the violators as against the structures that provoke the systematic commission of these violations."[27]

All these thinkers operated with a critical social perspective. According to Dussel, liberation theology was "critical" because it attempted to expose the social realities that cause injustice.[28] Again, the work of Karl Marx was used to explain the source of social injustice by appealing to his socioscientific critique, and not to adopt the philosophical ideas associated with him, such as atheism or dialectical materialism.[29]

The structural nature of sin subsequently emerged as a central idea within the broad movement of liberation theology.[30] This concept recognized how social structures were causal factors in poverty and violence. The oppression and exploitation of Latin American peoples were exposed as systematically present in institutions and the persons formed by those institutions.

The Third General Conference of the Latin American Episcopate—held at Puebla, Mexico, in 1979—marked another significant development of the concept. The Puebla document broke little new conceptual ground. However, the importance of the conference's final document is found in the frequency with which the bishops refer to the structural aspects of sin. Throughout the final document, the bishops underscore the connection of the poverty and oppression experienced by millions on the continent to the cultural mechanisms—along with economic, social, and political structures—that were put in place by the powerful. The bishops decry the institutionalized situation of sin that reigned in Latin America. They specifically cite the sinful cultural "mechanisms that are imbued with materialism rather than authentic humanism."[31] They argue that the structurally rooted materialism of Latin America is sinful because it creates and sustains poverty and injustice. Echoing Medellín, they proclaim that sin is both personal and structural.

The bishops observe that social realities profoundly influence personal moral development: "Culture is continually shaped and reshaped by the ongoing life and historical experience of peoples; and it is transmitted by tradition from generation to generation."[32] They warn that the culture that is transmitted could either inculcate authentic values or disvalues; it could promote just or unjust structures. In light of the influence of culture and social structures on the development of individual persons, they maintain that personal conversion is necessary and primary but insufficient. Social structures also need to be transformed.³³ They thus propose that the transformation of persons and structures should transpire through an infusing of evangelical values into Latin American society:

> The church calls for a new conversion on the level of cultural values, so that the structures of societal life may then be imbued with the spirit of the Gospel. And while it calls for a revitalization of evangelical values, it simultaneously urges a rapid and thoroughgoing transformation of structures. For by their very nature these structures are supposed to exert a restraining influence on the evil that arises in the human heart and manifests itself socially; and they are also meant to serve as conditioning pedagogical factors for an interior conversion on the plane of values.³⁴

Puebla marked a significant development in the bishops' approach to structural sin. They proposed that Gospel values could transform the culture and subsequently shape social structures. Here, structures are cultural products. Evangelical values were intended to have a dual effect. First, they were to transform the systemic injustices within Latin American society. Second, these structures were to function pedagogically. They were to convert Latin American persons to live justly. The bishops named the virtue of solidarity as the antidote to the "well-springs of injustice." Solidarity, or the sharing of the burdens and benefits of society among all of its members, emerged as the central virtue for liberation theologians.³⁵ Furthermore, at Puebla the bishops codified the preferential option for the poor as the principle whereby persons and institutions cultivate solidarity and also the principle whereby political and economic structures are to be judged. That is, they argued that all political and economic decisions should first and foremost promote the well-being of the poor and vulnerable of society.³⁶

THE MAGISTERIAL APPROPRIATION OF THE CONCEPT

The Roman Catholic Magisterium initially pushed back against liberation theology due to its occasional use of Marxist social analysis.³⁷ In addition, the Magisterium critiqued what it perceived to be a structural determinism in some of the formulations of structural sin in the writings of the liberation theologians. The pope and the Magisterium argued that if structures were regarded as the locus of moral responsibility, the category of personal sin would cease to have meaning.

Saint John Paul II and the Structures of Sin

However, John Paul realized that human agency could be preserved amid a theory of structural sin, and he incorporated the concept into official Catholic social teaching in the mid-1980s.[38] Three texts, in particular, are essential for the development of his notion of the structures of sin. Although the pope referred to "sinful structures" in his opening homily at the Third General Conference of the Latin American Episcopate in Puebla, Mexico, his most extensive treatment of the concept is found in his 1983 apostolic exhortation, *Reconciliatio et paenetentia*, which also marked the most systematic magisterial treatment of the topic. This document allowed the pope to respond to various articulations of the concept of structural sin that he found to be less than doctrinally accurate.[39]

Paragraph 16 of the exhortation establishes three central points. First, all sin is personal. Only moral agents can be the subject of moral acts. Thus, though a person may be "influenced" by external social factors, she is still a free moral agent. Responsibility for sinful action, therefore, rests with the person, not the social structure. Second, "social sin" has three legitimate meanings and one illegitimate one. According to John Paul, the concept of social sin rightly communicates the fact that every sin affects others insofar as it "drags down with itself the church and, in some way, the whole world."[40] The "law of descent" is opposed by the "law of ascent," whereby right actions inspire the human community. Furthermore, social sins are those directly against one's neighbor. These actions contradict the law of love, the common good, and the virtue of justice. Finally, there is a category of analogical social sins. These sins exist between human communities. Blocs of nations and social classes are principal actors here. Again, these collectives function analogically as agents, and therefore their "social sins" are likewise analogical.[41] The pope asserts that these social sins ultimately provide a moral challenge to the consciences of the individual moral agents who compose the community.

Third, the pope concludes paragraph 16 with a condemnation of any definition of social sin that "contrasts social sin and personal sin." He notes that such a dichotomy enervates, and possibly destroys, the concept of personal sin and replaces it with a theory of sin that is reduced to structurally determined social guilt and responsibility. In his condemnation, the pope provides one final insight into the nature of social sin. He notes that social sin is "the result of the accumulation and concentration of many personal sins." This point is developed in greater depth in the 1987 social encyclical *Sollicitudo rei socialis*.

Because of its higher degree of ecclesial authority, *Sollicitudo rei socialis* firmly establishes the notion of structures of sin in the Church's social teaching. The encyclical presupposes the definition of social sin presented in *Reconciliatio et paenetentia*. *Sollicitudo* also closely follows the Congregation for the Doctrine of the Faith's "Instruction on Christian Freedom and Liberation." This instruction, which was originally published a year before *Sollicitudo rei socialis*, tempered the Church's earlier critique of aspects of liberation theology.[42] Importantly, in its response to the liberationists' development of structural sin, the congregation defines the concept of social structure:

> These are the sets of institutions and practices which people find already existing or which they create on the national and international level, and which orientate or organize economic, social, and political life. Being necessary in themselves, they often tend to become fixed and fossilized as mechanisms relatively independent of the human will, thereby paralyzing or distorting social development and causing injustice. However, they always depend on human responsibility; human beings can alter them, and they are not dependent on an alleged determinism of history.[43]

This definition contains three crucial claims. The first is that structures are sets of institutions or practices. Unfortunately, the document does not define what institutions or practices are and how they are different kinds of structures. The second is that structures are often durable. At times, they take on a life independent of human agency. Third and finally, the definition asserts that structures can always be created or changed by human agency and are not finally independent of the free choice of human persons.

This account seems to have filtered into John Paul's thinking and enabled him to further refine the meaning of a sinful structure. *Sollicitudo rei socialis* refers to the "structures of sin" instead of "social sin." Like John Paul's definition of "social sin," "structures of sin" places the locus of moral responsibility in the person. Furthermore, this modification of language enables John Paul to explicitly engage the structural aspects of injustice. He defines structures of sin this way: "The sum total of negative factors working against a true awareness of the universal common good, and the need to further it, gives the impression of creating, in persons and institutions, an obstacle which is difficult to overcome."[44]

Sollicitudo rei socialis proposes an antidote to the structures of sin: solidarity. Following the Latin American bishops, and emerging from the Polish experience of Solidarność, John Paul sees solidarity as the virtue whereby the structures of sin are "conquered."[45] This constitutes a "diametrically opposed" attitude to the structures of sin, insofar as it directs the person to commit herself to the common good.[46] In addition, it could take hold in a person only with the aid of divine grace. In naming solidarity as the corrective to structures of sin, John Paul further illumines the concept. Like solidarity, structures of sin are moral attitudes, akin to vices, that can be willingly appropriated from society by the agent.

John Paul's inclusion of the law of ascent in *Reconcilatio et paenetentia* and solidarity in *Sollicitudo rei socialis* were essential additions to the tradition's theory of structures of sin. The introduction of these positive, correlative concepts better reflects the spirit of moral theology post–Vatican II. These concepts attune the agent not only to avoid evildoing but also to strive to do the good. Of particular interest for the current study is the pope's use of the language of virtue in his definition of solidarity. Unfortunately, John Paul did not flesh out the relationship of structures of sin and the virtues. His texts merely suggest that virtues overcome the structures of sin.

Even with these developments, John Paul's account of structural sin remained substantially sociologically underdeveloped. For this reason, Denis Goulet has called *Sollicitudo rei socialis* "not an exercise in social analysis, but a sermon."[47] Donal Dorr has critiqued the encyclical because "what is lacking is a social analysis which would take more seriously the causes of the class structure in society."[48] The pope lacked an incisive account of what a structure is, how it is formed, and how it shaped action and outcomes.

Four years later, the pope promulgated *Centessimus annus*. Therein, John Paul describes how human persons are formed by the structures of sin in their society:

> Man receives from God his essential dignity and with it the capacity to transcend every social order so as to move toward truth and goodness. But he is also conditioned by the social structure in which he lives, by the education he has received and by his environment. These elements can either help or hinder his living in accordance with the truth. The decisions which create a human environment can give rise to specific structures of sin which impede the full realization of those who are in any way oppressed by them. To destroy such structures and replace them with more authentic forms of living in community is a task which demands courage and patience.[49]

Here again, the pope's use of the concept is primarily in the context of personal moral formation. He maintains that social structures can facilitate or constrain education in the true and the good. The human agent remains free but is conditioned, primarily through education, by the structures of his society. For example, in a society of institutional racism, individual moral agents are conditioned to be racist. In fact, in such a society individual consciences are formed to assent to the perceived "rightness" of racism.

The 1995 encyclical *Evangelium vitae* marked John Paul's final significant development of the concept. One passage is noteworthy because a certain level of agency is ascribed to society:

> It is at the heart of the moral conscience that the eclipse of the sense of God and of man, with all its various and deadly consequences for life, is taking place. It is a question, above all, of the individual conscience, as it stands before God in its singleness and uniqueness. But it is also a question, in a certain sense, of the "moral conscience" of society: in a way it too is responsible, not only because it tolerates or fosters behavior contrary to life, but also because it encourages the "culture of death," creating and consolidating actual "structures of sin" which go against life. The moral conscience, both individual and social, is today subjected, also as a result of the penetrating influence of the media, to an extremely serious and mortal danger: that of confusion between good and evil, precisely in relation to the fundamental right to life.[50]

Notice the modified focus of this passage. *Evangelium vitae* heightened the profile of the moral quality of the social structure. For the first time, John Paul ascribes moral responsibility to a nonmoral agent: "the moral conscience of society." He qualifies this claim with the Latin *quodammodo*, translated as "in some way." The pope indicates that certain societies create structures that work against the good of life. Insofar as a society freely creates these structures, it functions as a moral agent and therefore has a kind of moral responsibility. In keeping with previous papal statements, the passage shows an awareness of the role of social structures in forming the consciences of individual moral agents. The pope maintains that a person's conscience could not be understood when abstracted from society's conscience. The individual conscience is formed, in part, by the conscience of society. This formation is mediated through both cultural and structural realities.

The conceptual development from *Reconciliatio et paenetentia* to *Evangelium vitae* was likely grounded in John Paul's experience of the Western world's creation of a "culture of death," which is related to structures that "go against life." Unfortunately, John Paul did not elaborate on how, and to what extent, culture acts. He did not explain the qualifier *quodammodo*. Nor did he unpack the relationship of society, culture, and structure. His final word on the subject did not clarify his position but only created further ambiguity.

Benedict XVI and the Dormancy of the Concept

Benedict XVI rarely employed the concept of structures of sin in his papal writings. His most prominent use of the term was toward the end of his papacy, when he noted that "over these fifty years, we have learned and experienced that original sin exists, and that it translates itself into personal sins which can become structures of sin."[51] This marked the resurrection of a concept that had been dormant since the death of John Paul II.

Benedict envisioned structures as more malleable and open to change through personal action than John Paul and the Latin American bishops. For Benedict, social, political, and economic structures were not durable realities that had a level of existence that was different from that of persons. Instead, he typically wrote of structures as the accumulated, collective actions of persons. Ultimately, for him, structures were reducible to individual actions. For this reason, he rarely referred to the existence of "unjust structures" and instead focused on vicious persons.[52]

Following John Paul, Benedict recognized that "instruments" can produce harmful effects. Also, he at least nominally recognized that sin can permeate social structures when he recalled that "the Church's wisdom has always pointed to the presence of original sin in social conditions and the structure of society."[53] However, he hesitated to offer a substantive moral judgment of impersonal instruments, institutions, or structures. Instead, his moral focus was trained on the individuals who created and sustained specific instruments and structures. In a passage that betrays his understanding of the ethical nature of impersonal structures, he writes,

> Admittedly, the market can be a negative force, not because it is so by nature, but because a certain ideology can make it so. It must be remembered that the market does not exist in the pure state. It is shaped by the cultural configurations which define it and give it direction. Economy and finance, as instruments, can be used badly when those at the helm are motivated by purely selfish ends. Instruments that are good in themselves can thereby be transformed into harmful ones. But it is man's darkened reason that produces these consequences, not the instruments per se. Therefore it is not the instrument

that must be called to account, but individuals, their moral conscience and their personal and social responsibility.[54]

There is a similar pattern of thought throughout the encyclical. The pope argues for the development and use of ethical structures, mechanisms, and institutions, while concomitantly underscoring that individuals create these realities.[55] Here, social structures are limited in their causal capacities to secure integral human development.[56] Benedict views the relationship between persons and structures not as a mutually influencing dialectic but rather as a unidirectional formation of structures by persons. In Benedict, we find a pope who emphasized the personal moral agency involved in creating and sustaining structures.[57]

Francis and Unjust Structures and Institutions

In a 2007 speech to his fellow Latin American bishops, Cardinal Bergoglio (now Pope Francis) gave a sign of things to come when he argued that "the unjust distribution of goods persists, creating a situation of social sin that cries out to heaven and limits the possibilities of a fuller life for so many of our brothers." This language has continued during his papacy.

Francis has written and spoken often on social, economic, and ecclesial structures. His focus on ecclesial structures, and the need to reform them, is novel in recent papal writings. Although his work on ecclesial structures is important, this study focuses on his analysis of social and economic structures. And though many works in Francis's corpus address social structural issues, the most developed are his 2013 encyclical, *Evangelii gaudium*, and his 2015 encyclical on the environment, *Laudato si'*.

In November 2013 Francis articulated his vision for the Catholic Church in his apostolic exhortation *Evangelii gaudium*. The exhortation repeatedly addresses social structures. Three themes emerge in his treatment on the topic. First, he notes that structures are real and have a moral nature:

> The socioeconomic system is unjust at its root. Just as goodness tends to spread, the toleration of evil, which is injustice, tends to expand its baneful influence and quietly to undermine any political and social system, no matter how solid it may appear. If every action has its consequences, an evil embedded in the structures of a society has a constant potential for disintegration and death. It is evil crystallized in unjust social structures, which cannot be the basis of hope for a better future.[58]

Notice that Francis does not refer to the structures as sinful but rather as evil and unjust. Unjust structures are evil because they produce "disintegration and death." Here, Francis finds fault in impersonal structures. The text implies that structures are not reducible to the accumulated actions of individual agents. Instead, structures have existence that goes beyond the singular actions of persons.

Second, Francis argues that unjust social structures cause poverty. In paragraph 188, he writes, "Jesus' command to his disciples: 'You yourselves give them something to eat!' (Mk 6:37): means working to eliminate the structural causes of poverty and to promote the integral development of the poor, as well as small daily acts of solidarity in meeting the real needs which we encounter."[59] In paragraph 202, he returns to this theme and expounds on it:

> The need to resolve the structural causes of poverty cannot be delayed, not only for the pragmatic reason of its urgency for the good order of society, but because society needs to be cured of a sickness which is weakening and frustrating it, and which can only lead to new crises. Welfare projects, which meet certain urgent needs, should be considered merely temporary responses. As long as the problems of the poor are not radically resolved by rejecting the absolute autonomy of markets and financial speculation and by attacking the structural causes of inequality, no solution will be found for the world's problems or, for that matter, to any problems. Inequality is the root of social ills.[60]

These quotations show that Francis has moved Church teaching closer to that of Gutiérrez and Boff and their notions of the "dialectical explanation of poverty." Although Francis has rejected their overtly Marxist language, he agrees with these thinkers insofar as they all maintain that systemic poverty and inequality are not accidents of history or the result of indolence.[61] His thought is also reminiscent of John Paul II in *Evangelium vitae*, paragraph 24, where the Polish pope recognizes the causal power of social structures. *Evangelii gaudium* argues that the moral development of individual persons is insufficient for justice to flourish. Structures, due to their "agency," also must change.

Third, Francis argues for a strong, mutually influencing dialectic between persons and structures. He notes that structures make it easier for agents to habituate vicious behaviors, such as "inordinate consumption."[62] He then follows John Paul II in arguing that when society is organized in a particular manner, it can hinder the acquisition of the virtues.[63] Francis has underscored that social structures direct and influence the development of personal action and character.

In concert with every pope from Leo XIII onward, he has argued that structures are not determined by an impersonal force, such as history. Francis notes that "what we need, then, is to give priority to actions which generate new processes in society and engage other persons and groups who can develop them to the point where they bear fruit in significant historical events."[64] In a move toward Benedict's approach, Francis argues that the human family creates its history through actions that produce new structures in society. In fact, through virtuous habits of solidarity, persons "open the way to other structural transformations and make them possible."[65] Here, personal virtues can create new social structures. Further, personal virtue must accompany structural change for the stability of the latter. In a sentence that echoes the Latin American bishops at Medellín, Francis argues that "changing structures without generating new convictions and attitudes will only ensure that those same structures will become, sooner or later, corrupt, oppressive and ineffectual."[66] In short, personal conversion is needed because vicious persons will eventually redirect structures to their selfish ends.

Laudato si' builds on *Evangelii gaudium*. First, whereas in *Evangelii gaudium* Francis writes of "structures," in *Laudato si'* he focuses on "culture" and "institutions." *Laudato si'* presents a contemporary global culture that has failed to address the ecological crisis. This is the case because "we lack leadership capable of striking out on new paths and meeting the needs of the present with concern for all and without prejudice towards coming generations."[67] The leadership deficit seems to be due to the two regnant moral cultures of the twenty-first century: relativism and utilitarianism.[68] Decisions are either informed by a lack of moral logic or by a purely instrumental logic. This leads Francis to call for a "cultural revolution," the creation of a "counterculture," and the creation of "new lifestyles."[69]

Second, *Laudato si'* modifies aspects of the interplay of personal action and social change that *Evangelii gaudium* endorsed. In *Laudato si'* Francis implores individuals to pursue moral transformation, to cultivate sound virtues, and to convert spiritually.[70] But the transformation of the world in *Laudato si'* is a societal, not individual, endeavor: "Isolated individuals can lose their ability and freedom to escape the utilitarian mind-set, and end up prey to an unethical consumerism bereft of social, or ecological awareness. Social problems must be addressed by community networks and not simply by the sum of individual good deeds."[71] Here, Francis strongly rejects an individualist approach to ecological justice. This constitutes a development from *Evangelii gaudium*'s claim that priority should be given to "actions which generate new processes in society" and Benedict's insistence that "it is not the instrument that must be called to account, but individuals ... and their personal and social responsibility." In *Laudato si'* Francis argues that mechanisms, or institutions, constrain personal agency. Thus, the solution to social problems is found in collective action and through the reformation of institutions. More specifically,

> political institutions and various other social groups are also entrusted with helping to raise people's awareness. So too is the Church. All Christian communities have an important role to play in ecological education. It is my hope that our seminaries and houses of formation will provide an education in responsible simplicity of life, in grateful contemplation of God's world, and in concern for the needs of the poor and the protection of the environment. Because the stakes are so high, we need institutions empowered to impose penalties for damage inflicted on the environment. But we also need the personal qualities of self-control and willingness to learn from one another.[72]

This passage contends that personal moral character is relevant to the ecological crisis but is an insufficient solution. The solution is both found in personal conversion and in the emergence of strong institutions in the political and religious spheres. To this end, *Laudato si'* proposes enforceable international agreements as a first-line therapy. Francis writes that it is "essential to devise stronger and more efficiently organized international institutions, with functionaries who are appointed fairly by agreement among national governments, and empowered to impose sanctions."[73] In focusing more on the causal power of institutions, and less on the causal power of individual actions, Francis's understanding of social change has developed since *Evangelii gaudium*.

In sum, Francis has reinvigorated the Church's ability to morally analyze impersonal social structures by placing his critique of oppressive and destructive structures and institutions at the center, not the periphery, of his ethics. His first and most important contribution has been the recognition that structures and institutions are real, have causal power, and have a moral nature. In this way, he has retrieved the thought of the later John Paul II. *Laudato si'*, his most authoritative document in moral theology, emphasizes a more institutional approach to global problem solving. Francis has been clear and consistent in his insistence that social structures and institutions can exert causal influence on moral agency. The overall trajectory of Francis's teaching regarding social structures is toward a moral theory that takes seriously social structures and institutions as analogical moral agents.

STRUCTURE, AGENCY, AND SIN IN THE WORK OF CONTEMPORARY THEOLOGIANS

Although magisterial accounts of the structure-agency problem have been inadequate, Christian ethicists have begun to develop a better understanding of the relation of social realities and personal moral agency and action. David Cloutier and William Mattison make the case that the communal formation of personal character is the area in most need of development in Catholic virtue ethics.[74] Along similar lines, Lisa Sowle Cahill has called for a reappraisal of moral agency. She argues that "the person is not an 'adequate' starting point because the communities and social relations that shape personal identity and agency are also essential. In addition to the person, we need to consider traditions and communities 'integrally and adequately.'"[75]

Cloutier, Mattison, and Cahill have identified a problem that has plagued theological ethics since the literature recognized the complex interplay among structures, culture, and agency in the work of the Latin American liberation theologians. However, the early work of North American Catholic theologians on social/structural sin has reflected the Magisterium's accounts of the relation of structure and agency. Unlike the liberation theologians, North Americans typically have not employed Marxist social analysis. Indeed, the latter group is still searching for a language with which to discuss what makes structural sin "structural."

For example, in a commentary on John Paul II's *Sollicitudo rei socialis*, Gregory Baum defines structural sin as "institutional realities, such as colonialism and imperialism, that create an unjust distribution of wealth, power, and recognition, and thus push a section of the population to the margin of society where their well-being or even their life is in danger."[76] Here, Baum reduces structures to what he calls institutions but fails to define the term. Such conceptual deficits significantly undercut his claim that colonialism and imperialism are "sinful." Although people agree that something is dehumanizing about these social realities, Baum does not explain the mechanics that render them so.

In a remarkable and provocative essay, Christine Gudorf argues that structures could directly sin and also coerce individuals into sinning against others. Here, we find a more advanced understanding of structure. She explains that structures are more than the sum of individual actions. She suggests but does not develop the notion that structures exist independently of human agents and agency. Further, she convincingly argues that structures, such as Jim Crow laws, once in place, constrain the agency of certain actors, such as judges, prosecutors, and police.[77]

Although the main thrust of her argument is that structures incur moral responsibility and guilt, she makes several additional points that pertain to the project at hand. First, she suggests that moral theology should penetrate the complexity of social structures and systems. To do so, she argues that social analysis would be increasingly important for the discipline if it is to "combat the sin which emanates" from social structures.[78] She does not, however, furnish a developed notion of what a structure is, or a solution to the structure-agency problem. Like Baum, "structure" is assumed to be a colloquial term and not an academic one. This assumption, I show in chapter 3, is mistaken.

Others have drawn more explicitly on social theory to explain what might make a sin "structural" or "social." Kenneth Himes and Mark O'Keefe each has turned to the dialectical solution to the structure-agency problem offered by Peter Berger and Thomas Luckmann in their important work *The Social Construction of Reality*.[79] Himes argues that to assess an individual's responsibility for social sin, one needs to understand "the dialectic between consciousness and society."[80] In summarizing the Berger-Luckmann approach, Himes writes that "on one hand, human beings shape and influence the spirit of the age while, on the other hand, we are all shaped by our social location. What has been objectified in the social structure of communal life can become internalized within a person's consciousness."[81]

Although Himes presents the broad outlines of Berger and Luckmann, Mark O'Keefe takes a more granular look at the text. In his book *What Are They Saying about Social Sin?* O'Keefe recounts the development of social sin in the Catholic tradition. The text is unique because it provides an extended discussion of how theologians have used social theory in their work. Like Gudorf, O'Keefe recognizes that specific terms, such as social structure, "are used without careful definitions and appropriate distinctions."[82] He argues that one should "offer some definitions for the most frequently used terms such as 'structures,' 'institutions,' and 'systems.'... When used according to more strictly sociological usage, these terms often connote differing 'levels' of social reality."[83]

In his chapter on sociological perspectives on social reality, O'Keefe notes that some theologians have turned to Berger and Luckmann to aid their work on a theology of social sin. O'Keefe quotes the shorthand for their theory, which states, "Society is a human product. Society is an objective reality. Man is a social product."[84] Interestingly, the chapter goes beyond a simple recounting of the work of other authors. True to his belief that sociological terms should be controlled and defined, O'Keefe offers his own definition of social structure, which draws on the work of Berger and Luckmann: "A social structure is an ordered pattern of relations that is established and becomes routine. Structures involve policies and institutions that make up the patterns of societal organization as well as the worldviews, perspectives, and value systems by which we interpret our experiences so as to bring coherence and meaning into our lives. Structures, therefore, are both external and internal to the individual person."[85]

O'Keefe's account of social structure is the most developed account in the theoethical literature until the middle of the second decade of the twenty-first century. But his account is not without its problems and limits. He argues that social structures are "both external and internal to the individual person." And he later explains that though persons are influenced by a structure, they remain free. These claims require explication, as the former suggests that the person lacks internal critical distance from the structure in which she participates. Here, O'Keefe claims that structure and agency exist in a dyad, where the structure so thoroughly seeps into the consciousness and conscience of the agent that the structure exists in the agency of the person herself. The moral agency of such a person would not be as free as O'Keefe's later claim would suggest.

Others have followed O'Keefe and Himes in their appropriation of Berger and Luckmann. Kristin Heyer has several works that are sensitive to social theory. In her work, one finds a transition to a more sociologically aware account of structure and agency. Drawing on Berger and Luckmann, Heyer notes that "structures are then both consequential and causal in nature, and we are subjectively responsible for sinful situations yet remain subject to external influences."[86]

My first attempt at developing an account of structural virtue and vice drew on Berger and Luckmann. There, like O'Keefe, I argued that their tripartite process of externalization, objectification, and internalization "would enable the tradition to more precisely define the moral nature and influence of structures and institutions."[87] As I show in chapter 3, I now believe that a better solution to the structure-agency problem is available.

Shaji George Kochuthara has lamented that one of the great failures of Catholic ethics is that it has not attended to structural problems, such as the dowry system in India.[88] Kochuthara endorses a dialectical relationship between the social structures and personal sins that is reminiscent of those who draw on Berger and Luckmann's approach. Ada María Isasi-Díaz draws on the work of Iris Marion Young to argue that social oppression refers to the systemic constraints that are embedded in cultural norms and institutional rules.[89] Isasi-Díaz urges theologians to differentiate among the various modes of oppression, such as exploitation, marginalization, and cultural imperialism. She argues that oppression should be clearly explained because this "forces us to make options concrete enough to play a central role in devising strategies for radical social change."[90]

Gerald Beyer's work has taken up structural issues as well. In an article on justice for workers, he writes that "numerous social structures, such as the market economy, do more or less stringently condition our actions today. Nonetheless, consumers, investors, and entrepreneurs still retain their freedom and responsibility if they know about the exploitation and injustices involved in their market transactions."[91]

Later, Beyer directly quotes the work of the social theorist Pierpaolo Donati, who has written that "moral responsibility is thus proportional to the degrees of freedom available."[92] Beyer rightly argues that consumers are both constrained by social structures and free to act or not act in specific ways. But this analysis could be made sharper by an account of how, exactly, the market economy conditions agency and free choice. As this section shows, contemporary Catholic ethics cries out for such social analysis.

In January 2017 the Annual Meeting of the Society of Christian Ethics took up the theme of structural evil. The conference proceedings contain many mentions of structure, structural evil, and social sin. But tellingly, only three papers in the proceedings define "structure." Wonchul Shin and Elizabeth Bounds draw on the work of two social theorists, Iris Marion Young and Pierre Bourdieu, to address the types of moral harm that befall those who inhabit vulnerable social positions. Young's work provides them with an account of sociostructural processes, which include a portrait of how social positions present constraints on agency. They also draw on Young's notion of shared responsibility for structural harm. The shared responsibility to repair the damage caused by social structures, they argue, should be "practiced on a structural or institutional level as well as an interpersonal level."[93] Shin and Bounds mine Bourdieu's thought for his notion of *habitus*. *Habitus*, according to Shin and Bounds, emerges when an individual unconsciously appropriates dispositions from social structures.[94] Shin and Bounds use Bourdieu's *habitus* to enable them to explain why and how persons in dominant social positions unconsciously reproduce types of social harm, such as racism and sexism.

David Cloutier's piece employs a critical realist account of a social structure.[95] There, Cloutier offers critical realism as a corrective to some of the work of William Cavanaugh and Katie Grimes. Cloutier argues that "Grimes and Cavanaugh would be helped by modifying their analyses ... in ways that more clearly name existing restrictions, enablements, and incentives that affect the interests and situational logics of various agents."[96] Here, Cloutier argues that Grimes and Cavanaugh need to produce sharper explanations of the relation of social realities and human agency. In short, they require a social theory.

Grimes's important book *Christ Divided: Antiblackness as Corporate Vice* introduces the notion of corporate virtue and vice. There, Grimes gestures toward, but does not develop, Bourdieu's notion of *habitus* to support her claim that antiblackness supremacy is a corporate vice. Grimes argues that antiblackness supremacy, "shaping bodies materially and contouring our perception of them, . . . encourages certain bodies to cleave together and others to remain apart."[97] However, though Grimes's notion of corporate vice is rhetorically powerful, the institutional mechanisms through the Church's corporate body can have an "appetite for racial stasis" remain unclear.[98] As Cloutier suggests regarding her earlier work, Grimes's account of corporate virtue and vice is ripe for further conceptual development.

In her presidential address, Society of Christian Ethics president Cristina Traina defines structural evil as the comprehensive complex of interdependent, overlapping systems that—by distributing risks, benefits, and harm unequally—generates an oversupply of violence, insecurity, and disadvantage for some and relative immunity from them for others. Because systems involve institutions, and institutions have actors, participation in structural evil is inescapable.[99]

Although her attention to structural evil is laudatory (as is her decision to focus the conference on structural evil), Traina's account could be rendered more precisely. What is a system? What is an institution? And what is the relation of institutions and "actors"? Further, because the theme of the conference was structural evil, Traina's piece would be enriched from a descriptive, morally neutral account of structure before she categorized certain structures as "evil." Thus, the proceedings of the Society of Christian Ethics show that theological ethicists are taking promising steps toward an understanding of social structures and that work remains to be done. Cloutier and Shin and Bounds indicate the way forward.

Finally, the recent research of Daniel Finn has been pathbreaking. It contains a decisively sociological answer to the question of what a social structure is and how structures causally affect human action. His work has argued that critical realist social theory provides the most accurate account of social reality. I prescind from a presentation of critical realism at the moment as it is taken up in depth in the next chapter. Finn's 2014 edited volume, *Distant Markets, Distant Harms: Economic Complicity and Christian Ethics* brings together critical realist social theorists and theologians on the structure-agency problem.[100] Next, Finn's 2016 article "What Is a Sinful Social Structure?" argues that Catholic social ethics "has no coherent account of what a social structure is" and thus should turn to critical realist social theory.[101] Finally, his 2019 monograph, *Consumer Ethics in a Global Economy*, contains an extended explanation and use of critical realism and other conceptual frameworks in social theory to analyze the ethical problems caused by a global market economy.[102] There, Finn argues that the social sciences offer "a re-conceived view of the market as a social structure that allows Christians to articulate the causal foundations for moral judgment about our responsibilities in a globalized world."[103] Finn's corpus in the second decade of the twenty-first century offers the most extensive accounts of social structures and their relation to human agency, institutions, and culture in the Catholic ethical tradition.

THE STATE OF THE QUESTION

Where does this leave theological ethics regarding a solution to the structure-agency problem? The emergence of the concept of the structures of sin in the work of Latin American liberation theologians provided a helpful account of the moral nature of social structures. Gutiérrez, Dussel, the Boff brothers, and others convinced many ethicists of the importance of using the social sciences. However, liberation theologians generally were not as interested in producing substantive theoretical accounts of social realities, such as social structures, as they were in naming the actual structures that dealt death and misery across the continent. Those who did so turned to Marx as a social critic, not a philosopher. However, though Marxist social analysis is vital in the development of the discipline of social theory, such analysis has been surpassed in contemporary social theory.

The magisterial appropriation of the "structures of sin" was, likewise, sociologically undertheorized. John Paul's claim that the structures of sin are the "sum total of negative factors" is much too imprecise to be of use when analyzing a situation such as sweatshop labor or global warming. The Magisterium's one attempt at a definition of "structure" was, likewise, inadequate. In the 1986 "Instruction on Liberation Theology," the Congregation for the Doctrine of the Faith defined social structures as "sets of institutions and practices... which orient or organize economic, social, and political life."[104] This account of the structure is unrecognizable from a sociological perspective. Also, the definition notes that human beings create and can alter social structures. Again, there is no elaboration on how such creation and alteration transpire.

This is a problem for a tradition in which understanding reality is a precondition for moral analysis. Just as one cannot make a cogent moral claim about abortion before one knows what a fetus, zygote, or blastocyst is, one cannot make strong socioethical claims if one does not know what a structure is and how structures and agency relate.

However, this chapter has shown that magisterial teaching is rife with implicit notions of what a structure is. John Paul's early thought saw structures as aggregated individual actions, while his later thought suggested that structures have a durable reality that is not simply the addition of personal actions. Benedict's implied notion of structure was consistent and mapped with the earlier statements of John Paul. Francis's thought has aligned with that of the later John Paul. He has suggested that structures and agency are distinct but not separate. Implicit within his view is that social structures are real and have causal power; they shape human and environmental outcomes. As one can see, these are underdeveloped, unreflective notions that, when viewed as a whole, are incoherent. What is the Church's official account of a structure? Well, that depends on whom you ask and how much you read between the lines.

Additionally, North American theologians consistently have failed to control sociological terms such as "structure" or "institution." If one quickly peruses works of theological ethics on social structures, one finds that these sociological concepts are used in colloquial, nonacademic ways. By contrast, medical ethicists typically define concepts such as "embryo," "congestive heart failure," and the like according to the standard definitions of the academic medical community. This chapter has shown that the work of Gudorf, Himes, O'Keefe, Heyer, Cloutier, Finn, and others is the exception, not the rule.

The shift to a more sociological account of social realities is in its infancy. This chapter has identified a number of schools of thought regarding structures within the discipline. Berger and Luckmann have informed the first generation of North American Catholic reflection on social or structural sin. Their approach continues to inform the work of prominent social ethicists such as Kristin Heyer. More recently, some have turned to Iris Marion Young and Pierre Bourdieu, while others have turned to critical realism, a school of social theory, to explain social reality.

The structure-agency problem wrestles with questions such as these: How do people form structures? How do structures form people? What is the relationship between culture and structures? There are two kinds of questions here. The first kind involve the nature of social structures—what they are, how they function in the world, and how they are shaped and transformed. These questions are essential for Christian ethics because they ask how structures causally contribute to human outcomes, such as health, education, and political liberty. The second kind of questions regard how personal moral agency is affected by social structures. Personal character is formed, to a certain degree, by the structures of society. Then how, exactly, do social structures play a causal role in how people act and who they become? These kinds of questions are important for Christian ethics because they pertain to how social structures shape the virtues and vices of moral agents.

THE NEED FOR A BETTER ACCOUNT

This chapter has shown the need for a better account of the relationship between structure and agency in the Catholic tradition. Specifically, the explanatory capacity and output power of Catholic ethics as a whole have been diminished because the discipline lacks a solution to the structure-agency problem.

Francis's focus on the structures that cause global poverty and the destruction of the climate presents the Church with an especially appropriate moment to pursue a more refined ethical understanding of social, political, and economic structures. Vatican II signaled a break with the narrow ethics of sin avoidance that was present in the manuals and championed a more socially aware ethics that recognized the importance of structures. However, the tradition requires further development. For instance, the Rana Plaza case still poses significant challenges to Catholic ethical concepts and methods. Francis no more easily answers the questions that I posed at the outset of this chapter than they might have been by Benedict. The work of both pontiffs lacks a developed social theory. As the chapter has shown, the same is true for the work of many Catholic theologians.

The way forward requires Catholic ethicists to heed the call of Ada María Isasi-Díaz to be specific regarding what constitutes systemic injustice. This will require a more profound engagement among social theory and social ethics. As I argued in chapter 1, the moral dynamics of structures and agency should be one of the "growing end(s) of the tradition."[105] Catholic theologians are only now beginning to deliver a substantive treatment on the moral nature of structures and institutions and how these realities relate to human agency and action. As they continue to do so, they will need to draw deeply on sociological, economic, and political thought. Further, the discipline requires a solution to the structure-agency problem that comports with core Christian commitments. Nicholas Wolterstorff's book, *Reason within the Bounds of Religion*, argues that Christians should approach disciplines such as psychology with control beliefs in mind. That is, their previous religious commitments to, for example, the nature of human freedom within human agency compel them to reject theories of neurological determinism that claim that human persons are not truly free moral agents.[106]

As I argue in the next chapter, critical realism provides a social theory that insightfully explains the complex interplay between free moral agents and objective social structures. If the Church is to offer true and convincing ethical claims, it must provide a keener analysis of the moral nature of structures in contemporary life.

NOTES

1. I am grateful that *New Blackfriars* permitted me to use material from my article "Structures of Virtue and Vice." I am also grateful that Lexington Books permitted me to use material from a previously published chapter, "Confronting the 'Normative Abyss': The Challenges and Resources in Catholic Ethics for the Global Age."
2. Leo XIII, *Rerum novarum*, 27.
3. Leo XIII, 22.
4. Pfeil, "Magisterial Use," 134.
5. Marciano Vidal argues this point in "Structural Sin," 183. Maurizio Ragazzi provides a helpful summary of magisterial use and development on the social and structural nature of sin; see Ragazzi, "Concept."
6. Second Vatican Council, *Lumen gentium*, chapter II, 36.
7. See Second Vatican Council, *Gaudium et spes*.
8. Second Vatican Council, 1–10.
9. Second Vatican Council, 68, 74.
10. Second Vatican Council, 26.
11. Second Vatican Council, 25.
12. "When the structure of affairs is flawed by the consequence of sin, man, already born with a bend toward evil, finds there new inducements to sin, which cannot be overcome without strenuous efforts and the assistance of grace." Second Vatican Council, 25.
13. See Carroll, "Church," 164–69.
14. Keenan, "Vatican II," 190.
15. Latin American Bishops, *Church*, I: 2.
16. Latin American Bishops, I: 2.
17. Latin American Bishops, I: 2.
18. Latin American Bishops, I: 3.
19. Synod of Bishops, *Justicia in mundo*, 290.
20. Synod of Bishops, 296.
21. Gutiérrez, *Theology*, 100–101.
22. Gutiérrez, 102.
23. Gutiérrez, 5.
24. Dussel, "Theology," 87.
25. Boff and Boff, *Introducing Liberation Theology*, 25–28.
26. Petrella, *Future*, 27.
27. Segundo, "Human Rights," 66.
28. Dussel, "Theology," 86.
29. Dussel, 86–87.
30. Archbishop Óscar Romero often wrote and spoke of "institutionalized violence," "structures of sin," and "social sin." See Romero, *Voice*, 68, 143, 183.

31. Latin American Bishops, *Evangelization*, 1264.
32. Latin American Bishops, 385–96.
33. Latin American Bishops, 436–38; see also 362. There the bishops write that "evangelization should penetrate deeply into the hearts of human beings and peoples. Thus its dynamism aims at personal conversion and social transformation."
34. Latin American Bishops, 438.
35. Brackley and Schubeck, "Moral Theology," 123–60.
36. Latin American Bishops, *Evangelization*, 1134–66.
37. See Congregation for the Doctrine of the Faith, "Instruction on Certain Aspects"; and Congregation for the Doctrine of the Faith, "Instruction on Christian Freedom."
38. See John Paul II, *Reconciliatio et paenetentia*, 16; and John Paul II, *Sollicitudo rei socialis*, 36.
39. Pfeil, "Magisterial Use," 140.
40. John Paul II, *Reconciliatio et paenetentia*, 16.
41. The analogical nature of social sin is reminiscent of the Church's teaching on original sin. Paragraph 404 of *The Catechism of the Catholic Church* remarks that "original sin is called 'sin' only in an analogical sense: it is a sin 'contracted' and not 'committed'—a state and not an act."
42. See Congregation for the Doctrine of the Faith, "Instruction on Christian Freedom," as well as the earlier document, Congregation for the Doctrine of the Faith, "Instruction on Certain Aspects."
43. Congregation for the Doctrine of the Faith, "Instruction on Christian Freedom," 74.
44. John Paul II, *Sollicitudo rei socialis*, 36. See Second Vatican Council, *Gaudium et spes*, 25, quoted above. See also Congregation for the Doctrine of the Faith, "Instruction on Certain Aspects," 14, 15.
45. For a theo-ethical treatment of the solidarity movement in Poland, see Beyer, *Recovering Solidarity*.
46. John Paul II, *Sollicitudo rei socialis*, 38.
47. Goulet, "Search," 130.
48. Dorr, *Option*, 299.
49. John Paul II, *Centessimus annus*, 38.
50. John Paul II, *Evangelium vitae*, 24. The original Latin reads, "*Ipsa in intima morali conscientia perficitur Dei hominisque sensus obscuratio, multiplicibus suis perniciosisque de vita consecutionibus. Ante omnia cuiusque conscientia in medio ponitur, quae una et non iterabilis sola Dei in conspectu stat* [cf. Second Vatican Council, *Gaudium et spes*, no. 16]. *At agitur quoque ratione quadam de societatis 'conscientia morali'; ipsa quodammodo est responsalis non modo quia tolerat vel consuetudinibus vitae adversantibus favet, verum quia et 'mortis culturam' alit, quippe quae ipsas 'structuras peccati' adversum vitam efficiat et confirmet. Conscientia moralis, tum personalis tum socialis, etiam ob instrumentorum socialis communicationis praepotentes virtutes, pergravi mortiferoque periculo hodie subditur: permixtionis scilicet boni malique, quod attinet ad idem fundamentale vitae ius.*"
51. Benedict XVI, "Benediction."
52. See Benedict XVI, "World Day of Peace Message, 2013." There he wrote that "mankind can overcome that progressive dimming and rejection of peace which is sin in all its forms: selfishness and violence, greed and the will to power and dominion, intolerance, hatred and unjust structures," paragraph 3.
53. Benedict XVI, *Caritas*, 34.
54. Benedict XVI, 36.
55. Benedict XVI, 42, 68.

56. Benedict XVI, 11, 20.
57. Daly, "Structures," 352.
58. Francis, *Evangelii gaudium*, 59.
59. Francis, 188.
60. Francis, 202.
61. Caño and Ordaz, "Peligro."
62. Caño and Ordaz, 60.
63. Francis, *Evangelii gaudium*, 196, quoting John Paul II, *Centessimus annus*, 41.
64. Francis, 223.
65. Francis, 189.
66. Francis. See Latin American Bishops, *Church*, I: 3.
67. Francis, *Laudato si'*, 53.
68. Francis, 101, 123.
69. Francis, 114, 108, 203.
70. Francis, 211, 217.
71. Francis, 219.
72. Francis, 214.
73. Francis, 175.
74. Cloutier and Mattison, "Resurgence," 231.
75. Cahill, "Reframing Catholic Ethics," responding to Selling, *Reframing Catholic Ethics*.
76. Baum, "Structures," 110–26.
77. Gudorf, "Admonishing Sinners," 4.
78. Gudorf, 14–22.
79. Himes, "Social Sin." See also Berger and Luckmann, *Social Construction*.
80. Himes, "Social Sin," 192.
81. Himes.
82. O'Keefe, *Social Sin?* 45.
83. O'Keefe, 46.
84. O'Keefe, 43, citing Berger and Luckmann, *Social Construction*, 61. The more developed account by Berger and Luckmann is found in the concepts of externalization, objectification, and internalization. In a later work, *The Sacred Canopy*, Berger summarizes the account like this (p. 4): "Externalization is the ongoing outpouring of human being into the world ... objectification is the attainment by the products of this activity of a reality that confronts its original producers as a facticity external to and other than themselves. Internalization is the re-appropriation by men of this same reality, transforming it once again from structure of the objective world into structures of subjective consciousness."
85. O'Keefe, *Social Sin?* 46.
86. Heyer, "Social Sin," 425. Here, Heyer seems to marry Berger and Luckmann with a modification of a line in the Congregation for the Doctrine of the Faith's 1984 "Instruction on Certain Aspects." In part IV, paragraph 15 of the congregation's document, the authors write that "structures, whether good or bad, are the result of human actions and so are more consequences than causes." Heyer's point is that structures are both and equally consequences and causes, as Berger and Luckmann would have it.
87. Daly, "Structures," 353.
88. Kochuthara, "Dowry," 114.
89. Isasi-Díaz, "Spirituality," 253.
90. Isasi-Díaz, 254.

91. Beyer, "Advocating Worker Justice," 234.
92. Beyer.
93. Shin and Bounds, "Treating Moral Harm," 166.
94. Shin and Bounds, 160, quoting Bourdieu, *Distinction*, 170.
95. At this point, I forgo an explanation of the central tenets of critical realism because it is the topic of chapter 3.
96. Cloutier, "Cavanaugh and Grimes," 72. There, Cloutier reflected on these works by Cavanaugh: *Theopolitical Imagination*; "Future"; *Migrations*; and *Field Hospital*. He also considered these works by Grimes: "Breaking"; "Racialized Humility"; "Butler Interprets Aquinas"; and "But Do the Lord Care?"
97. Grimes, *Christ Divided*, 181. Grimes makes a passing reference to Bourdieu on p. xxiv.
98. Grimes, 182.
99. Traina, "'This Is the Year,'" 4.
100. Finn, *Distant Markets*.
101. Finn, "What Is a Sinful Social Structure?" 138.
102. Finn, *Consumer Ethics*.
103. Finn, 108.
104. Congregation for the Doctrine of the Faith, "Instruction on Christian Freedom," 74.
105. Murray, "Problem," 561.
106. Wolterstorff, *Reason within the Bounds*, chap. 11.

PART II

Resources

CHAPTER 3

The Critical Realist Solution to the Structure-Agency Problem

The sociologist Michael Landon has argued that the emergence of the concept of social sin in liberation theology was predicated on presupposed, and largely unarticulated, social theories.¹ One can legitimately make the same claim regarding most work in Catholic social ethics today. As chapter 2 showed, magisterial and theological ethics has operated with an underdeveloped understanding of the relationship between social realities and personal moral character. What is needed is an in-depth account of what a structure is and a plausible solution to the structure-agency problem. The goal of this chapter is to identify a social theory that (1) provides an accurate description of reality and (2) comports with Catholic commitments regarding the nature of the person and society.

The chapter proceeds in four sections. The first one argues that a social ethics, especially one concerned with social change and personal conversion, contains an implied understanding of social structures. The second section argues that Catholic ethics must be critical regarding its social theory and should employ a social theory that accurately describes reality and comports with core Catholic theological beliefs—called "control beliefs." The third section surveys prominent contemporary social theories and critiques them in light of Catholic control beliefs. An argument for critical realist social theory is the purpose of the fourth section. There I draw on key critical realist scholars such as Margaret Archer and Dave Elder-Vass to explain their solution to the structure-agency problem. Further, I show how it meets the two conditions of a good social theory that I laid out in the chapter's second section. The material covered in this section is essential to the synthetic argument that is constructed in chapter 6.

One distinction is in order before I begin. As I noted in the introduction, this book focuses more on social structure than culture. Culture has received far more attention than structure in theological ethics. However, I think it is important for theological ethicists to have a more developed account of both structure and culture, and, to this end, I develop a notion of culture and employ it where appropriate. My goal, however, is to show how culture relates to structure and agency, not to address culture for its own sake.

Although the chapter unpacks both structure and culture, it is helpful to briefly consider the distinction between the two. A social structure consists of webs of relations among preexisting social positions. A university is a social structure comprising networks of relations between students, administrators, and faculty. Culture pertains to the ideas, practices, and understandings that a social group holds in common. Although many universities share a similar structure—consisting of relations between students, deans, faculty members, department chairs, and others—the very same universities have distinctive cultures regarding, for instance, the importance of athletics or the arts. Following critical realist thinkers, I contend that structure and culture are distinct social realities but are not separable. Each influences the other.

THE RELATIONSHIP OF CHRISTIAN SOCIAL ETHICS AND SOCIAL THEORY

As James Hunter argues in a chapter titled "Christian Faith and the Task of World Changing," there is an implicit social theory at play in much of religious ethics.[2] Hunter claims that many religious communities hold the "common view" of structural change. The common view maintains that structures are the accumulation of persons' values and worldviews. In this reading, social transformation is the product of personal transformation. This is reflected in the adage that "structural change arises from the bottom up, not from the top down." Hunter argues that these claims rest on a contemporary iteration of Hegelian idealism. That is, ideas directly guide action and thereby move human history and effect social change.

The moral solution, in this view, is for each person to practice the virtues. That is, structures are sustained through the aggregation of the actions of the individual actors in society. In this account, structures are "what people do." Academic structures, such as the relations between professors and students, are simply the aggregation of what professors and students do. The fact that students typically respect professors is simply the result of the actions that students typically perform. This approach, though implicit in some forms of religious ethics, is its own school of social theory: methodological individualism. As Hunter has written, "This account is almost wholly mistaken."

EXPLANATORY POWER AND CONTROL BELIEFS

Chapter 1 argued that true theories, whether social or ethical, should have explanatory capacity. More specifically, a robust social theory should provide an insightful explanation of the world as it is. This explanation should be organized and internally coherent, and it should withstand testing through a variety of examples. No single theory will entirely explain social reality, as complex as it is. Instead, we should follow Charles Taylor's lead in searching for the "best account" of social reality.[3] But understanding the "world as it is" presupposes an already-existing intellectual framework. One does not approach a new question without knowledge of how one has asked and answered previous questions. Here, the work of Nicholas Wolterstorff is helpful. In his book *Reason within the Bounds of Religion*, Wolterstorff argues that "in weighing a theory one always brings along the whole complex of one's beliefs."[4] For example, materialists will reject any theory that claims that human action arises from within the relation of the body and soul. This preexisting intellectual commitment serves as a filter through which the materialist evaluates new truth claims. One would be incapable of assessing any truth claim without such prior commitments. For instance, if one is not committed to a notion that one's experience mediates reality (however imperfectly) to one, one cannot commit to truth claims regarding reality.

More specifically, Wolterstorff claims that "the religious beliefs of the Christian scholar ought to function as control beliefs within his devising and weighing of theories." Christian "control beliefs"—namely, the core theological commitments of Christianity—serve as the canon by which theories are judged. He added that "these beliefs also shape his views on what it is important to have theories about."[5] For example, if one's social ethics advocates social transformation, it is essential to have a theory regarding how social transformation transpires.

Control beliefs function both positively and negatively. Christian faith should support and devise theories that comport with Christian beliefs and reject those that undermine and conflict with core theological commitments. The neuroscientist Sam Harris, for example, has argued that "free will *is* an illusion."[6] For Harris, human thought and action emerge "from background causes of which we are unaware and over which we exert no conscious control," much of it determined by neural activity. Although a Catholic may have a number of reasons for rejecting Harris's account of the relationship of neural activity with thought and action, surely one of them would be that Catholicism is committed to free moral agency. Therefore, if we are going to find a suitable understanding of social structures, and how structures and human agency relate, we need to be sure that these explanations comport with the key beliefs of Catholicism.

CATHOLIC CONTROL BELIEFS

Chapter 4 presents some of the core theoanthropological commitments of Catholicism. Here, I sketch three faith commitments of Catholicism to enable a critical evaluation of social theories.

Catholic thought is grounded in its commitment to the "knowability" of reality. From the beginning of the Christian tradition, it was assumed that reality could be accessed and imperfectly understood through the workings of both *fides* and *ratio*. The reverence and respect for the use of reason is first found in Saint Paul's Letter to the Romans, where he famously argues that "the Gentiles who do not have the law by nature observe the prescriptions of the law" because "they show the demands of the law are written on their hears, while their conscience also bears witness and their conflicting thoughts accuse or even defend them."[7] Even without the benefit of explicit revelation, the Gentiles, according to Paul, had access to some of the moral insights of the Jewish people. Justin Martyr repeats Paul's idea when he writes of those virtuous persons who, without divine revelation, did the good that is "universal, natural, and eternal."[8]

The first full synthesis of faith and reason was wrought in the thought of Saint Thomas Aquinas. In the first article of the first question of the *Summa theologiae*, Aquinas stakes his ground when he asks "whether, besides philosophy, any further doctrine is required?" Philosophy, for Aquinas, includes all sciences that employ reason in the pursuit of truth, such as astronomy and physics.[9] He answers that philosophical science is insufficient to know the truth about God and salvation, so faith in divine revelation is needed. Revelation is required because even though reason can be perfected through the acquisition of intellectual virtue, it remains prone to errors due to the fall of humanity.[10] At the end of the first question, he explicitly endorses both faith and reason as tools for theology: "Since therefore grace does not destroy nature, but perfects it, natural reason should minister to faith as the natural bent of the will ministers to charity. . . . Hence, sacred doctrine makes use also of the authority of philosophers in those questions in which they were able to know the truth by natural reason."[11]

The *Summa* is the result of Aquinas's ability to "make use of the authority of philosophers" in their specified areas in addition to revelation. What emerges in the text is a more complex, and more accurate, picture of reality. For Aquinas, reality is multilayered. First, he argues that physical reality exists and can be encountered through the experiences of the body. Aquinas assumes that persons have direct access to reality through their "corporeal organs."[12] His epistemology operates with the presupposition that objects external to the human mind are real and human experiences generally are to be trusted. Second, the ideas, or universals, that arise from human experience are real but immaterial. He writes, "Through the intellect, the soul knows bodies by a knowledge which is immaterial, universal, and necessary."[13] Further, these ideas are correct, insofar as he believes that "truth is the equation of thought and thing."[14] A realist epistemology is one of the foundations of his thought.[15] Finally, he maintains that spiritual realities exist and can be experienced through their activities. I know I have an intellect (which, for him, is a power of a person's spiritual soul) because I encounter it in the act of thinking.[16] I can reflect on my thinking and can thereby experience this immaterial aspect of personhood. Aquinas's portrait of reality is physical, ideational, and spiritual.

Gaudium et spes echoes Aquinas's use of faith and reason as well as his realism. There, the council fathers implicitly critique both the twentieth century's growing rationalism along with epistemological skepticism, when they write that "for (humanity's) intelligence is not confined to observable data alone, but can with genuine certitude attain to reality itself as knowable, though in consequence of sin that certitude is partly obscured and weakened."[17] According to the council fathers, the human intellect can grasp immaterial realities that go beyond the physically observable. Although human knowledge is always imperfect, due to the condition of sin, persons still can know reality in its various complex dimensions. Further, they underscore the fact that the Church learns from the nontheological sciences:

> The experience of past ages, the progress of the sciences, and the treasures hidden in the various forms of human culture, by all of which the nature of man himself is more clearly revealed and new roads to truth are opened, these profit the Church, too. For, from the beginning of her history, she has learned to express the message of Christ with the help of the ideas and terminology of various philosophers, and has tried to clarify it with their wisdom, too.[18]

Nontheological sciences help the Church to both understand and express its message. Humanity understands itself better through these sciences.

The most recent codification of the relation between faith and reason in the official tradition is Saint John Paul II's encyclical *Fides et ratio*, whose central argument is the harmony that exists between faith and reason. In an important footnote, the pope cites Galileo: "[Galileo] declared explicitly that the two truths, of faith and of science, can never contradict each other, 'Sacred Scripture and the natural world proceeding equally from the divine Word, the first as dictated by the Holy Spirit, the second as a very faithful executor of the commands of God,' as he wrote in his letter to Father Benedetto Castelli on 21 December 1613."[19]

Like the council fathers, John Paul draws on Aquinas for his synthesis of these two fonts of knowledge: "Nonetheless, in the light of faith which finds in Jesus Christ this ultimate meaning, I cannot but encourage philosophers—be they Christian or not—to trust in the power of human reason and not to set themselves goals that are too modest in their philosophizing."[20]

Further, he endorses a "realism ... of what is."[21] John Paul, like Aquinas and the council fathers, argues for an optimistic epistemology, which maintains that human reason can grasp what is real. In a related move, John Paul condemns fideism, which he argues "fails to recognize the importance of rational knowledge and philosophical discourse for the understanding of faith, indeed for the very possibility of belief in God."[22]

Finally, John Paul makes an argument on the necessity of employing philosophical anthropology and the social sciences in moral theology. He writes, "In other words, moral theology requires a sound philosophical vision of human nature and society, as well as of the general principles of ethical decision-making."[23] Although contemporary moral theology has turned to philosophical anthropology as a resource, it has less frequently and fruitfully used the social sciences in its deliberations.

In sum, any social theory that will be of use to Catholic ethics must profess to present a picture of objective reality, however imperfect. We are searching for a realist social theory. Contrast this with constructivist notions that argue that reality itself is constructed in the human mind. Such an account would hold that there is no reality independent of human "knowing" of it.[24] Further, a philosophical (including social scientific) theory must trust human reason to grasp reality, but it must not limit human knowledge to that which is gained through empirically verified experience. Materialist social theories would fail this control belief.

Chapter 4 develops a detailed account of the human person; but for this chapter, let three points suffice. The overarching anthropological commitment is to the centrality of the person. This is a personalist approach, which begins with actually existing persons. Here, the focus is on the whole person. Personalism makes three interrelated claims about persons. First, persons are "substance in relation," and relationality is the essence of personhood.

Second, all persons possess human dignity, which means that they are transcendently valuable. The source of this value is that each person has been created by, images, and is loved by God. Third and finally, many, but not all, persons have agency, which enables them to freely act and enter into relationships with others. Because these claims function as acceptance-governing principles, social theories that undercut these theoanthropological commitments need to be rejected.

PROMINENT CONTEMPORARY SOCIAL THEORIES

Before turning to critical realism, I briefly discuss and critique several competing social theories. This section is not comprehensive but instead aims to explain several prominent and influential sociological approaches.

The social theorist Pierpaolo Donati has offered a three-part typology of social structures—individualistic, holistic, and relational explanations of social reality. Although social theories cannot be reduced to these three types, the others that vie for influence have been either discredited or are difficult to take seriously. For instance, those that would make a theory out of the supposed "pure" linguistics of Jacques Derrida, in which there is nothing outside the text, or the "pure" sociology of Donald Black, essentially reduce the question of social structure and human agency to either the text or social structures.[25] The person-as-agent disappears entirely in these approaches. Let us now turn to the theories contained in Donati's typology.

Individualist Theories

Donati's first type is methodological individualism. The founder of critical realist theory, Roy Bhaskar, writes that "methodological individualism is the doctrine that facts about societies and social phenomena are to be explained solely in terms of facts about individuals."[26] This is the "micro approach" to social structures.[27] For example, this approach to structures and communities leads to statements such as Bentham's famous dictum that "the community is a fictitious body, composed of the individual persons,"[28] and Ian Jarvie's claim that "army is the plural of soldier."[29] Structures, like Bentham's community and Jarvie's army, are reducible to individual actors and their actions, and they have no existence independent of the accumulated actions of persons.

This approach is the implicit social theory of contemporary neoclassical economic theory. The neoclassical approach typically explains structures as the aggregate of the actions of rational actors. Informed by rational choice theory,[30] many economists maintain that all rational actors decide individually what is in their own best interest.[31] This occurs by weighing one's various desires and beliefs against each other to determine one's action. For example, let us imagine that on a Saturday, Brendan desires to work overtime to make extra money, and he may also desire to spend the day at the beach with his family. For the rational choice theorist, Brendan acts as a free agent, with the ability to weigh and compare these desires to arrive at his intended action. The notion that this man is a free agent, without any reference to his relation to the preexisting social structure, yields the notion that social structures are the accumulated choices of free, rational persons.

Although human agency is respected in this theory, it fails to explain how structures influence and constrain agency. Here, social structures have no unique reality. The person has been preserved in such an account, but impersonal social realities have been eliminated. This is a problem because personal choice is limited by social structures. For instance, in her book *Law's Virtues*, the legal/moral scholar Cathleen Kaveny presents the example of knighthood. She notes that in today's age, one cannot decide to become a knight.[32] Even if a person desired knighthood, contemporary social structures do not facilitate or allow for persons to assume that position in relation to others. Further, consider a person who wishes to purchase a "fair trade" sweatshirt. Finding none on the open market, she is faced with either not purchasing clothing at all or purchasing a sweatshirt that was manufactured by people who were treated unjustly. Let us assume that she bought the sweatshirt because the weather was turning colder. Rational choice economists and methodological individualists cannot fully explain this person's actions. Although she freely chose to purchase the sweatshirt, she did not freely choose the conditions under which she exercised free choice. Those conditions served to constrain her ability to buy fairly traded clothing and to enable her to purchase clothing that is less than fairly traded.

Ironically, many religious ethical systems understand social structures in this way. There is an implicit and unacknowledged individualist social theory in the writings of many churches. Recall Hunter's articulation of the "common view" of social change. This common view is predicated on an individualist presupposition, which denies the intrinsic reality of social structures and instead understands structures as reducible to the acts of individual agents. At times, Pope Benedict XVI fell victim to this perspective. In his critique of the workings of the market economy and finance, he writes that "it is not the instrument that must be called to account, but individuals, their moral consciences and their personal and social responsibility."[33] Benedict is right to hold individuals morally responsible but wrong to dismiss a moral account of "instruments" or institutions. For Benedict, the CEO of a multinational apparel company is solely to blame for the unjust wages that his corporation offers its seamstresses. The structures that compose free market capitalism are not accounted for in this mode of analysis.

There are many problems in such an analysis, beginning with the fact that here Benedict's thought does not mesh neatly with that of the later Pope John Paul II and that of Pope Francis. Again, recall the previous chapter. John Paul and Francis implicitly reject methodological individualism by recognizing structures as realities of one kind or another. This section yields two points. First, it reminds us that all religious social ethics contains an implicit social theory. My critique is that instead of remaining implicit, such theories should be explicitly acknowledged and debated.

Second, methodological individualism stands in disagreement with Catholic social thought regarding the nature of the person and the community. Specifically, it undercuts the notion that persons are interdependent and realize their own good in and through the community.[34] Catholicism rejects any pure individualist explanation of human reality because human persons are "substance in relation"; the individual is always relational. The human person is always influenced by the community. Methodological individualism reduces the person to a creature who does not exist: an unencumbered self.

Holistic Theories

Holistic social theories understand social structures, their effects, and human agency as a tightly woven web. I mention two variants here. The most prominent holistic social theory is Anthony Gidden's structuration theory. Giddens's project is partly a rejection of the dualisms that he finds in functionalism and structuralism.[35] He argues that these two prominent mid-twentieth-century theories are dualist insofar as they each maintain that social structures have causal priority over agents and their actions.[36] His goal is to avoid the reductionisms inherent in the abovementioned theories, and to preserve the importance of both structure and agency, while showing how these concepts are interdependent.

Giddens grounds this interdependence on the recursive nature of human social activities.[37] That is, social actors continually apply the rules that constitute a social structure, such that they recreate the conditions that enabled them to act at all. Language serves as his prime example. The English language allows persons to communicate. When a person employs the language and follows the rules of grammar and pronunciation, she reproduces the language. Unintentionally, she further codifies the grammar and syntax of English. For Giddens, this is evidence that structures and agents exist in duality, not dualism. He writes that "the constitution of agents and structures are not two independently given sets of phenomena, a dualism, but represent a duality."[38] Metaphorically, this is symbolized by the coin: structure and agency represent two sides of the same coin. The duality of a structure is the central proposition of structuration theory. That is, structuration theory maintains that individuals draw on social rules and resources to act in the world, and, in doing so, reproduces the social structures that confront them.[39] Structures and agents, in this account, compose a whole. Persons come to embody structures to the point that structures exist within persons. A social structure is inscribed in human bodies and minds, which allows for the production, reproduction, and transformation of structures.[40]

Giddens's most prominent critic, Margaret Archer, has argued that structuration theory conflates structure and agency. According to her, and other critics of structuration, structuration oversocializes agents who have thoroughly interiorized their social conditions. Structuration theory, then, contains two fundamental problems. First, agents cannot be distinguished from their social circumstances. Here, social structures so deeply penetrate the agent that her agency is partly composed of the structures themselves. This robs the agent of the fullness of agency. Second, "agents and structures are so closely elided that responsibility for outcomes cannot be apportioned to them."[41] Once robbed of her agency, an agent can no longer be held responsible for her "freely willed" actions. Thus, Archer argues that structure and agency do not constitute a duality but are distinct entities. As I show below, she and other critical realists do not separate structure and agency—but they do ontologically distinguish between them.

The second holistic theory is determinism, which can be neurological or sociological. The neurological version maintains that human actions arise from brain events and neural firing, not free and rational deliberation.[42] For example, actions such as shopping *happen to* the person and are not rationally chosen by her. Sociological determinism finds that society, and not a person's neural networks, are the mechanical cause of her thoughts and actions. A person's internal deliberations about buying a new pair of shoes are not properly hers. Instead, these internal deliberations (and the actions that arise from them) are "derivative from society's conversation."[43] A person's entire personality is formed and directed by social factors. There is no unique contribution of the person in her inner and outer life.

Structuration and determinism fail to satisfy the acceptance-governing principles of Catholicism. Either the person is reduced to a part of a larger social whole (structuration) or is little more than her brain chemistry (neurological determinism) or is a cog in the social wheel (sociological determinism). These approaches challenge, if not outright deny, moral freedom.

CRITICAL REALIST SOCIAL THEORY

We now turn to critical realist social theory. I argue that critical realism comports with Catholic control beliefs and provides an insightful social theory that can aid in the development of Catholic ethics. The purpose of this section is to sketch a picture of critical realism and to show how it coheres with Catholic theological commitments. This sketch and analysis are instrumental in the argument that is constructed in chapter 6.

Five aspects of critical realism, for our purposes, deserve attention. Critical realism maintains that reality exists independently of human consciousness and can be known through reason; that reality is complex and irreducible in type; that structures are realities that emerge within relations of persons and groups; that structures shape, but do not determine, agency and action; and finally, that structures and culture are mutually influencing.

The Realism of Critical Realism

Although I treated realism above in discussing the Catholic epistemological tradition, what is realism in the critical realist paradigm? Realism for the latter group is best described as the belief that material and immaterial objects external to human consciousness truly exist independent of human consciousness. Reality is objective for critical realists rather than a construct of personal subjectivity. John Searle has defined realism as "the view that the world exists independently of our representation of it."[44] This is the fundamental ontological claim of critical realism. As I show below, it is essential to distinguish this ontological claim from epistemological claims regarding how, and to what extent, reality is intelligible to the human knower. A crucial second claim is that persons can directly experience various types of realities. For instance, a person directly experiences the chair in which she sits. This raw, unreflective experience is not mediated through language or concepts but, rather, is directly present to the person. For these reasons Kevin Schilbrack argues for the notion of "embodied critical realism," a term referring to the fact that "there is no gap between mind and body and persons are never separated or divorced from reality in the first place."[45] The direct access to reality that is available to the person does not, however, lead to direct access to knowledge of reality. Knowledge of reality is mediated through language and traditions. Notice that critical realism does not conflate ontology with epistemology. Simply because human knowers understand reality through the mediation of language and community does not mean that reality is constructed by language and society.

Critical realists view reality as complex and emergent. For instance, a computer, the thought that I am thinking at this moment, and calculus are all real. However, they are real in different ways. The physical world, the mental world, and the world of intelligibles are all equally real. Social structures are intelligible realities. They are not physical, nor are they merely mental phenomena. They are nonphysical but empirically verifiable social realities.[46]

A critical realist approach avoids the reductionisms inherent in materialist and idealist ontologies. The physical and ideational worlds are real. A Catholic appropriation of critical realism would need to be committed to the reality of spiritual aspects of the person and spiritual beings. Persons and God are not mere ideas or intelligible categories. They are transcendent beings whose reality, by definition, cannot be reduced to matter or intellectual categories. Of course, a sociologically produced social theory will not include the spiritual aspects of reality within its purview. However, a social theory that comports with Catholic control beliefs must not dismiss the existence of spiritual realities.

The Critical Realist Account of Social Structure

A distinctive mark of critical realism is its insistence on the relational and emergent nature of reality, particularly of social structures. Critical realists use the concepts of relation and emergence technically, so let us begin by unpacking these. "Relation" is a broad category, which Porpora has defined as "a reciprocal action among two entities."[47] Christian Smith has used the example of a computer to demonstrate the point. It is in the relation of the microchips, screen, keyboard, battery, and plastic casing that a computer emerges. It is only when all these components are in right relation with each other that the reality of a computer comes into existence and the computer functions as a computer.

Critical realism makes an essential distinction between the concepts of relation and interaction. These terms should not be used interchangeably. Bhaskar has noted that relations include but do not all consist of interactions.[48] Porpora has written that "relations are not the same as interaction. Relations exist even if no interaction exists." He illustrates this with the example of the principal–student relation. "A principal can always expel a student, even if he does not."⁴⁹ The relation of a particular student and a principal typically lacks interaction. Most students, especially those in large school systems, rarely interact with their principals. However, all students enter into a relation with a principal, whereby a principal has the potency to alter the student's educational experience. This is why critical realists consistently claim that the category of relation is not between two specified individual persons but rather between the social positions that persons assume.⁵⁰ With this technical definition of relation in mind, we are prepared to define "social structure."

The most concise definition of social structure is that structures are "social relations among preexisting social positions."⁵¹ Structures are webs of social relations. Pierpaolo Donati emphasizes this point when he defines a social structure as "institutionalized social relations, which are the product of networks of relations."⁵² For Donati, structures emerge within the relation of social relations with each other. Donati maintains that multiple relations make up a structure. Again, an established social relation exists between the positions of student and professor. The student–professor relation does not, by itself, compose the structure that is American higher education. There are other relations—such as between the positions of deans and students, deans and professors, professors and college presidents, professors and boards of trustees, and so on—that interrelate to compose the structure.

Donati argues that structures are made *by* individuals, not *of* individuals. Instead, social structures are made of relations:⁵³ "Social mechanisms are *relational* in the sense that they are made of social relations that are enacted by individuals and by the super-individual social subjects that individuals create."⁵⁴ Margaret Archer notes that structures are relations between preestablished social positions.⁵⁵ Smith agrees, and goes further, furnishing an extensive definition of social structures: "Social structures are durable patterns of human social relations, generated and reproduced through social interactions and accumulated and transformed historically over time, that are expressed through lived bodily practices, which are defined by culturally meaningful cognitive categories, motivated in part by normative and moral valuations and guides, capacitated by and imprinted in material resources and artifacts, controlled and reinforced by regulative sanctions, which therefore promote cooperation and conformity and discourage resistance and opposition."⁵⁶

While echoing the relational aspects of structures, Smith's definition elucidates the fact that structures implicate many aspects of human social life, including the cognitive, normative, and material. What we find is that there is a strong consensus among critical realists that structures are made of durable human social relations among social positions.

All this raises questions about social positions. Namely, though structures are relations among social positions, what are individual social positions? Here, Bhaskar's work on the position-practice system is helpful. Bhaskar first defines "position," then moves to what positions prescribe:

> We need a system of mediating concepts ... designating the slots, as it were, in the social structure into which active subjects must slip in order to reproduce it; that is, a system of concepts designating the point of contact between human agency and social structures. Such a point, liking acting to structure, must both endure and be immediately occupied by individuals. It is clear that the mediating system we need is that of the positions (places, functions, rules, tasks, duties, rights, etc.) occupied (filled, assumed, enacted, etc.) by individuals and of the practices (activities, etc.) in which, in virtue of their occupancy of these positions they engage. I shall call this mediating system the position-practice system. Now such positions and practices, if they are to be individuated at all, can only be done so relationally.[57]

Bhaskar understands that relations are among the positions that people assume. A given social position contains practices that are endorsed and enforced by other position holders. Structures are activated in and through the activities of persons, who act through their positions in relation to others.[58]

For example, the position of professor is a relational reality.[59] As noted above, it involves a relation to the positions of students, administrators, and other professors. Further, there are practices that one automatically assumes that a professor will perform: lecturing, grading, meeting with students, researching and writing, and attending graduation. Thus, if a professor decides to stop grading exams and papers, she will be met with resistance from students, the department chair, and ultimately, the dean. The students, in their social positions, are enabled to complain to the professor and appeal to the chair and dean if the professor fails to perform the prescribed practices of her position. The dean will be able to demand that the professor grade student work. She will also have the capacity to terminate the professor for nonperformance of duties. Each position enables its inhabitants to carry out specific actions and constrains them from other actions. Students are empowered to complain to and about, but not terminate, a given professor. Professors are required to execute certain practices, such as grading, and can suffer ridicule or be removed from the position if they neglect to do so.

Social Structures as Emergent Realities

Importantly, the critical realist perspective does not view structures as the aggregate of relations. Instead, critical realists argue that social structures are emergent realities. Many critical realists have argued that "emergence" is a crucial concept in the theory. Douglas Porpora has argued that emergence is one of the chief concepts of critical realism.[60] Archer supports an emergentist vision of reality at the outset of her book on the relationship of structures and agency.[61] Christian Smith places emergence at the core of his critical realist theory. Smith argues both for the emergent nature of personhood and the emergent nature of social structures.[62] The concept of emergence is a technical one and deserves explication. Smith defines emergence as "the process of constituting a new entity with its own particular characteristics through the interactive combination of other, different entities that are necessary to create the new entity but that do not contain the characteristics of the new entity."[63]

Emergence exists when two entities at a lower level combine or interact and a third, higher entity is created from the relationship of the two lower ones.[64] This third entity is real, but its reality is constituted through the relationship of the two lower entities and is not merely a reality that exists in the composition of the two lower realities. This form of emergence is "strong" or "ontological" because new realities come to be from within the relation of the parts.[65] Again, a computer is a unique, higher-level reality that transcends any of its component parts, and it exists as a computer only when each part is in proper relation with all others.

Water provides a stock example of ontological emergence. Water forms through the combination of two hydrogen (H) atoms and one (O) oxygen atom. But water is not merely the simple addition of two H atoms and one O atom. Water is a new reality that emerges out of the relation of these elements. Its properties, such as wetness, materialize within the relation of the elements. Although the H and O remain H and O, they are also changed through their relationship. When combined, they exist in a state that transcends each individually. Thus, if you separate the O from the Hs, water ceases to exist. Water cannot be reduced to its parts and remain water. Further, water's properties of liquidity at room temperature, wetness to the touch, visibility to the human eye, and capacity to extinguish fire are unpredictable based strictly on a knowledge of its parts. Both H and O are gaseous at room temperature, are odorless and undetectable to the touch, are invisible to the human eye, and are highly flammable. Something genuinely *new* exists when H and O enter a particular relation with each other.

Smith argues that "what gives rise to emergent properties are not just particular parts, but the way those parts are arranged, their structure, their interrelations."[66] Thus, new realities emerge from within the relations of previously existing realities. Consider a pencil. A thin, graphite rod on its own is an imperfect writing instrument. The moment one presses the rod on the page, it snaps. But when a graphite rod is adequately encased in a cylinder of wood, and the end of the pencil is shaped into a cone, a useful writing instrument emerges. These two simple parts, put in proper relation with each other (namely, that one houses the other), and shaped in a specific way, produce an object capable of clearly and consistently writing on paper.

Like computers, water, and pencils, structures are emergent realities that emerge from within relations.[67] Recall that structures are relations among social positions. The positions that compose a structure cannot be understood in isolation. The position of "professor" is understood only in relation to the position of "student." Individual persons assume social positions and relate to other social positions in characteristic ways by practicing the normative actions of the position. When, over time, such relations draw others in—and are supported by material conditions, cognitive categories, and normative claims—a social structure emerges. This is true of higher education. Higher education transcends its parts, and thus it cannot be reduced to any of them.

Another aspect of ontological emergence is what social theorists call downward causation. This means that "higher-level realities causally affect their lower-level constituents."[68] Once new realities emerge, they possess downward causal capacities to organize and direct the properties of their parts. When an oxygen atom joins with two hydrogen atoms, the oxygen atom ceases to possess flammable properties. Similarly, stars exert downward causation on the atoms that compose them. Atoms that alone are not light-emitting emit light when related to other atoms within stars. The new reality—the star—causes the parts to express different properties.[69] So, stars act on their parts and alter the activities of their parts. As I show below, social structures possess the downward causal capacity to influence human relations, consciousness, actions, and ultimately, outcomes from a level above persons.[70]

Norm Circles

Now that we have explored the fundamental tenets of critical realism, let us delve deeper into the theory's account of social structures. Consider the fact that "professor" and "mother" are social positions that partially compose larger structures (the university and the family, respectively) but differ in key ways. "Professor" is a professional position in highly organized institutions of higher education, while "mother" is a position within the social structure of a nonorganizational social unit called the family. The position of mother also seems to contain many cultural notions of who a mother is, what she should do, and what it means to be a good mother. To understand how "professor" and "mother" are both social positions, we need to describe what the critical realist scholar Dave Elder-Vass has called a "norm circle," which is a "broad type of social structure."[71] For Elder-Vass all social structures are based on norm circles. As I show below, Elder-Vass has also argued that culture depends on norm circles.

A norm circle is a group of people whose members, due to their relation with each other, both endorse and enforce certain defined practices with each other.[72] Over time, such normative conformity leads people in the group to share the same beliefs and dispositions. The practices and behaviors that the circle incentivizes and penalizes shape the consciousness of its members.[73] When outsiders interact with those who are in a norm circle, they experience certain constraints on their actions. For example, when walking down the street in an American city, it is presumed that one will walk on the right-hand side of the sidewalk. The mechanics of this simple social interaction look like this:

Social position: pedestrian in an American city
Norm: walk on the right-hand side

By walking in an American city, one encounters a norm circle in which nearly every other person in the city is a member in relation with other members. Now imagine that a person from England begins to walk on the left side of the sidewalk. Such a person is likely to encounter difficulty in getting to her destination as well as dirty looks from the members of the norm circle. Members of the "walk on the right-hand side of the sidewalk" norm circle may even catch each other's eyes and silently engage in a moment of shared disdain for the Englishwoman who flouts the circle's accepted practice. This is the case because the members of the norm circle "are aware that other members of the circle share their commitment" and "feel an obligation to them to endorse and enforce the norm concerned." And the members of the norm circle also "have an expectation of others that they will support them in that endorsement and enforcement."[74] Elder-Vass's notion of norm circle maps neatly with the position-practice theory of Bhaskar and other critical realists, and it adds an emphasis on the shaping of the beliefs and dispositions of persons in social positions.

The Two Kinds of Social Structures

Walking on the right is what Elder-Vass terms a normative social institution, which emerges from within a norm circle. A normative social institution develops to enforce the content of a norm circle. That is, a group of like-minded people institutionalize their vision of what to believe, how to act, and how to be disposed to act. Elder-Vass offers queuing as an example of a normative social institution. People in the United States, for example, generally share an agreement that customers should line up for service. "Line cutters" will typically be chastised by many members of the line, even those who are unaffected by the "cutting." Here, lining up is both endorsed and enforced by members of the norm circle, who in this case are Americans. Parents of small children will both endorse and enforce lining up. This example shows that normative social institutions influence people such that they "act differently than they would do otherwise."[75] Some people desire to "cut" a line but do not because they fear the social sanctioning of those who enforce the norm circle.

As this example suggests, normative social institutions are structures; they are composed of relations among social positions, and these positions entail norms and practices. Basic normative social institutions neither possess a high level of organization nor relations in which some positions are endowed with more authority than others. Everyone in a line is equally authoritative to endorse and enforce line etiquette. Elder-Vass has suggested that all structures contain normative social institutions. In short, all structures ultimately reflect the beliefs and practices of a norm circle.

However, imagine a scenario in which a group of citizens became concerned that Millennials were flouting queuing conventions. These citizens belong to the norm circle of lining up and endorse and enforce its norms and practices. This line-enforcing group may then decide to start meeting at a local coffee shop to discuss the loss of proper lining-up practice in the younger generation. By formally meeting, the group has become, in the typology of Elder-Vass, an association. Associations emerge when people not only belong to a norm circle but also then commit themselves to a group of identifiable people regarding a specific norm circle. Elder-Vass notes that romantic couples, "nerd girls," and barbershop quartets are all associations.[76] Nerd girls become associates because of their "nerd" status. Because an association is a kind of normative social institution, an association is also a norm circle that influences the behaviors of the members. Nerd girls, for example, are sanctioned if they begin to dress, speak, and act like "cool kids," or athletes.

Now imagine that the lining-up association decides that to more effectively preach the good news of proper lining up, they need to formalize their group. They draft by-laws, elect a president and vice president, and create processes whereby new members are accepted into the association. According to Elder-Vass, this association has become an organization. Organizations are complex associations containing highly structured positions, some of which possess authority in relation to others.[77] Positions in an organization are relationally determined by the set of practices that are specific to the position.[78]

The power of organizations to shape agency is seen through the practice of "upselling," an example that both Porpora and Elder-Vass employ.[79] Salespeople upsell when they attempt to sell a customer a more expensive item than the customer initially desired. Imagine there is a customer, Curt, who wishes to buy a set of speakers. He meets the salesperson, Sally, who represents the organization, Speaker City. Speaker City has incentivized Sally to sell expensive speakers because (1) she is paid based on commission and (2) she has been trained in the art of "upselling" by her manager, Marty. Here Sally is a member of a norm circle, consisting of Marty and the other members of the management team. This circle endorses upselling practices and rewards successful sales work. The organization, Speaker City, has intentionally created and sustained a norm circle that places salespeople like Sally in a particular relation to customers such as Curt. So, what does Sally do? Although she is not mechanically moved to upsell in this case, she is incentivized to do so. But such an incentive may conflict with norms embedded in her value system. She may, as a result, decide to sell Curt a set of speakers that fits his personal and budgetary requirements.

Critical Realism and Culture

With an understanding of norm circles and the kinds of social structures in hand, we can now turn to a critical realist account of culture. As I argued at the outset of the book, my work on culture is in service to an understanding of social structure. For critical realists, an account of social structure requires an understanding of the cultural aspects of society that contribute to social structures.

Although I endorse Elder-Vass's understanding of culture, Margaret Archer has provided the standard critical realist account. Archer has argued that culture as a whole is taken to refer to "all intelligibilia, that is, to any item which has the dispositional capacity of being understood by someone."[80] This aspect of culture is what Archer has termed the "cultural system," which comprises the full corpus of ideas available at any one time. For Archer, culture is whatever is contained in libraries, on the internet, and in the world of existing ideas. This necessarily includes books that have not been read in decades or Web pages that have never had any visitors.⁸¹ This makes Archer a cultural realist; cultural reality exists independently of the persons who participate in culture. Intelligibilia need not gain communal support; they simply need to exist for them to attain cultural reality.

Archer's second aspect of culture is sociocultural interaction. This refers to how people draw on the cultural system in their interactions with others. Some ideas have more currency and power within a culture at any one time. It is the dynamic between the cultural system and sociocultural interaction that leads to cultural elaboration. Like structures, Archer maintains that culture both enables and constrains human action and agency.⁸²

Although Elder-Vass has drawn on aspects of Archer's account, he has contested her definition of what counts as culture. Instead, he develops a nonrealist approach to culture. Culture refers to "'practices, rituals, institutions and material artefacts, as well as texts, ideas and images.'"⁸³ But cultural reality is not purely objective for Elder-Vass; it is not necessarily present in a book on a library shelf. Culture has a subjective component as well: "Culture is a shared set of practices and understandings."⁸⁴ The intelligibilia that constitutes culture is such only if it is shared among members of a norm circle. Recall that a norm circle is a group of people committed to endorsing and enforcing a particular standard of behavior.⁸⁵ As Elder-Vass explains, "Culture is not merely belief, but socially endorsed belief, and that social endorsement can only be brought about by a group—a norm circle."⁸⁶

Consider that though the United Kingdom and the United States have access to the same set of intelligibilia, they do not have the same culture. It is the collective endorsement of the artifacts of a society that render them cultural.⁸⁷ The UK primarily endorses one set of artifacts as "cultural" regarding the reality of evolution, though there is a subculture in the US that supports another. Culture, then, is sociologically significant because it is a proxy term for the causal influence of norm circles, not because the ideational content of culture is independently capable of exerting a causal influence.

To demonstrate this, Elder-Vass has engaged a thought-experiment made famous by Karl Popper. Popper argues that one could reasonably reconstruct a culture if everything but the society's libraries was destroyed. Elder-Vass disagrees, arguing, "We could only reconstruct a culture if we had, not only readable texts containing the ideas at large amongst the members of that culture, but also information about which of those ideas were endorsed within the culture and how widely, and indeed how those patterns of endorsement varied and interacted across the social space."[88] Archer's cultural system, then, is not "cultural" at all. Because specific ideas are not shared, endorsed, or enforced by communities, they cease to exist on a *cultural* level. Unread books and the ideas contained therein do exist ontologically but do not exist culturally.

As the above example shows, culture cross-cuts as well. Although there is a subculture of creationists, the majority of Americans believe in the Big Bang and evolution. A pluralist nation-state will have many socially endorsed beliefs that contradict each other.

Thus far, I have shown how culture emerges from within the most basic kind of social structure, a norm circle. For an idea or belief to be genuinely "cultural," it must be endorsed by many members of a social group. However, though culture emerges from social structures, it is also true that cultural realities play a causal role in the emergence of social structures. Below, I show how cognitive categories (e.g., Black persons possess the same dignity as white persons) and moral beliefs (e.g., racism is evil) are key social realities in the reproduction and transformation of social structures. There is, then, a dialectic among cultural realities and social structures for those in the Elder-Vass school of critical realism.

A portrait of social reality has begun to take shape. This section has explored the essential claims of critical realism. Structures are nonmaterial social realities that are social relations among social positions. The professor–student relation has provided a ready example of this. Also, structures cannot be reduced to the aggregation of individual personal actions. Instead, structures emerge from within the relation of social positions, exist at a level "above" persons, and then exert downward causation on the activities and practices of the persons who assume social positions. The section has shown that there are two kinds of social structures, each of which contains norm circles: normative social institutions and organizations. Although each possesses all the abovementioned characteristics, the former has porous borders and lacks authority figures, whereas the latter includes only certain members who stand in relation to positions of leadership. Finally, the section showed that cultural realities are products of a basic social structure called a norm circle.

Before this portrait can aid in addressing the issues for theological ethics identified in chapter 1, I need to make two additional points. The first concerns the critical realist approach to the reproduction and transformation of social structures. The second concerns the inner workings of how structures exert causal influence on human agency and action.

The Reproduction and Transformation of Social Structures

Critical realism offers an important account of the reproduction and transformation of social structures. In this view, it is impossible to identify the emergence of an entirely new structure, ex nihilo. Instead, critical realists write of the emergence of structures from existing ones.

Structures exist in societies, which are "massive conglomerations of distinct but tightly linked social structures in larger structural environments."[89] The existence of webs of structures explains both the durability of structures and how structures actually change. First, structures are durable because they involve many different aspects of social reality.[90] Recall Smith's multifaceted definition of a social structure. Structures involve the historical emergence of specific relational patterns that include culturally endorsed beliefs. The complexity of a structure means that a change in just one area of relationality among social positions or culture does not finally alter the structure. For a structure to change, change needs to transpire in many aspects of social reality, including cultural realities.

Although structural transformations can and do happen, more often one finds preexisting structures reiterated and sustained through human activity. Take, for instance, marriage. This structure traditionally has consisted of a well-defined relation of the position of husband and position of wife. It is a symmetrically internal relation, in which a husband and wife only become a husband and a wife with the other.

Because the categories of husband and wife are socially constructed, their meaning has evolved. These changes in cognitive categories notwithstanding, the relation of husband and wife contained stable elements from the founding of the United States to the 1990s. It had been understood that the relation was between one man and one woman, children should be a fruit of the marriage relation, marriage would be recognized in the civil sphere, a marriage ceremony in which vows are made is required for the marriage to exist, and that such an event must be officiated by an agent of the government. But as Bhaskar has written, women and men do not marry to perpetuate the structure of marriage; instead, this perpetuation is an unintended consequence of couples who marry.[91] Porpora has written that people are often unaware of the social relations into which they have entered.[92]

Archer has emphasized that people sustain structures (and the positions and relations that structures comprise) when they pursue certain human projects, goals, and desires, such as committing one's life to another person. She has argued that structural powers rely on human projects to exist.[93] It is precisely when a person pursues a project that she meets a social structure.

The preexisting positions and relations of society provide smooth pathways to carry out their projects, such as having a family. Further, when persons pursue their projects in a manner in which they participate in the already-existing structures of society (i.e., they enter into the positions that are available in society and enact the practices that are internal to these positions), the structure is perpetuated. Each structure's existence is predicated on if and how persons enter preexisting social relations and perform the characteristic practices of social positions.

But just as individuals and groups sustain structures when they pursue their projects, goals, and desires, individuals and groups can set the stage for the transformation of structures when they find that their projects are frustrated by an existing structure. Although frustrated persons and groups may be necessary for structural change, they are insufficient. Predictably, critical realists have argued that multiple social realities lead to structural transformation. This is the case because the transformation of structures is an emergent process; it does not transpire quickly or easily.[94] Therefore, structural change rarely transpires when a single group protests or one or two areas of social life are developed and or altered.

Christian Smith has identified seven areas of social life that contribute to the transformation of social structures. First, "social structures are often transformed when new relationships between different groups are initiated and when old relationships are severely weakened or terminated."[95] For example, the social worlds of the indigenous peoples of the Americas were altered fundamentally with the introduction of European peoples after the late fifteenth century. Smith noted that the social world of the Celts was transformed with the Roman conquest of Britain in AD 43. Second, "social structures are often transformed when the basic cognitive categories that help to constitute and justify them are altered."[96] Consider the structural transformations that have occurred since the 1960s regarding the capacities and abilities of women. The realization that women are neither intellectually inferior nor physically weak has played a causal role in the development of opportunities for women to pursue the professions and athletics. Third, "social structures are often transformed when sustaining material resources are significantly reduced (and sometimes when they are increased)."[97] History has shown that dramatic reductions in material resources within a society often lead to revolutions that radically transform social structures. The welfare state of the United States, for example, emerged from the ashes of the Great Depression.

Fourth, "social structures can be transformed as a result of changes in the moral and normative beliefs of affected people and in the practices, procedures, rules, and laws those beliefs underwrite."[98] The institution of slavery, for example, was abolished when, as Smith explains, "enough of the right people came to believe that slavery is . . . a reprehensible evil."[99] Fifth, "social structures can be transformed when enough of their participants simply . . . stop sanctioning noncompliance, deviance, and rebellion."[100] The #MeToo movement that began in 2017 provides an example of this. The movement started when women who had been sexually harassed or assaulted began publicly sharing their stories of abuse at the hands of powerful men. Historically, women have been punished for such public resistance. For example, to penalize Anita Hill for testifying against then–Supreme Court nominee Clarence Thomas, members of the Oklahoma state legislature introduced legislation to shutter her employer, the University of Oklahoma Law School.[101] Although women who speak out against their abusers continue to suffer negative consequences as a result of their actions, the #MeToo movement has made it more difficult for powerful men to punish the "noncompliance, deviance, and rebellion" of those who report sexual assault and harassment.[102]

Sixth, "social structures can change when new or newly mobilized systems of communication decrease the intractability of coordinated interactions."[103] For example, the creation and adoption of the printing press was a key factor enabling Martin Luther's movement to spread across Europe.[104] In our own time, the ubiquity of the internet has contributed to many structural changes. Seventh, "social structures can be transformed as a result of disruptions of normal reiterated bodily practices and collective activity currents."[105] For example, "a relatively small number of civil rights activists . . . instigated havoc in the established structure of Jim Crow race relations in the American South by sitting their bodies at off-limits lunch counters, occupying certain unacceptable seats on public buses, and spending time standing their bodies in certain forbidden transportation terminals."[106] The disruptive bodily practices of Rosa Parks and others played a causal role in the emergence of new social structures regarding race.

Because many aspects of social life have a causal influence on the transformation of social structures, Smith argues that "people acting collectively and in great numbers have limited control over the character of society and the course of history. Most often, the forces that transform structures are animated by other causal forces beyond anyone's purposive control or foresight."[107]

Here, Smith endorses the notion that social structures are emergent realities. Structures are not the result of the aggregate of human actions but dynamically take shape when the many aspects of social life come into contact with each other. In this way, structural transformation cannot be predicted easily. However, Smith emphasizes that "no social structure is transformed without some purposive human action intending change."[108] The only hope for positive sociostructural change is collective action to transform some or all the seven areas described above.

Case Study: The Emergence of Gay Marriage

The rapid transformation of the structure of marriage in the United States in the twenty-first century offers a contemporary example of how structures are transformed. This subsection neither states nor implies anything regarding a normative position regarding gay and lesbian relationships and actions. Such an inquiry goes beyond the scope of the current project. Instead, this example is used because it illumines the recent and dramatic transformation of a social structure. The influence of cultural realities on the development of a social structure also is evident in this example.

The first area of social existence that influences structural change involves the transformation of relationships between people and groups. In the past thirty years, there has been an increasing acceptance of LGBTQ people inhabiting various positions in society. Most influentially, there has been a growing acceptance of gay and lesbian relationships in society. For the first time, gay men and lesbian women could openly inhabit the position of "boyfriend" or "girlfriend" with their same-sex partner.

Second, cultural conceptual developments contribute to structural change. Same-sex attraction was formerly regarded as an abnormal state. Now, sexual orientation is largely understood as an unchosen, identity characteristic of a person. A 2014 study of 409 pairs of gay brothers supported the existence of two parts of the genome that influence male sexual orientation.[109] Although the idea of a "gay gene" has generated controversy, the public's perception of the issue of how people come to be gay has developed over the past forty years. In 1978 only 13 percent thought that people were "born gay." In 2014 that number was 42 percent.[110] This cultural change has played a causal role in the transformation of the structure of marriage.

Third, cultural changes in normative beliefs contribute to structural developments. This change is especially pertinent regarding the development of structures supporting same-sex relationships. When Gallup asked Americans in 2012, "Do you personally believe gay or lesbian relations are morally acceptable or morally wrong?" 54 percent responded that such relations were acceptable and 42 percent said such relations were wrong. When the same question was posed in 2001, the results were inverted; only 40 percent responded "acceptable," whereas 53 percent said such relations were morally wrong.[111]

Fourth, the expansion or contraction of material goods often plays a role in structural change. For example, the increased economic autonomy of women has enabled lesbian couples to become economically self-supporting. In previous eras, it was difficult for two women to support a household. The economic liberation of women, which continues to grow in Western nations, has facilitated the emergence of lesbian relationships.[112]

Fifth, structural transformation often relies on the cessation of punishing noncompliance or deviance in an area of life. The cultural consensus in the middle to late twentieth century viewed gay and lesbian behavior as deviant, and it was often punished as a crime. Gay men and lesbian women also experienced many types of noncriminal social punishment. For example, families often shunned their gay sons and lesbian daughters. Although gay men and lesbian women still face social punishment, the social costs for being openly gay have diminished over the past few decades.[113] For example, many Catholic colleges have nondiscrimination policies that include sexual orientation.[114]

Sixth, structures are more apt to change when new systems of communication emerge. Again, a well-documented example was the invention of the printing press and the social changes that it helped to unleash.[115] Anecdotal evidence suggests that the invention and the adoption of the internet as a tool of communication enabled gays and lesbians to find support, build community, and further organize the gay/lesbian rights movement in the period leading up to the legalization of gay marriage.[116]

Seventh, Smith argues that disruptions of bodily practices and collective activity currents can play a role in social change. Like the concurrent civil rights movement of the 1960s, the gay rights movement organized marches in major metropolitan areas. Further, the taboo of same-sex couples kissing in public and on television was challenged by activists who sought to normalize the lived experience of gay people. Gay men and lesbian women also began to make their presences felt by going to courthouses and churches to request marriage.

The example shows that gay marriage emerged out of a multiplicity of roughly simultaneous cultural and institutional changes. Some of these changes directly intended to create a morally and legally recognized category of relation among gay people. However, most of these social changes were not about gay and lesbian relationships at all. For instance, the expansion of economic opportunities for women in the second half of the twentieth century was not primarily intended to free women to pursue lesbian relationships. Yet it had the unintended effect of facilitating the emergence of such relationships. This example shows that the emergence of structures is complex and interwoven with cultural changes regarding ideas that are endorsed and enforced by norm circles.

Social Structures, Causality, and Moral Agency

Although Christian theological ethics has recognized a relationship between social structures and personal agency, chapter 2 showed that the theorizing of this relationship has remained superficial at best and incorrect at worst. However, the critical realist approach may help provide a solution to this problem.

At the outset of her book *Structure, Agency, and the Internal Conversation*, Archer poses the question that drives her project: "How does structure influence agents?"[117] Her stated goal in the book is to describe the "single narrative" regarding the relationship between persons and structures. Specifically, she is concerned with causality—how do structures "cause" persons to act in specific ways? Her project is important because the stock sociological answers either have located causality entirely within the person, as in methodological individualism, or have conflated the distinction between objective structures and the human subject, as in holism. The holistic account has maintained that the agent is reduced to a product of the objective social structure. In this mode of thinking, the agent is moved "hydraulically" to act in certain prescribed ways. Causality, in this account, is a blunt force. But though many or most agents might act in similar ways, such a reduction leaves little space for moral subjectivity.

In order to discover the relationship between agency and structures, Archer argues that "it is essential to distinguish between the existence of structural properties and the exercise of their causal powers."[118] According to Archer, social structures do not move persons in a physical or hydraulic way. Instead, the causal power of social structures flows through human relations to direct human activity. Recall that we do not meet hydrogen and oxygen head-on in water—we meet the emergent properties of water. So, too, we do not meet structural properties head-on—we meet their features in certain situations. Structural emergent properties enable and constrain a person's agency and action. The fact that structures enable and constrain a person's action is critical for Archer.[119] For Archer, structures exercise their causal power through the kinds of actions that they either constrain or enable. Because structures are relations among social positions, it is the *relation* that produces the enablement or constraint.

When a person enters a social relation, she finds that her action is both enabled and constrained.[120] Tenure-track professors are enabled to do research and publish articles and are constrained from taking vacations during September. Imagine a situation where a tenure review committee learns that a faculty member has canceled classes during the first two weeks of the semester to relax on the beaches of Aruba. The tenure committee's relation to the offending faculty member enables the members of the committee to punish her. The faculty member is certainly free to take the trip but knows that her tenure is in jeopardy if she does. This relation (tenure candidate–tenure committee) constrains the faculty member's agency in real ways. If she intends to secure tenure and enjoy a good reputation with her colleagues and students, she will not take a vacation during this time. Crucially, the tenure candidate does not know which individuals will be on the tenure committee. But the composition of the tenure committee is immaterial in this case. Though certain individuals may have slightly different interpretations of tenure guidelines, the tenure candidate knows that *whoever* inhabits the position of tenure committee member will follow a prescribed set of practices and norms. Here, the tenure candidate's relation to another *social position* (viz., a tenure committee member) has causal power to shape the actions of the tenure candidate.

What this shows is that "structures actually exist, but they do not literally act. They direct action within human and group relations. Structural powers rely on human projects to exist. No projects, no powers, no enablements."[121] For example, if a woman's "life project" is to be a surgeon, she will pursue certain activities and practices and will reject others. Aspiring surgeons should develop their fine motor skills through playing the guitar or sewing, while avoiding recreational drugs that may produce jittery hands. Although an aspiring surgeon is free to use drugs that induce an unsteady hand, she should not expect to be a surgeon for long. Here, we begin to understand how structures causally contribute to human decisions. Structures encourage and reward certain actions and discourage and punish other actions.

Agents choose among positions through what Archer termed the "internal conversation."[122] Agents approach already-existing social structures with their personal concerns and moral values. That is, persons bring their already-existing personhood into dialogue with the world as it is. Specifically, a person is concerned with how to pursue and fulfill her life goals. An individual's course of action is produced through her reflexive deliberations. After surveying the various positions that are open to her, including the constraints and enablements of the positions, she determines her practical projects. These projects should enable her to realize her life goals within the social situation. Here, the causality of social structures is real but indirect. Structures do not determine human action any more than an acceptance letter to a college determines an applicant's enrollment. The acceptance letter enables the applicant to inhabit a position (student) and facilitates her enrollment. The applicant still must discern whether enrollment in college is a project that fits her life concerns and whether enrolling in *this* college will promote her life agenda. Structures enable and facilitate, or constrain and penalize, persons from acting in specific ways.

Archer has argued that reflexivity mediates social structures to agents. Reflexivity is the missing link in how structures are mediated to persons. It is through reflexivity that the moral agent can "deliberate internally upon what to do in situations that were not of our making."[123] Reflexivity is where Archer's critical realism differs from Giddens's structuration. Although Giddens emphasizes the duality of structures and agents and the recursive nature of social action, Archer underscores the reflexive nature of agents. Structures and agents exist in the same dimension of reality for Giddens but not for Archer. Critical realists like Archer maintain an ontological distinction between agents and structures, whereas Giddens's structuration theory blurs the line between the two. For Archer, persons can stand at a critical distance from the structure, and there they can evaluate how their life projects and goals are either realized or frustrated by the position and relations that they might assume. Further, how one practices a position is free and involves an internal conversation. This point is taken up in greater depth in chapter 6.

An Emergentist Theory of Human Action

The portrait of human action developed by Archer suggests that action arises from within a complex set of realities—some personal, some social. Although the act is always fully the person's, it is also the case that his action arises from within the relationship of his goals and the social opportunities that are presented to him. Drawing on Archer, Elder-Vass has argued that the human act is an emergent reality. Human action is multiply caused.[124] Like Archer, Elder-Vass has argued that human action may be affected by social structures without being determined by them.[125] Elder-Vass has likened action to a leaf falling to the ground. And though the leaf's relation to the Earth pulls the leaf to the Earth's surface, air pressure, moisture, and wind currents cause the leaf to fall in a zigzag fashion. The leaf's movement can only be explained by referencing all these causes. In a similar way, human action is caused by conscious decisions as well as the constraints and enablements of social structures, cultural values, and what Elder-Vass has termed "stored decisions."

With his notion of stored decisions, Elder-Vass moves beyond Archer. He argues that stored decisions arise from previous decisions in which the agent decided to act in a similar manner when confronted by similar circumstances in the future. To demonstrate this, Elder-Vass offers the example of the tennis player who has less than a quarter of a second to return a serve. Conscious decision-making takes *at least* a quarter of a second. So how do players return a serve? Elder-Vass argues that they have to rely on stored decisions to return a serve without the benefit of rational reflection. In a similar manner, the person walking down the street does not have time to consider whether she should pull the small child out of the way of a speeding car or intervene to stop a physical assault; she acts, to some degree, in line with her stored decisions.

An emergentist account of human action is necessarily nonreductionist. The human act is irreducible to conscious decision-making, stored decisions, or structural causality. Each of these is a different kind of reality, and each provides its own distinct cause for the action. Although structures are not sufficient causes of action, neither are conscious decisions. Elder-Vass, for one, maintains that conscious decisions are only indirect and partial causes of our behavior.[126] I return to and develop a fuller account of an emergentist account of human action in chapter 5.

SUMMARY

The first two chapters of this book argued that contemporary Christian ethics has had difficulty analyzing structural problems because it is conceptually dated and has inadequately addressed the structure-agency problem. Theologians have yet to follow the guidance of Mark O'Keefe in offering "some definitions for ... terms such as 'structures,' 'institutions,' and 'systems.'"[127] This chapter has attempted to answer the call by providing a better account of social structures and the relationship of structures and agency. It also demonstrated how culture intersects with social structures.

The insights gained in this chapter serve as the ground on which a more insightful ethics can be constructed. First, unlike Marxism, which directly undercuts Christian control beliefs, critical realism comports with the ontological, epistemological, and anthropological commitments of Christianity. Second, critical realism has explanatory capacity. Unlike individualist explanations, which overrate the influence of the individual and underrate the role of structures, the critical realist approach presents an account of structures and agency that makes space for both realities. For instance, the tenure-candidate example showed how preexisting relations, positions, and practices function to enable and constrain personal action. Third, critical realism maintains that structures are real and emerge within relations. Here structures generate "causal powers" when people enter into relations that prescribe and proscribe certain practices. Structures are "activated" through the presence and action of individual agents. Fourth, structures enable persons to act in prescribed ways and constrain them from acting otherwise. In short, the possibilities of human action occur within a social context. Critical realism maintains that though agents are free, structures provide pathways to certain kinds of lives and actions and prevent other types of lives and actions. Structures do not determine actions; rather, structures enable and constrain action. Because critical realist thought maintains that there is ontological distance between structures and persons, it preserves space for the person to conduct an internal conversation regarding what she should do given the circumstances.

The chapter has yielded a conceptual bundle that has significant implications for Christian ethics. We have found that the relations among social positions enable and constrain the action of those who inhabit any given social positions. This leads to questions regarding the moral quality of the relations that make up social structures. If structures are made of relations, and if human action is enabled and constrained by relations, then what kinds of actions are our relations enabling? Do our structures enable good and virtuous actions? That is, do they recognize human dignity and promote human well-being and the common good? Or do these relations constrain that kind of action and instead enable persons to oppress each other, despoil the environment, and create "common bads?"

These questions are taken up in chapter 6. But first, I need to sketch an adequate ethical lens with which to scrutinize them.

NOTES

1. Landon, "Social Presuppositions."
2. Hunter, *To Change the World.*
3. Taylor, *Sources,* 7.
4. Wolterstorff, *Reason within the Bounds,* 62.
5. Wolterstorff, 63.
6. Harris, *Free Will,* 5.
7. Saint Paul, *Letter to the Romans,* 2:14–15.
8. Justin Martyr, *Dialogue with Trypho,* chap. 45.
9. Aquinas, *Summa theologiae,* I, 1.1 ad 2. There, he implies that astronomy and physics are philosophical sciences.
10. Aquinas, I-II, 85.3: "Therefore in so far as the reason is deprived of its order to the true, there is the wound of ignorance."
11. Aquinas, I, 1.8.
12. Aquinas, I, 84.7.

13. Aquinas, I, 84.1. See also I, 87.4: "Whereas the proper object of the human intellect, which is united to a body, is a quiddity or nature existing in corporeal matter; and through such nature of visible things it rises to a certain knowledge of things invisible."
14. Aquinas, I, 16.1.
15. On Thomistic realism, see Gilson, *Christian Philosophy*, 231–35.
16. Aquinas, *Summa theologiae*, I, 87.1: "Therefore the intellect knows itself not by its essence, but by its act."
17. Second Vatican Council, *Gaudium et spes*, 15.
18. Second Vatican Council, 44.
19. John Paul II, *Fides et ratio*, n. 29.
20. John Paul II, 56.
21. John Paul II, 44.
22. John Paul II, 55.
23. John Paul II, 68.
24. Smith, *What Is a Person?* chap. 3.
25. Derrida, *Of Grammatology*, 158; Black, "Dreams of Pure Sociology."
26. Bhaskar, *Possibility*, 208.
27. Porpora, "Four Concepts," 240.
28. Bentham, *Introduction*, 7.
29. Ian C. Jarvie, cited by Bunge, "Clarifying," 371.
30. Archer, *Structure*, chap. 1.
31. Donati, "Morality," 59.
32. Kaveny, *Law's Virtues*, 27.
33. Benedict XVI, *Caritas*, 36.
34. Hirschfeld, "How a Thomistic Moral Framework Can Take Social Causality Seriously."
35. Anthony Giddens addresses both functionalism and structuralism on the first page of his *Constitution*.
36. Giddens, *Constitution*, 1–2.
37. Giddens, 2.
38. Giddens, 25.
39. King, "Odd Couple."
40. See Elder-Vass, *Causal Power*, 79.
41. Archer, "Structural Conditioning," 26.
42. Harris, *Free Will*. See also Archer, *Structure*, 10–11.
43. Archer, *Structure*, 13.
44. Searle, *Construction*, 153.
45. See Schilbrack, "Embodied Critical Realism," 174. In this paper, Schilbrack synthesizes critical reality with the embodied realism of George Lakoff and Mark Johnson.
46. Archer, *Structure*, 36.
47. Porpora, "Who Is Responsible?" 14.
48. Bhaskar, *Possibility*, 221.
49. Porpora, "Who Is Responsible?" 14.
50. Bhaskar, *Possibility*, 221.
51. Porpora, "Who Is Responsible?" 14. Archer, "Structural Conditioning."
52. Donati, "Morality," 57.
53. Donati.
54. Donati.

55. Archer, "Structural Conditioning," 28.
56. Smith, *What Is a Person?* 326.
57. Bhaskar, *Possibility*, 221.
58. Bhaskar, 218.
59. I am indebted to Daniel Finn for this example. See Finn, *Consumer Ethics*, 68–70.
60. Porpora, "Who Is Responsible?" 5.
61. Archer, *Structure*, 2.
62. See Smith, *What Is a Person?* chap. 1.
63. Smith, 26.
64. Bhaskar, *Possibility*, 125.
65. Clayton, "Conceptual Foundations," 1–34, 8–10.
66. Porpora, "Who Is Responsible?" 14.
67. Smith, *What Is a Person?* 2.
68. Clayton, "Conceptual Foundations," 2.
69. Elder-Vass, *Causal Power*, 59.
70. Smith, *What Is a Person?* 356.
71. Elder-Vass, *Reality*, 15.
72. Elder-Vass, *Causal Power*, 123.
73. Elder-Vass, 125.
74. Elder-Vass, *Reality*, 26.
75. Elder-Vass, *Causal Power*, 124.
76. Elder-Vass, 149–52.
77. Elder-Vass, 152.
78. Elder-Vass, 196.
79. See Elder-Vass, chap. 8.
80. Archer, *Culture*, xviii.
81. Archer and Elder-Vass, "Cultural System," 95.
82. Archer and Elder-Vass, 96.
83. Elder-Vass, *Reality*, 38.
84. Elder-Vass, 39.
85. Elder-Vass, 48.
86. Elder-Vass, 44.
87. Elder-Vass, 46.
88. Elder-Vass.
89. Elder-Vass, 357.
90. Elder-Vass, 354.
91. Bhaskar, *Possibility*, 215.
92. Porpora, "Who Is Responsible?" 14.
93. Archer, *Structure*, 6–9.
94. Smith, *What Is a Person?* 378.
95. Smith, 369.
96. Smith, 370.
97. Smith, 371.
98. Smith, 372.
99. Smith, 373.
100. Smith, 374.
101. Thomas, "Anita Hill Plans to Leave."

102. E.g., in 2018 Christine Blasey Ford testified to the Judiciary Committee of the United States Senate that the nominee for the Supreme Court, Brett Kavanaugh, had sexually assaulted her while both were in high school. Blasey Ford received death threats because of her testimony.
103. Smith, *What Is a Person?* 375.
104. Pettegree, *Brand Luther.*
105. Smith, *What Is a Person?* 376.
106. Smith.
107. Smith, 378.
108. Smith.
109. Sanders et al., "Genome-Wide Scan."
110. McCarthy, "Americans' Views on Homosexuality."
111. Gallup, "US Acceptance."
112. Matthaei, "Sexual Division of Labor," 217: "Economic independence from men made it economically feasible for some women to structure their lives around lesbian relationships."
113. This is not to claim that gays and lesbians are no longer the victims of unjust discrimination. It is only to claim that such discrimination has diminished relative to previous eras.
114. Saint Anselm College in Manchester, New Hampshire, for example, includes sexual orientation in its nondiscrimination policy.
115. Einstein, *Printing Press.*
116. Johnson, "Nurturing a Community."
117. Archer, *Structure*, 1.
118. Archer, 7.
119. Archer, introduction.
120. Archer, 132.
121. Archer, 6.
122. Archer, chap. 4.
123. Archer, 342.
124. Elder-Vass, *Causal Power*, 191.
125. Elder-Vass, 87, and chap. 5.
126. Elder-Vass, 95.
127. O'Keefe, *Social Sin?* 45.

CHAPTER 4

The Growing Ends of Catholic Theological and Ethical Traditions in the Age of Pope Francis

The last chapter provided a solution to some of the sociological deficiencies that have plagued theological ethics. However, as chapter 1 showed, the difficulty of grappling with structural evils for theological ethicists is not solely due to their undertheorized accounts of social structures. Part of the problem has been the inadequacy of the ethical concepts, such as the principles of double effect and cooperation and human rights theory, which theologians have employed in order to evaluate structural issues. A new approach is needed. This chapter identifies the resources within the recent theoethical tradition that will be useful in constructing a revised ethical approach to social structures.

This chapter is not merely a recapitulation of the direction of the Catholic tradition but is also an argument about what the growing end of the tradition should be. The work here draws on the official writings of Saint John Paul II, Pope Benedict XVI, and Pope Francis, while acknowledging the theological influences that helped to develop their thought. The focus on magisterial teaching is to show that these theological movements, which were first developed in the writings of theologians, have been appropriated into the Church's teaching. We find that, in three developments, the work of a critical mass of theologians and the writings of recent papal magisteria have moved toward a theocentric, personalist, and virtue approach to various questions in theology.

The first development is the rise of a theocentric vision. The Church's ethics have become more theological since the election of Pope Benedict XVI, and Pope Francis has deepened this vision. The second development is the emergence of personalism. Pope John Paul II cemented the personalist turn that he helped usher in at the Second Vatican Council. This turn is marked by a focus on actually existing persons, their human dignity, and their relationality. The third development is the return of virtue ethics as the Church's moral methodology. This movement has its roots in the ethics of Aquinas, was resurrected in the 1980s and 1990s, and, as I argue below, is the central moral lens of Pope Francis.

The result of this chapter's analysis is a triad of concepts that supply a more insightful portrait of the person and moral life. Only then will ethicists be able to make substantive normative claims about how persons should act in a highly structured world. What begins to be delineated in this chapter is more fully developed in chapter 5. The current chapter assembles the building blocks for a theocentric, personalist virtue theory that is the focus of the following chapter. This chapter argues that these three theological trajectories are the center of Catholic ethics in the postconciliar era.

THEOCENTRISM

Since Vatican II, the Church's ethics has become more theological and theocentric. Aquinas argued that theology was the noblest science because it can offer the fullest and most complete understanding of reality.[1] However, how does theology provide the most profound understanding of the real? Aquinas provides an answer in the first question, seventh article, of the first part of the *Summa theologiae*, where he asks, "Whether the object of this science [theology] is God?" In his *respondeo*, Aquinas writes, "Whatever other conclusions are reached in this sacred science are comprehended under God, not as parts or species or accidents but as in some way related to Him."[2] Here, Aquinas argues for nothing more than viewing all of reality as it relates to God. A theological ethics should develop from an understanding of God's relationship with God's creatures and creation. In this account, any understanding of creation that ignores God is descriptively and morally incomplete.

However, Aquinas's theologically deep ethics were lost during the era of the manuals, which stretched roughly from the seventeenth century to the time of the Second Vatican Council.[3] During this long period, Church documents and theological inquiry, and especially ethics, were dominated by philosophical reasoning.[4] Theological claims were thin and were often appended as rhetorical supports. Consider, for instance, Pope Pius XI's 1931 encyclical *Quadragesimo anno*. In arguing for a more just economic order, the pope implicitly draws on the natural law tradition:

Since the present system of economy is founded chiefly upon ownership and labor, the principles of right reason, that is, of Christian social philosophy, must be kept in mind regarding ownership and labor and their association together, and must be put into actual practice.... First, so as to avoid the reefs of individualism and collectivism, the twofold character, that is individual and social, both of capital or ownership and of work or labor must be given due and rightful weight. Relations of one to the other must be made to conform to the laws of strictest justice—commutative justice, as it is called—with the support, however, of Christian charity.[5]

Note that Pope Pius XI defines "Christian social philosophy" as "the principles of right reason." Further, Christian charity functions to "support" the claims of justice. Charity, that most Christian of all virtues, does not drive the social-ethical analysis.

The Second Vatican Council serves as a point of rupture with the manualist mentality. It appropriates the move to a more theological ethics that had begun in the work of Fritz Tillman, Gerard Gilleman, and Bernhard Haring. Haring, in particular, shepherded the council's move toward theocentrism. His landmark book *The Law of Christ* argues for a theocentric/Christocentric ethics:[6] "We understand moral theology as the doctrine of the imitation of Christ, as in life in, with, and through Christ; ... the point of departure in Catholic moral theology is Christ."[7] In his role as a council *peritus*, Haring integrates his theological approach into documents such as *Optatam totius*, and he has been called the quasi-father of *Gaudium et spes*.[8] Hours after the pastoral constitution was promulgated, Paul VI closed the council by noting that "we prefer to point out that charity has been the principal religious feature of this Council."[9] David Hollenbach notes that *Gaudium et spes* "makes a major new contribution to modern Catholic social teaching by presenting more explicitly developed theological grounds for the Church's social engagement than are found in the earlier social encyclicals."[10] Similarly, Charles Curran has argued that "the major influence of Vatican II was to make moral theology more theological."[11]

However, Curran shows that papal social encyclicals did not fully realize the theological moral vision of the council until *Caritas in veritate*. John Paul's social teaching, for instance, privileged philosophical over theological argumentation. Only one of the seven sections of *Sollicitudo rei socialis* is devoted to an explicitly theological analysis of the social situation.

The work of Pope Benedict XVI presents a palpable methodological development. During his papacy, the Congregation for the Doctrine of the

Faith promulgated *Dignitas personae*, an instruction on reproductive ethics. The document grounds its central moral value, the dignity of the human person, theologically: "By taking the interrelationship of these two dimensions, the human and the divine, as the starting point, one understands better why it is that man has unassailable value: he possesses an eternal vocation and is called to share in the trinitarian love of the living God."[12]

The turn toward a more theological ethics hit its apex in Pope Benedict's lone social encyclical, *Caritas in veritate*. Curran has argued that "*Caritas in veritate* breaks new ground by proposing a coherent and integrated theological approach to the discussion of social and economic issues in the tradition of Catholic social teaching."[13] James Keenan has remarked that because *Caritas in veritate* is deeply rooted in the Scriptures, it exemplifies the move toward a more theological ethics that has transpired over the past seventy years.[14] And David Cloutier has argued that in *Caritas*, Benedict fully theologizes Catholic social teaching.[15] It is, in short, the most theologically developed work of moral theology by a pope since Vatican II.

Benedict explicitly argues from theological premises in the document. First, he claims that "charity is at the heart of the Church's social doctrine."[16] Further, he contextualizes justice when he writes that "charity transcends justice and completes it."[17] Whereas John Paul employs charity and love as critical orienting principles, and then analyzes issues in light of justice, Benedict focuses on charity throughout the document and analyzes issues through the lens of charity. For example, John Paul mentions charity, love, and justice 13, 5, and 38 times, respectively, in *Centessimus annus*; Benedict uses the same terms 89, 78, and 42 times in *Caritas in veritate*.[18]

This theological turn was not meant to pull the Church away from engagement with the world. Instead, Benedict argues that Christianity, and other religions, should have a place in the public realm.[19] *Caritas in veritate* is Benedict's attempt to make the Catholic voice in the public square more distinctively theological.

As a student of Aquinas, of the Second Vatican Council, and of Benedict, Francis has continued the Magisterium's trajectory toward a more theocentric ethics. For example, when asked if he "approved of gay persons," Pope Francis responded with a theologically rich question: "Tell me: when God looks at a gay person, does he endorse the existence of this person with love, or reject and condemn this person? We must always consider the person. Here, we enter into the mystery of the human being. In life, God accompanies persons, and we must accompany them, starting from their situation. It is necessary to accompany them with mercy. When that happens, the Holy Spirit inspires the priest to say the right thing."[20]

The pope's statement is indicative of his overall moral approach. Note that he begins his answer by asking a question regarding God's vision of the person. It is God's vision that should inform how a believer sees a gay person.

"Vision" has emerged as the key theological theme of Francis's papacy. For him, Christian faith reveals reality to the believer. This serves as the central theme of his coauthored encyclical, *Lumen fidei*. There, Pope Benedict and Pope Francis write, "The light of faith is unique, since it is capable of illuminating *every aspect* of human existence" (emphasis in the original).[21] Further, they argue that every aspect of human existence is illumined in relationship with Jesus: "Faith does not merely gaze at Jesus, but sees things as Jesus himself sees them, with his own eyes: it is a participation in his way of seeing."[22] The believer not only has a relationship with God; this relationship provides a lens through which the believer views and interprets the world. And this seeing with Christ does not blind the believer to reality but instead "enables us to grasp reality's deepest meaning and to see how much God loves this world."[23]

Francis has continued to underscore this theme in his writings and speeches. In his 2014 World Day of Peace speech, he argues that the basis for universal fraternity between persons is God's love, offered to all.[24] Francis claims that the relationship with God as Father of all transforms the relationship between all persons. Instead of being set against each other, those who recognize God's love and fatherhood find in Him the realization that all persons are children of God and thereby should exist as brothers and sisters to each other.[25]

This theme is strong in *Laudato si'*, the pope's encyclical on care for creation. Throughout the text, Francis urges all people of goodwill to see and understand creation as in relation to God. All creatures have a "value of their own in God's eyes."[26] The moral argument of the encyclical rests on an ontology of creation: creation is best understood in relation to God, finds its fulfillment in God,[27] and reflects God's goodness.[28] The pope argues that the environmental crisis is a moral crisis, in many ways, because it results from a reductive anthropocentrism. Humankind views the created order in light of its usefulness, not as bearing intrinsic value and communicating God's goodness.

PERSONALISM

Personalism is the second characteristic of post–Vatican II theology. It is the person, not abstract human nature, who is a central reality in contemporary Catholic ethics. As an explicit theological movement, personalism finds its roots in the great Thomists of the mid–twentieth century, such as Réginald Garrigou-Lagrange and Jacques Maritain, and was codified in Church teaching at Vatican II.[29] The first chapter of *Gaudium et spes* is devoted to a treatment of "The Dignity of the Human Person." There, in paragraph 12, the council fathers immediately connect personhood to human dignity and interpersonal relationality. The person, according to this account, is intrinsically valuable and social. The document is personalist insofar as it grounds its arguments on the person and her dignity.

Karol Wojytwa / Saint John Paul II's use of personalism has been well documented.[30] As a student of Garrigou-LaGrange, Wojytwa takes a phenomenological approach to personalism. His most important book, *The Acting Person*, seeks to find the person through the person's actions. In the introduction, he writes that "this book is not a study in ethics. The person is not presupposed.... The source of our knowledge of the reality that is the person lies in action, but even more so in the dynamic or existential aspects of morality."[31] Wojytwa's personalism is philosophically derived from within the dialectic of personhood and moral action. Action and experience yield a progressively more complete portrait of what it means to be a person. This portrait is of a free, rational, and responsible moral agent.[32]

After his ascension to the Chair of Saint Peter, John Paul II's personalism became less phenomenological and more focused on the relational aspects of personhood. For instance, his theology of the body buttresses traditional arguments within Catholic sexual ethics, which he continues to espouse, with a more relational logic. He develops the kernels of personalist argumentation that he sees contained in *Humanae vitae*. This approach focuses on what is good for the person and the relationship, not on the person's faculties.[33]

John Paul's personalism extends into his social ethics as well. *Centessimus annus* gives a glimpse of his approach. There, echoing *Gaudium et spes*, he argues that the guiding principle "of all of the Church's social doctrine is a *correct view of the human person*."[34] Later, he emphasizes that it is the reality of the person to which the Church attends:[35] "We are not dealing here with man in the 'abstract,' but with the real, 'concrete,' 'historical' man. We are dealing with *each individual*" (emphasis in the original).[36] Here, personalism has become woven into the Church's official teaching.

Before his election to the papacy, Josef Cardinal Ratzinger espoused a radically personalist position.[37] He maintains that a correct definition of the person "sees that in its theological meaning, 'person' does not lie on the level of essence, but of existence."[38] Second, he notes that personhood is not a "substance" but a relation.[39] That is, to be a person is to exist in relation to others and God. In this way, Ratzinger's privileging of the relational goes beyond that of the noted personalist Norris Clarke, who claims that the Christian tradition maintains that a person is "substance in relation."[40] Clarke argues that the term *person* is "bipolar," as the person is present in herself and oriented toward others. Ratzinger reduces personhood to relationality, whereas most personalists, like Clarke, include space for the substantial self as well.

During his pontificate, Benedict XVI tempered his radical personalism. His most interesting use of personalism is found in the encyclical *Spe salvi*. There, he argues against individualism on several fronts. First, he trains his focus on the individual notion of salvation that has plagued the contemporary mind-set. Following Henri de Lubac, Benedict notes that salvation is communal and is a "'social' reality."[41] The pope also diagnoses a perennial theospiritual problem when he asks, "How did we arrive at this interpretation of the 'salvation of the soul' as a flight from responsibility for the whole, and how did we come to conceive the Christian project as a selfish search for salvation which rejects the idea of serving others?"[42] His solution is thoroughly personalistic. He notes that the reality of existence is "that we escape from the prison of our 'I,' because only in the openness of this universal subject does our gaze open out to the source of joy, to love itself—to God."[43] It is only in interpersonal relationships of love that persons overcome the turned-in self, which stifles the person. Nothing is individual for the human person. Even salvation is a social reality.

Although Pope Francis has not used the term "personalism," his approach is decidedly personalist. First, he asserts the moral primacy of the person over ideology.[44] Throughout his writings, he gives the existing person epistemological priority over ideas about the person's nature. As he has written in *Evangelii gaudium*, "Reality is more important than ideas."[45] Thus, the person reveals the reality of the person more than abstract claims about human nature reveal about the person. Recall Francis's response to the question about gay persons. His focus remains on the existing person and her relationship with God, and he does not turn to discussions of human nature or other abstractions.

In his book on Francis, Walter Cardinal Kasper provides important context for Francis's personalist vision. Kasper notes that Francis's theological mentor was his fellow Argentinian Lucio Gera, an early and influential liberation theologian. Argentinian liberation theology, which formed Bergoglio, "proceeds from a historical analysis of the culture of the people, who are united by a common ethos. It is a theology of people and culture.[46] Unlike Brazilian liberation theology, which drew deeply from social theory, Argentinian liberationists like Gera began with the person living in community. Thomas Massaro has noted that Francis's theology turns "to the actual religious practices of faithful church people . . . as a primary source of theology."[47]

Like Benedict's, Francis's fundamental anthropological claim has been that the person is relational. In *Laudato si'*, he emphasizes that personal existence is grounded in relations with God, others, and the whole of creation.[48] Further, he argues that persons must understand themselves in and through their relations.[49] The encyclical also argues that the biblical account of humanity understands human value in relation to God, and not separated from God.[50] The actual reality and value of the human person should be understood in relation to God and creation.[51]

In addition to tacitly arguing for a personalist vision, Pope Francis has consistently identified an anthropological crisis in the contemporary worldview. In his address to participants in the International Seminar on *Evangelii gaudium*, he notes that "this moment is the most pronounced time of anthropological reductionism."[52] He has continued his critique of contemporary anthropology in *Laudato si'*, where he notes that the crisis is, at root, the failure to see the person as a person. Throughout *Laudato si'*, he cites the combination of anthropocentrism, individualism, and a consumerist vision of the person as a fundamental intellectual and moral error of our time.[53]

In the background stands a relational ontology. In *Lumen fidei*, Francis writes in favor of a "relational way of viewing the world." This vision is further specified in *Laudato si'*. There, he notes that the universe is a relational reality and that "we need to grasp the variety of things in their multiple relationships. We understand better the importance and meaning of each creature if we contemplate it within the entirety of God's plan."[54] He closes the encyclical with a mini-treatise on the relation of the human person and the Trinity:

> The divine Persons are subsistent relations, and the world, created according to the divine model, is a web of relationships. Creatures tend towards God, and in turn it is proper to every living being to tend towards other things, so that throughout the universe we can find any number of constant and secretly interwoven relationships. This leads us not only to marvel at the manifold connections existing among creatures, but also to discover a key to our own fulfilment. The human person grows more, matures more and is sanctified more to the extent that he or she enters into relationships, going out from themselves to live in communion with God, with others and with all creatures. In this way, they make their own that trinitarian dynamism which God imprinted in them when they were created. Everything is interconnected, and this invites us to develop a spirituality of that global solidarity which flows from the mystery of the Trinity.[55]

Thus, the Trinity, creation as a whole, and all creatures are best understood as relational realities.

Conspicuous by their absence from the writings of Pope Francis are references to the faculties of the person—the soul, intellect, will, and appetites. Instead, he writes of the person in relation. A focus on the abstracted "parts" or faculties of the person has finally fallen away. In Francis, one finds a certain "givenness" of the personalist approach; it no longer needs explanation or justification. Instead, it is simply used.

DIGNITY

Finally, persons are relational, free moral agents who possess human dignity. The connection between personhood and dignity finds its origins in the work of Aquinas. In his discussion of personhood, he argues that "personality pertains of necessity to the dignity of a thing, and to its perfection so far as it pertains to the dignity and perfection of that thing to exist by itself (which is understood by the word 'person'). Now it is a greater dignity to exist in something nobler than oneself than to exist by oneself."[56]

Further, Aquinas notes that "thence by some the definition of person is given as 'hypostasis distinct by reason of dignity.' And because subsistence in a rational nature is of high dignity, therefore every individual of the rational nature is called a 'person.'"[57] This is a curious move by Aquinas. As Augustine Anthony has noted, "The predicate dignity here qualifies and identifies the subject, namely, the person."[58] For Aquinas, the concepts of dignity and person mutually implicate.

The twentieth century saw the concept of dignity assume a central place in Christian ethics. The centrality of dignity coincided, naturally, with the refinement of its definition.[59] For instance, in *Gaudium et spes* "dignity" was often mentioned but never clearly defined. However, the theological community, the US Catholic bishops, Saint John Paul II, and Pope Benedict XVI have further specified this core concept. The US Catholic bishops have defined dignity as the "transcendent worth" of each person.[60] Personal worth, according to this account, cannot be finally measured. Along the same lines, Pope John Paul II has stated that human dignity means that each person possesses inestimable value and incomparable worth.[61] This notion of dignity grounds his moral theology. His arguments on the rights of workers, sexual ethics, the use of in vitro fertilization, and the like derive their force from the value of each human person.[62] In *Dignitas personae*, Pope Benedict argues that "man has unassailable value without distinction. At every state man is in the image of God."⁶³ This is the case because "God sees divine image in each being; embryo, disabled, etc."⁶⁴ He further refines his definition by calling the world to recognize the transcendent value of each person.⁶⁵

Pope Francis has frequently mentioned human dignity but has not given a unique definition of the concept. Instead, he has drawn on already-established definitions. In *Evangelii gaudium*, citing John Paul II, Francis writes that "to believe in a Father who loves all men and women with an infinite love means realizing that 'he thereby confers upon them an infinite dignity.'"⁶⁶ In *Laudato si'*, Francis cites the *Catechism of the Catholic Church* when he writes that "this shows us the immense dignity of each person, who is not just something, but someone. He is capable of self-knowledge, of self-possession, and of freely giving himself and entering into communion with other persons."⁶⁷ These post–Vatican II definitions coalesce around two interlocking themes: Persons have transcendent value because they have been created and loved by God. And like all things personal, dignity is a relational reality.

The definition of dignity given above focuses on inherent and normative dignity. Darlene Fozard Weaver has argued that Catholic theology contains four interrelated meanings of dignity: inherent dignity, consequent dignity, normative dignity, and emblematic dignity.⁶⁸ Inherent dignity is about the worth of a human person. Consequent dignity pertains to how a person has lived; here, a person "attains" dignity through the virtuous life. Third, dignity serves as a normative guide—dignity guides people to treat others *this* way, not *that* way. Fourth and finally, the tradition has understood dignity as an expression of the fullness of the person, an expression that resists reductionism to an aspect of the person. Weaver has termed this "emblematic" dignity. The current study draws on only the first and third meanings. In fact, at the heart of my argument is a commitment to the transcendent value of all persons (inherent dignity), which gives rise to an ethics that morally requires persons and institutions to treat all persons as transcendently valuable (normative dignity).

These notions of dignity provide the grounding principle of Catholic ethics today.⁶⁹ Pope Benedict writes that "on this subject the Church's social doctrine can make a specific contribution, since it is based on man's creation 'in the image of God' (Gen 1:27), a datum which gives rise to the inviolable dignity of the human person and the transcendent value of natural moral norms."⁷⁰ On this point, there is a growing consensus among the Magisterium and the theological class. The theologians Todd Salzman and Michael Lawler acknowledge that dignity is widely recognized as the central moral principle in Christian ethics.⁷¹ To be more precise, the combination of inherent and normative dignity is the central moral concept in Christian ethics.

VIRTUE

The emergence of a more theocentric and personalist theology prepared the ground for the third movement in postconciliar theology: the turn to virtue. These movements made it possible to retrieve an ethics of virtue, which contextualized human action within the person, her character, and the quality of her relations to God and others. Linda Hogan states as much when she argues that personalism requires that moral theology attend to the character of a person and not merely analyze discrete actions.[72]

The rise of virtue has been well documented. In the early 1990s, William Spohn noted that virtue was "becoming an industry giant."[73] In 2004 James Kennan wrote that virtue has been, and is once again becoming, the dominant language of the Catholic moral tradition.[74] Nine years later, Todd Salzman and Michael Lawler noted that there had been a move from analyzing actions to the analysis of persons.[75] And in their 2014 article titled "The Resurgence of Virtue in Recent Moral Theology," David Cloutier and William Mattison noted that "virtue again plays a prominent role in Catholic moral theology."[76]

Virtue has informed much of the recent work of Catholic theological ethicists. Official church teaching has been less informed by such an approach. A lasting vestige of the manuals has been the continued presence of a norm-centered moral theology in papal writings. *Veritatis splendor*, John Paul's encyclical on moral theology, focuses more on the natural law, norms, and obedience than on virtue. The virtues have received scant mention in other major moral and social encyclicals, such as *Sollicitudo rei socialis* and *Evangelium vitae*. Charles Curran has argued that John Paul II "puts the heaviest emphasis on the legal model of ethics."[77]

Although Pope Benedict's series of encyclicals on the theological virtues reintroduced the language of the virtues into magisterial moral teaching, these documents present something less than a developed virtue ethics. *Spe salvi* is Benedict's most robust articulation and use of virtue ethics. At the outset of the text, he appropriates Aquinas's notion that faith is a *habitus*.[78] He emphasized that it is through the stable disposition of faith that the person is substantially altered.

In *Caritas in veritate*, Benedict largely refashions the virtues as principles of action. There, charity is recast as an external source of moral truth. The pope notes that charity "is the principle not only of micro-relationships, but also of macro-relationships."[79] He reiterates this point later, writing that "*caritas in veritate* is the principle around which the Church's social doctrine turns, a principle that takes on practical form in the criteria that govern moral action."⁸⁰ Here, charity is reduced to a principle. Further, it is charity as a principle, not as a virtue, that guides action. The moral norm of Christian action is not a developed way of living and being in relation to others but rather an external precept.

Pope Francis

In contrast to John Paul and Benedict, the virtues primarily drive Francis's moral analyses. This is seen, first, in *Evangelii gaudium*. After arguing that "the biggest problem is when the message we preach then seems identified with those secondary aspects which, important as they are, do not in and of themselves convey the heart of Christ's message," Francis turns to his moral focus: the virtue of mercy.⁸¹ There, Francis retrieves Aquinas's notion that the Church's moral teaching has its own hierarchy, with mercy near the top:

> Saint Thomas Aquinas taught that the Church's moral teaching has its own "hierarchy," in the virtues and in the acts which proceed from them. What counts above all else is "faith working through love" (Gal 5:6). Works of love directed to one's neighbor are the most perfect external manifestation of the interior grace of the Spirit: "The foundation of the New Law is in the grace of the Holy Spirit, who is manifested in the faith which works through love." Thomas thus explains that, as far as external works are concerned, mercy is the greatest of all the virtues: "In itself, mercy is the greatest of the virtues, since all the others revolve around it and, more than this, it makes up for their deficiencies. This is particular to the superior virtue, and as such, it is proper to God to have mercy, through which his omnipotence is manifested to the greatest degree."⁸²

Three points deserve to be noted here. First, and most obviously, Francis's ethical approach is to turn to the virtues. The virtues serve as the organizing concepts for his moral reflection. In a similar vein, Kate Ward has argued that Francis has analyzed inequality through a virtue/vice paradigm.⁸³ Second, Francis claims that acts proceed from virtues. Again, for Francis human action is contextualized and adequately understood in its relation to personal character. Finally, following Aquinas, Francis claims that mercy is the greatest of the virtues regarding external works. I return to this point below.

Pope Francis's 2018 apostolic exhortation *Gaudete et exsultate* follows a similar line of thought. After critiquing those who express "an obsession with the law, ... a punctilious concern for the Church's ... doctrine," the pope writes that "to avoid this we do well to keep reminding ourselves that there is a hierarchy of virtues.... The primary belongs to the theological virtues.... At the centre is charity."[84] Here, Francis argues for a virtue ethics that avoids the dangerous excesses of a law-centered approach to the moral life. Francis affirms this approach in *Amoris laetitia*, noting that "it is reductive simply to consider whether or not an individual's actions correspond to a general law or rule, because that is not enough to discern and ensure full fidelity to God in the concrete life of a human being."[85] He then calls for prudential discernment in using rules to guide decision-making. Ultimately, the pope urges the faithful to follow the *via caritatis*, the virtue of charity, as the first and overriding law of God.[86]

The virtues also enabled Francis to emphasize moral maturation and growth. In *Evangelii gaudium*, he locates moral growth in the cultivation of the virtues, guided by the double love commandment.[87] The focus on personal moral growth privileges the virtues, which attend to the relationship of a person's character and her actions. This focus continues in *Laudato si'*. There, Francis's virtue ethics comes to full flower. Although it does not offer a systematic virtue theory, the encyclical does address the relationship of acts and habits, the role of moral education and habit formation, and the interplay between structures and habits. After arguing for the need for better environmental education, the pope concedes that

> this education aimed at creating an ecological citizenship is at times limited to providing information, and fails to instill good habits. The existence of laws ... is insufficient ... to curb bad conduct.... Only by cultivating sound virtues will people be able to make a selfless ecological commitment.... Education in environmental responsibility can encourage ways of acting which directly and significantly affect the world around us, such as avoiding the use of paper and plastic, reducing water consumption, separating refuse, cooking only what can reasonably be consumed, showing care for other living beings, using public transport or car-pooling, planting trees, turning off unnecessary lights, or any number of other practices.[88]

Here, Francis underscores the power of habit in shaping human action. In this way, he rejects idealist moral theory, which views moral development as primarily intellectual. Thus, though the world's people have a "growing ecological sensitivity," they have not succeeded in "changing their harmful habits of consumption."[89] Like a true virtue ethicist, Francis understands that intentional action arises from the settled habits of the person.

After asserting that acts follow from habits, Francis addresses habit formation. As noted above, education that is concentrated on passing along information is ultimately ineffective. Moral formation—or, better, education in practice—is the effective way "to curb bad conduct." The practice of recycling, or separating out refuse, provides a helpful example. Over the past thirty years, many communities and institutions have encouraged their members to recycle by prescribing specific actions and by facilitating those prescribed actions by placing recycling bins next to trash cans. Likewise, parents have begun directing their children to throw paper and plastic in recycling bins. The result of these practices has been a radical change in behavior. Whereas thirty years ago, most families threw the Sunday paper in the trash, today over two-thirds of the paper consumed in the United States is recycled.[90] Although awareness of ecological problems is necessary to motivate people to change their habits, it is insufficient. People need to be held accountable to a set of practices for behavioral change to occur. It is only through practice that the agent acquires the "sound virtues," which enable her to live a life of environmental respect and material simplicity. And though such practices will not, by themselves, heal the ecological crisis, the creation of "new lifestyles," among other things, will.

Francis frequently has used the concept of "lifestyle" in his writings as a moral category describing the assemblage of a person's habits. In his 2014 World Day of Peace address, he closely aligned one's lifestyle with a person's virtues. There, following Pope John Paul II and Pope Benedict XVI, he called for a changed lifestyle that rediscovered the virtues of prudence, temperance, justice, and strength. He noted that, "above all, these virtues are necessary for building and preserving a society in accord with human dignity."[91]

Laudato si' reiterates this theme. There, Francis's complete solution to the ecological crisis is what he calls a "new culture."[92] This involves civic and political leadership, legal frameworks, and new structures as well as new relationships and lifestyles.[93] The practice of the virtues is central to these ends. The encyclical also showed an awareness of the complexities of moral growth and social change:

> Nevertheless, self-improvement on the part of individuals will not by itself remedy the extremely complex situation facing our world today. Isolated individuals can lose their ability and freedom to escape the utilitarian mindset, and end up prey to an unethical consumerism bereft of social or ecological awareness. Social problems must be addressed by community networks and not simply by the sum of individual good deeds. This task "will make such tremendous demands

of man that he could never achieve it by individual initiative or even by the united effort of men bred in an individualistic way. The work of dominating the world calls for a union of skills and a unity of achievement that can only grow from quite a different attitude." The ecological conversion needed to bring about lasting change is also a community conversion.[94]

Francis makes two points here. The first is that it is difficult to become good alone. The isolated person is apt to follow the prevailing moral mindset. Second, social problems are only solved by collective efforts—that is, by a conversion of a *community* to the life of virtue. In short, Francis recognizes that the moral quality of the community has a bearing on both the acquisition of virtue and building the common good. These points are taken up in greater depth in chapter 6.

Francis's Contextual Virtue Ethics

In his characteristic way, Francis does not approach the virtues theoretically (i.e., as being about human functions and powers) but rather in response to contemporary moral reality. As Cathleen Kaveny has put it, "He is not producing abstract and ahistorical treatises, but rather proffers concrete ethical guidance for people confronting today's challenges."[95] Chapter 4 of *Gaudete et exsultate* is premised on this very approach. His purpose in this chapter is to use the framework of the Beatitudes and Matthew 25:31–46 to underscore certain aspects of the life of holiness. However, he asserts that "the signs I wish to highlight are not the sum total of a model of holiness, but they are five great expressions of love of God and neighbor that I consider of particular importance in the light of certain dangers and limitations present in today's culture."[96]

Francis's focus on "certain dangers and limitations present in today's culture" has often led him to critique what might be called the vice of indifference. He has argued that a pervasive "culture of indifference" is the "great sickness of our time."[97] Clearly, indifference is not something new; every period of history has known people who close their hearts to the needs of others, who close their eyes to what is happening around them, and who turn aside to avoid encountering other people's problems. But in our day, indifference has ceased to be a purely personal matter and has taken on broader dimensions, producing a "globalization of indifference."[98]

Because Francis has identified indifference to suffering as a widespread moral sickness of the early twenty-first century, he often returns to this theme in his writings and homilies. Also, he identifies its cause:

Some people prefer not to ask questions or seek answers; they lead lives of comfort, deaf to the cry of those who suffer. Almost imperceptibly, we grow incapable of feeling compassion for others and for their problems; we have no interest in caring for them, as if their troubles were their own responsibility, and none of our business. "When we are healthy and comfortable, we forget about others (something God the Father never does): we are unconcerned with their problems, their sufferings and the injustices they endure... Our heart grows cold. As long as I am relatively healthy and comfortable, I don't think about those less well off."[99]

According to Francis, health and comfort, two by-products of affluence and consumerism, render people immune to the pain of others. As he writes in his 2019 *Urbi et orbi* speech, "It is injustice that turns [the poor] away from places where they might have hope for a dignified life, but instead find themselves before walls of indifference."[100] Put differently, migrants flee injustice in their homelands only to meet indifference to their suffering in the developed nations that are supposed to be beacons of hope. Wealth often malforms moral character. Many of the young "have grown up in a milieu of extreme consumerism and affluence which makes it difficult to develop other habits."[101] In short, consumer culture is an obstacle to the acquisition of a truly Christian character.

Francis's solution to this situation of indifference is a bundle of Christian virtues: "We too, then, are called to make compassion, love, mercy, and solidarity a true way of life, a rule of conduct in our relationships with one another."[102] This is a contextual virtue ethics. Francis argues that these traits are required today to combat the culturally given moral failings that offend the dignity of the poor and suffering. It is also a medicinal virtue ethics; the virtues provide the cure for contemporary moral ailments. Finally, a virtue approach recommends virtues based on their capacity to build up the common good in today's world.

Charity

Pope Francis has followed the tradition in asserting the primacy of charity, asserting that "what counts above all else is faith working through love"[103] and that "all of the virtues are at the service of this response of love."[104] The primacy of charity should be telegraphed in all that the Church does. Francis has argued that "if in the course of the liturgical year a parish priest speaks about temperance ten times but only mentions charity and justice two or three times, an imbalance results, and precisely those virtues which ought to be most present in preaching and catechesis are overlooked."[105]

In *Evangelii gaudium*, Francis employs a traditional account of love, contending that love "is the beginning of a true concern for the person which inspires me effectively to seek their good."[106] Further, he underscores the relational aspects of love when he notes that love "engages our affectivity, but in order to open it to the beloved and thus to blaze a trail leading away from self-centredness and towards another person, in order to build a lasting relationship; love aims at union with the beloved."[107] Love is not impersonal "do-gooding" but realizes its perfection in friendship and fraternity. The Christian spirit of fraternity yields the "duty of universal charity" for both individuals and nations.[108] Francis follows Benedict's insight that charity should be lived in micro, or interpersonal, relationships as well as in macro, or structural/political, relationships.[109]

However, though Pope Francis affirms the primacy of charity, he writes comparatively little about it. Instead, he has chosen to emphasize the virtues that are at the service of charity: mercy and solidarity.

Mercy

In a world of personal indifference to the poor and suffering, Pope Francis has called for the practice of mercy. Francis telegraphed the importance of mercy for his papacy when he chose his papal coat of arms: "*Miserando et eligendo*: by gazing upon me with the eyes of his mercy, he has chosen me."[110] He deepened his commitment to mercy by declaring an Extraordinary Jubilee Year of Mercy starting on December 8, 2015.[111] In the bull declaring the jubilee, Francis noted that the antidote of the indifference of the rich to the suffering is to rediscover the corporal and spiritual works of mercy.[112] Again, recall that in *Evangelii gaudium* Francis follows Aquinas's claim that mercy is the greatest of all the virtues regarding external works.[113] There, he draws on Pope John XXIII's words at the opening of the Second Vatican Council, in which he urged the Church to use the medicine of mercy, not judgment.[114] Further, at the opening of the Synod on the Family, Francis argues that the Church's first duty is to proclaim God's mercy.

Because Francis's theology has been more pastoral than systematic, he has not produced textbook definitions of concepts such as mercy. However, on two occasions he has offered more precise articulations of the virtue. During the homily for a Mass celebrating Our Lady of Guadalupe, he noted that mercy is that "love which embraces the misery of the human person."[115] Earlier, in 2015, in a homily at a penitentiary, he stated that mercy is "carrying the burden of a brother or sister and helping them walk."[116] This account roughly maps with Aquinas's understanding of mercy. Aquinas defines mercy as "being affected with sorrow at the misery of another as though it were his own. It follows that he endeavors to dispel the misery of this other as if it were his and this is the effect of mercy."[117]

In late 2016, Pope Francis announced a new series of catecheses, in which he would focus on the corporal and spiritual works of mercy:

> In the following Catecheses, we will reflect on these works which the Church presents to us as the concrete way of living out mercy. Over the course of centuries, many simple people have put this into practice, giving their sincere witness of faith. The Church, after all, faithful to her Lord, nourishes a preferential love for the weakest. Often it is the people closest to us who need our help. We should not go out in search of some unknown business to accomplish. It is better to begin with the simplest, which the Lord tells us is the most urgent. In a world which, unfortunately, has been damaged by the virus of indifference, the works of mercy are the best antidote.[118]

Notice again that Francis turns to the "concrete way of living out mercy" through the works of mercy. For him, pastoral direction and applications trump theological treatises. Further, he has envisioned mercy as medicinal in an age "damaged by the virus of indifference." Mercy is not only a core Christian virtue but is also an urgently needed one. Indeed, mercy is a key to Francis's moral theology and his pontificate.

Solidarity

To those who are indifferent to communities of those who are poor and suffer, Pope Francis has offered the virtue of solidarity. Whereas mercy is directed to certain specific individuals, solidarity is directed toward groups. For example, during his World Food Day 2013 address, he noted that solidarity is the solution to the problem of global indifference to those who are hungry.[119]

Francis has followed John Paul's definition of solidarity as "a firm and persevering determination to commit oneself to the common good."[120] Francis put his stamp on solidarity when he wrote that "solidarity represents the moral and social attitude which best corresponds to an awareness of the scourges of our day."[121]

For Francis, the central scourge of the early twenty-first century is indifference to those who suffer. Notice, again, that the virtues he emphasizes emerge from a particular social context and are not offered either due to their place in the tradition or as the result of a preexisting anthropological vision. For instance, in his 2020 World Day of Peace Message, Francis notes that a world marked by fear and mistrust can be healed only by a "global ethic of solidarity and cooperation."[122]

In addition to his basic definition of the concept, he uses solidarity in several different ways, sometimes in the same paragraph:

> Solidarity is a spontaneous reaction by those who recognize that the social function of property and the universal destination of goods are realities that come before private property. The private ownership of goods is justified by the need to protect and increase them so that they can better serve the common good; for this reason, solidarity must be lived as the decision to restore to the poor what belongs to them. These convictions and habits of solidarity, when they are put into practice, open the way to other structural transformations, and make them possible. Changing structures without generating new convictions and attitudes will only ensure that those same structures will become, sooner or later, corrupt, oppressive, and ineffectual.[123]

There are two sides of solidarity at play here. Like John Paul, Francis presents solidarity as a virtue that "spontaneously" produces actions that serve the poor and the common good.[124] Further, he notes that "habits of solidarity" need to be practiced. His is a more granular notion of solidarity, which emphasizes what one might call the practices or works of solidarity.[125] Second, the passage quoted above shows how solidarity contributes to the common good. It does not produce the structures that make up the common good, but it does "open the way to other structural transformations and make them possible."[126] The social effect of solidarity is a movement toward changed structures and the emergence of the common good.

We have seen that Pope Francis has used the virtues as medicines to cure persons of the vices that have infected large swaths of global society. Where relations among people have gone awry, Francis has proposed a new set of works, practices, and habits to rehabilitate these relations. Charity has served as the mother of the virtuous life, which Francis has suggested is concretely practiced through mercy and solidarity. As I have argued above, these virtues correct the two ways in which people in the twenty-first century are often indifferent to suffering.

CONCLUSION

This chapter has argued for two key points. First, Catholic theology and ethics have become more theocentric and personalist, and virtue ethics has emerged as the tradition's central ethical methodology. These are not fringe movements but are at the heart of magisterial teaching—the leading edges of the Church's theoethical tradition. Second, I have shown the ways in which there is an organic unity to these three developments. As noted above, Linda Hogan has argued that a personalist approach required attention to moral character and not merely an ethics of action.[127] This is the case because personalism attends to the whole person and not only to one's faculties, powers, or abstracted acts. In addition, personalism invites a focus on relationality. The virtue ethics of Francis, for instance, centers on how Christians should be in right relation with others in today's moral context. Charity, mercy, and solidarity are relational character traits. They are directed to others and to building a loving relationship with them. Francis's virtue ethics is, then, a relational ethics. In the tradition of Aquinas, it is also a theocentric ethics. The virtues aim to enable the person to relate to others in light of the relationship that God has with the other.

The same theocentric spirit is present in Christian personalism. Above, I have shown how the primary relation of the person, and the foundation for all other relations, is the relationship with God. As the image of God, the person reflects the relationality of the Trinity. Human dignity results from this imaging. For these reasons, these three theological trajectories—theocentrism, personalism, and virtue—furnish the conceptual architecture for the constructive proposal that is presented in subsequent chapters.

Moreover, the theocentric and personalist turns in Catholic ethics have yet to be fully integrated within virtue theory. However, I contend that Catholic virtue theory should have an explicitly theocentric and personalist architecture. Theologians have suggested just such an approach (as taken especially by James Keenan and Charles Curran), but work remains to develop a truly theocentric and personalist virtue theory. This synthesis is the goal of the next chapter.

NOTES

1. Aquinas, *Summa theologiae*, I, 1.3, 1.3 ad 2, 1.5.
2. Aquinas, I, 1.7 ad 2.
3. Curran, *Moral Theology*, 66.
4. See Pinckaers, *Sources*, chap. 11; and Gallagher, *Time Past*, chap. 2.

5. Pius XI, *Quadragesimo anno*, 110.
6. Haring, *Law of Christ*, 1.
7. Haring, 61.
8. Curran, "Obituary."
9. Paul VI, "Speech."
10. Hollenbach, "Commentary," 266.
11. Curran, "Risks," 410.
12. Benedict XVI, *Dignitas personae*, 8.
13. Curran, *Catholic Social Teaching*, chap. 2.
14. Keenan, *History*, 242.
15. Cloutier, *Vice*, 121, 126.
16. Benedict XVI, *Caritas*, 2.
17. Benedict XVI, 6.
18. The difference is not due to the length of the documents. *Centessimus annus* is 25,621 words, whereas *Caritas in veritate* is 27,882 words.
19. Benedict XVI, *Caritas*, 56.
20. Spardaro, "Big Heart."
21. Francis, *Lumen fidei*, 4.
22. Francis, 18.
23. Francis.
24. Francis, "World Day of Peace, 2014," 3.
25. Francis, 4.
26. Francis, *Laudato si'*, 69.
27. Francis, 83.
28. Francis, 86.
29. John Coburn argued that the council produced "one Personalist constitution or decree after another." See Coburn, *Personalism*, 75.
30. See Curran, *Moral Theology*, chaps. 3 and 5; and Spinello, "Enduring Relevance."
31. Wojtyla, *Acting Person*, 13.
32. Clark, *Vision*, 24–25.
33. John Paul II, *Theology*, 421–22.
34. John Paul II, *Centessimus annus*, 11.
35. John Paul II, 12.
36. John Paul II, 53.
37. Ratzinger, "Concerning the Notion."
38. Ratzinger, 439.
39. Ratzinger, 445.
40. Clarke, "Person," 607.
41. Benedict XVI, *Spe salvi*, 14.
42. Benedict XVI, 16.
43. Benedict XVI, 14.
44. Francis, *Evangelii gaudium*, 55.
45. Francis, 231.
46. Kasper, *Pope Francis' Revolution*, 16.
47. Massaro, *Mercy*, 143. See also Scannone, "Pope Francis."
48. Francis, *Laudato si'*, 66.
49. Francis, 85.

50. Francis, 68–69.
51. Francis, 119.
52. Francis, "Address to Participants in the International Seminar."
53. See especially Francis, *Laudato si'*, 116, 144.
54. Francis, 86.
55. Francis, 240. See also O'Meara, "Community"; O'Meara concludes this piece by stating that "community seems intrinsic to being. This is not a deductive proof of astrophysics or of faith but an intimation linking being to community. In all directions reality often seems to be communal" (p. 446).
56. Aquinas, *Summa theologiae*, III, 2.2 ad 2.
57. Aquinas, I, 29.3 ad 2.
58. Anthony, "Human Dignity," 37.
59. Although the concept of dignity has been refined since the Second Vatican Council, it remains true that "the Magisterium has yet to define what it means by dignity in a comprehensive and systematic way." See Petrusek, "Relevance," 535.
60. US Conference of Catholic Bishops, *Economic Justice*, 28.
61. John Paul II, *Evangelium vitae*, 2, 96.
62. Curran, *Moral Theology*, 94.
63. Benedict XVI, *Dignitas personae*, 7.
64. Benedict XVI, 16.
65. Benedict, "United Nations Address."
66. Francis, *Evangelii gaudium*, 178, quoting John Paul II.
67. Francis, *Laudato si'*, 65, here citing *Catechism*, 357.
68. Weaver, "Christian Anthropology," 2. For a more extended discussion of the various ways in which dignity has been defined and employed, see *Dignity and Conflict*, ed. Rothchild and Petrusek.
69. See, e.g., John XXIII, *Mater et magister*, 220; and Pontifical Council for Justice and Peace, *Compendium*, 107.
70. Benedict XVI, *Caritas*, 45.
71. Salzman and Lawler, "Method," 911.
72. Hogan, "Toward a Personalist Theology."
73. Spohn, "Return," 60.
74. Keenan, "Notes," 111.
75. Keenan, 915.
76. Cloutier and Mattison, "Resurgence," 228.
77. Curran, *Moral Theology*, 104.
78. Benedict XVI, *Spe salvi*, 7.
79. Benedict XVI, *Caritas*, 2.
80. Benedict XVI, 6.
81. Francis, *Evangelii gaudium*, 34, 38. There, he notes that Christians should not talk more about secondary virtues, such as temperance, more than the primary virtue of charity.
82. Francis, 37, citing Aquinas, *Summa theologiae*, I-II, 66.4–6, on hierarchy of moral teaching; and II-II, 30.4, on the centrality of mercy.
83. Ward, "Jesuit and Feminist Hospitality."
84. Francis, *Gaudete et exsultate*, 57, 60.
85. Francis, *Amoris laetitia*, 304.

86. Francis, 306.
87. Francis, *Evangelii gaudium*, 160–61.
88. Francis, *Laudato si'*, 211.
89. Francis, 55.
90. Statistics are taken from Earth911.com.
91. Francis, "World Day of Peace, 2014," 6.
92. Francis, *Laudato si'*, 53, 114.
93. Francis, 164, 167, 174, 181.
94. Francis, 219.
95. Kaveny, "Pope Francis," 187.
96. Francis, *Gaudete et exsultate*, 111.
97. Di Bussolo, "Pope at Mass"; Francis, "World Day of Prayer for Peace, Assisi."
98. Francis, "World Day of Peace Message, 2016."
99. Francis, "World Day of Peace, 2015."
100. Francis, "*Urbi et orbi*," 2019.
101. Francis, *Laudato si'*, 209.
102. Francis.
103. Francis, *Evangelii gaudium*, 37. See also Francis, *Gaudete et exsultate*, 60.
104. Francis, *Evangelii gaudium*, 39.
105. Francis, 38.
106. Francis, 199.
107. Francis, 27.
108. Francis, "World Day of Peace, 2014."
109. Benedict XVI, *Caritas*, 7. Francis, *Evangelii gaudium*, 205; Francis, *Laudato si'*, 231.
110. Kasper, *Pope Francis' Revolution*, 31.
111. Francis, *Misericordiae vultus*.
112. Francis, 15.
113. Francis, *Evangelii gaudium*, 37. See also Francis, *Gaudete et exsultate*, 106, where he drew on the same passage in the *Summa theologiae* to claim that the best way to show our love of God is through "the works of mercy towards our neighbor, even more than our acts of worship."
114. John XXIII, "Opening Address of Vatican II."
115. Francis, "Homily, December 12, 2015."
116. Francis, "Homily, March 12, 2015."
117. Aquinas, *Summa theologiae*, I, 23.1.
118. Francis, "General Audience," October 12, 2016.
119. Francis, "World Food Day 2013 Address."
120. Francis, "World Day of Peace Message, 2016," 6. See also John Paul II, *Sollicitudo rei socialis*, 38.
121. Francis, "World Day of Peace Message, 2016," 5.
122. Francis, "World Day of Peace Message, 2020," 1. There, quoting Francis, "Address of the Holy Father on Nuclear Weapons."
123. Francis, *Evangelii gaudium*, 189.
124. Francis. See also Francis, "World Day of Peace, 2016," 5.
125. Francis, "World Day of Peace, 2016," 7. There, he writes, "Many positive initiatives which testify to the compassion, mercy and solidarity of which we are capable. Here I would

offer some examples of praiseworthy commitment, which demonstrate how all of us can overcome indifference in choosing not to close our eyes to our neighbour. These represent good practices on the way to a more humane society."
126. Francis, *Evangelii gaudium*, 189.
127. Hogan, "Toward a Personalist Theology."

PART III

Synthesis and Application

CHAPTER 5

A Theocentric, Personalist Virtue Ethics

The last chapter argued that Catholic magisterial teaching has become more theocentric, personalist, and focused on virtue. The chapter did not present a developed account of virtue or delineate a theocentric, personalist approach to virtue. Such an account is the aim of this chapter. This work is necessitated by the fact that Catholic virtue theory is not sufficiently informed by the theocentric and personalist turns of the postconciliar era. However, space permits treatment of only the central facets of this theory rather than a comprehensive account.

This account is mine but draws deeply from Thomistic virtue theory. Because I take it as a given that a Catholic virtue theory develops from within the stream of thought that began with Aquinas, I focus less on a defense of his theoretical underpinnings and more on an explanation and contemporary appropriation of them. Further, the account emerges from developments in two bodies of literature. First, theological virtue ethicists—such as William Spohn, James Keenan, and Charles Curran—have moved virtue in a decisively relational direction. And second, contemporary philosophers of virtue theory, such as Julia Annas and Linda Zagzebski, have recently produced deep treatments of the inner workings of virtue and vice. Specifically, they have developed theories regarding how the virtues are formed and how the virtues guide action.

The chapter begins by naming a number of the strengths and weaknesses of contemporary virtue ethics. It then introduces a personalist virtue approach—an approach that grounds the virtues in the relationality of the person. The chapter's third section provides an account of the nature of habits and dispositions, drawing on traditional and contemporary philosophical treatments of these concepts in order to gain clarity on them. Finally, the chapter investigates the formation of habits and how they relate to human action. There, I argue for a multimodal approach to the formation and cultivation of the virtues.

STRENGTHS AND WEAKNESSES OF VIRTUE ETHICS

Why virtue ethics? There are at least six reasons why Christians should turn to virtue. First, virtue ethics provides the best account of ethics because it has explanatory power. That is, it provides an insightful explanation of moral reality. Virtue ethics conceptualizes the universal human experience of habituated action. Human actions do not arise at random but, rather, with regularity due to the causal power of habits. Mundane but morally important examples include what and how much one eats, how one drives, and how one interacts with persons suffering from homelessness. These are moral traits because they pertain to how one relates to self, others, and creation. Moreover, they are habituated ways of acting. Most people eat, drive, and interact with others in regularized ways. Aggressive drivers regularly drive aggressively. And because it is their "second nature" to drive aggressively, they have difficulty driving in a more relaxed and courteous manner. The point here is that a virtue approach to the moral life resonates with and helps explain moral experience.

Second, a virtue approach offers a full picture of the moral life. As Aquinas writes, "We may reduce the whole of moral matters to the consideration of the virtues." He continues, "Hence in treating about each cardinal virtue we shall treat also of all the virtues which, in any way whatever, belong to that virtue as also of the opposing vices. In this way no matter pertaining to morals will be overlooked."[1] We should not misinterpret his claim that moral matters can be "reduced" to the virtues. Aquinas's point here is that moral matters can be organized around the virtues because the virtues offer a full picture of the moral life. A virtue approach does not reduce ethical analysis to considerations of character, as if discrete actions, laws, precepts, and commandments lack moral standing. But it is quite the opposite; the virtues offer Aquinas the opportunity to integrate and organize all moral realities and guides into his moral theology.[2]

As Nicholas Austin has argued, virtue emerged in the mid–twentieth century in order to provide thicker moral analyses of action.[3] Whereas the manualist approach focused on "acts mandated by laws and rules" and "ignored questions of personal virtue," a virtue approach accounts for both moral character and action.[4] The virtues exist in an interdependent relationship with action. Each causally influences the other. Virtue ethics offers the most comprehensive approach to the moral life because it provides a coherent path to pursue the good, and it incorporates and contextualizes human action and normative action guides.

Virtue ethics also pertains to every *area* of the moral life. Virtue ethics attends to the mundane aspects of life, thus avoiding the reduction of ethics to moral quandaries. Consider the fact that principles and rules often have little to contribute to the mundane aspects of the moral life. For instance, there is neither a principle nor a norm that guides a mother's care for her disobedient child. Here, she rightly turns to exemplars of the virtues of love, patience, and courage to guide her action. Alternatively, and more directly, she may appeal to the virtues themselves to discern a loving response. She may ask herself: what would a patient mother do in such a situation?

Third, virtue attends to moral obligation and moral minimums, but also to moral excellence and supererogation. A virtue approach recurrently asks, What would a person of high moral character do in this situation? What is the loving, merciful, and just action to do? Such questions fit within a Christian ethics that has as its goal the life of universal love. Further, such questions will help guide a person's action when she meets unjust social structures. As the examples in this book have shown, structures present complex moral challenges to agents—challenges that manualist era principles cannot address. Unlike the principle of double effect and the principle of cooperation, a virtue approach enables a person to distinguish between prohibited actions, exemplary actions, and actions that are not exemplary but are still permitted.

Fourth, as has already been suggested, virtue is useful. Virtue ethics is capable of providing both action guidance ("What should I do in this situation?") and action assessment ("Did I act virtuously?"). Agents are guided by the virtues when they ask, "What is the just/chaste/temperate act in these circumstances?" Here the agent adverts to character, not rules, in discovering the right action. Put differently, the "direction of analysis" is from the virtues to action.[5] This aspect of virtue ethics is taken up in greater depth later in the chapter. Action assessment through a virtue lens is retrospective, inviting the agent to ask, for example, Who am I becoming, or who have I become, now that I have repeatedly lied to my friend?

One of the reasons virtue is useful is that it offers a thick analysis of human action by further specifying the right action as just, or loving, or merciful.[6] Other modes of ethical analysis either contain a thin notion of the good or right or turn to virtue terms, such as love and justice, to thicken their normative claims. In her pathbreaking article "Modern Moral Philosophy," Elizabeth Anscombe emphasizes this point: "It would be a great improvement if, instead of 'morally wrong,' one always named a genus such as 'untruthful,' 'unchaste,' 'unjust.' We should no longer ask whether doing something was 'wrong,' passing directly from some description of an action to this notion; we should ask whether, e.g., it was unjust; and the answer would sometimes be clear at once."[7]

Fifth, the concept of virtue is especially important in Christian ethics because it provides an account of how God's grace is operative in the moral life. Grace infused into the habits of a person forms her character so that she can freely execute acts of faith, hope, and charity.[8] These virtues orient her to God, and in doing so, direct all her acts to cultivate a loving friendship with God and God's beloved.

Sixth and finally, virtue ethics is especially fitting in a Christian context because the final and full human good is the person's loving relationship with God and neighbor. Virtue captures the moral reality of the person because it recognizes that there is a whole in the moral life, the person. When human acts are abstracted from the acting person, neither is sufficiently understood. The human person is in relation to family, friends, and God, not a person's actions. It is the person who is in union with God and neighbor through the virtue of charity, not her actions. It is the person who is saved, not her actions. It is the person who is capable of accepting the gift of salvation—who is capable of receiving the gift of divine love and mercy. Although actions mediate all these realities, there exists a person who is more than the sum of her actions. Thus, whom one becomes—a loving parent, a faithful spouse, a merciful friend—and not merely what one does is of supreme moral importance.

Although virtue ethics is the best approach to Christian ethics, it is not without deficiencies. Chief among these is the fact that virtue ethics is undertheorized. Contemporary Christian virtue ethics typically spills little ink on virtue theory. To clarify the concepts, virtue ethics is a normative ethical methodology in which virtue is the central normative concept whereby other normative concepts are defined or understood. A virtue theory seeks to explain and justify virtue. Deontological or utilitarian ethics could, for example, contain a theory of virtue. For the former, the virtues enable the person to carry out her duty. For the latter, the virtues capacitate the person to calculate the greatest overall pleasure for those affected by an action. Although a utilitarian may or may not rely on a virtue theory, it is imperative that a strong and insightful virtue ethics draws on a well-developed theory of virtue.[9]

In order to quickly move to normative analyses, Catholic ethicists often give short shrift to virtue theory by drawing on a thin body of literature on the topic. Catholic ethicists continue to, rightly I believe, draw from the well of Aquinas on all matters ethical. In particular, his virtue theory continues to provide a strong foundation for contemporary virtue ethics. However,

Aquinas's powers-based approach to the virtues does not comport with contemporary theological anthropology.

Many theological ethicists have contemporized their virtue theory by using Alasdair MacIntyre's work. Jennifer Herdt has noted that Christian ethicists have embraced his work to a greater degree than philosophers of virtue.[10] Christopher Vogt has argued that "the majority of Christian ethicists working today" use MacIntyre's three sources for virtue formation: practices, tradition, and narrative.[11] However, the conversation regarding what a virtue is and how a virtue is formed did not end with MacIntyre's *After Virtue*. Philosophers of virtue continue to develop insightful accounts regarding what a virtue is, how it is formed, and how the virtue-action dynamic transpires. There is much to be gained for Christian, and especially Catholic, virtue ethicists in these developments. A turn to the philosophy of virtue will aid Christian virtue ethicists in developing contemporary theories of virtue.

As I noted at the outset, what follows is not a comprehensive virtue theory. That will need to wait for another time. Instead, this chapter integrates some of the recent developments in theological ethics and philosophical virtue theory into what aims to be an outline of a contemporary Christian virtue theory. Such an account is needed to analyze how social structures shape personal moral character.

PERSONALIST VIRTUE THEORY

Virtue theory is a diverse field. There are the communitarian theories of Alasdair MacIntyre and Stanley Hauerwas, the pure virtue theories of Michael Slote and Linda Zagzebski, and the anthropologically based theories that arise from within the Thomistic tradition.[12] My approach develops out of the Thomistic tradition. Although Aquinas makes a significant contribution to virtue theory by grounding his virtues in an anthropological context, his thirteenth-century theological anthropology does not fully comport with the best theological accounts of the person today.[13] Chapter 4 showed that magisterial teachings increasingly have emphasized the relational aspects of the human person. And though Aristotle and Aquinas each emphasizes relational virtues, their anthropologies are not fundamentally relational.[14]

The post–Vatican II era has produced several accounts of virtue based on a relational portrait of the person. William Spohn argues that friendship is "the primary adult context for the development of moral judgment and character."[15] Paul Waddell notes that "the moral life is what happens to us in relationship with others."[16] James Keenan's 1995 article "Proposing Cardinal

Virtues" recasts the cardinal virtues in terms of a relational anthropology. There, human relationality is architectonic for Keenan. Relations are not just important; they provide the entire architecture for his approach to virtue. The same is not true of Aristotle, Aquinas, or other contemporary virtue theorists. Keenan claims that the traditional four cardinal virtues of prudence, justice, temperance, and fortitude were inadequate. He argues that the virtues do not perfect powers or "things" inside us but rather the ways that we are.[17] We are, Keenan notes, "beings in relationship." Keenan's solution is a revised set of virtues that are based on how persons are relational. For Keenan, justice perfects how persons are relational with all other persons in general. Fidelity perfects the ways in which persons are relational within close interpersonal relationships. Self-care perfects how a person relates uniquely to herself. Keenan retains prudence as the virtue by which one rightly determines how to live out the three others in a given situation.

Charles Curran has taken a similar approach to the virtues. In his *The Catholic Moral Tradition Today: A Synthesis*, he views the virtues through his relationality-responsibility lens and writes, "The relationality-responsibility model influences how one understands the virtues—both the general virtues that affect our basic orientation and all our relationships and the particular virtues that modify our particular relationships with God, neighbor, self, and world."[18] He then treats both general virtues, such as faith and creativity, and particular virtues, which are distinguished according to how people are relational.[19] In Keenan and Curran, one finds an explicit shift away from a faculty-based approach to the virtues and toward a relational approach.

My account of the virtues draws on these thinkers and is especially inspired by Keenan's move to relationality as the matrix for the virtues. However, mine is more explicitly personalist than theirs and requires some groundwork, which I present in three subsections. First, I present the anthropological and theological commitments, which lead to a personalist virtue theory. I then make the argument that a personalist approach to virtue is relational and not limited to interpersonal relationships. Third, I turn to foundational issues in virtue that require clarification, such as the definition of virtue, the nature of habits and dispositions, and the formation of moral character. Thus, the goal of this section of the chapter is to outline a Christian virtue theory, which is then used in the remaining chapters of the book.

Relational, Not Interactive, Personalism

Up to this point, I have noted that persons are relational and have written less about human relationships. Here is the difference. A relationship is with an identifiable person, such as a spouse or one's physician, and involves interaction. A relation is not necessarily with an identifiable person; nor is it necessarily interactive. Human relationality is about "reciprocal action among two entities."[20] Thus, one can be in a relation with another without interacting with that person. As an illustration, every citizen of the United States has a relation with elected officials, such as the nation's president. Although the vast majority of citizens lack a relationship with the president, there is reciprocal action between a president and a citizen. A citizen can organize a protest against a policy of the president, while a president can sign legislation that affects a citizen's taxes. A relation may be between two people, or a person and an institution or organization. For example, American taxpayers are in relation to the Internal Revenue Service. So, though all relationships are relations, not all relations are relationships.

This distinction comports with collective contemporary experience. As the Rana Plaza example showed, people are increasingly aware that they have some relation with distant others, such as those who sew their clothes, even if they never meet those persons. Along these lines, Julie Hanlon Rubio has argued that "we can no longer limit our discussion of justice to direct relationships with shopkeepers, neighbors, and employers."[21] Further, it is more accurate to speak of a relation with the created world than of a relationship with the created world. The concept of relationship seems strained and stretched if it can accommodate, for instance, both a spousal relationship and a relationship with the oceans. Although both these relations are morally important, they are different and require different concepts to explain them. Personalism ought to be able to account for and distinguish between both forms of relationality.

Human persons, then, have four kinds of relations, each of which will need to be guided by the virtues. A person is in relation with God, herself, her neighbor, and creation. My project differs from Keenan's insofar as mine is not focused on an articulation of contemporary cardinal virtues but endeavors to develop a theocentric virtue theory. Therefore, I want to discuss the ways in which persons are relational with self, others, *and* God. Further, as I noted above, I want to recognize the existence of a relation among persons and the nonhuman created world. Certainly, Keenan's approach to human relationality refines my account by distinguishing close interpersonal relationships from less intimate ones.

Personhood, the Good, and Love

A personalist approach focuses on the actually exiting person, not the parts of the person abstracted from her being. This perspective maintains that each person images God, is transcendently valuable, is substance-in-relation with God and others, and possesses free will. Such a portrait of the person is essential for any coherent virtue theory because one needs to know what the virtues perfect. For Aquinas, the virtues were perfections of powers. In my account, the virtues are excellences of a person regarding her relations to God, self, others, and creation.

Once we know what the virtues perfect, we need to know what the perfect or excellent is. That is, we need to know the goods that the virtues enable the person to realize. Questions regarding the good have been essential for virtue theorists who have drawn from the Aristotelian account of virtue. For Aquinas, the virtues are specified according to the good or end of each power. MacIntyre and Hauerwas, for example, have argued that the concept of a virtue always follows from some prior notion of the good.[22] MacIntyre emphasizes that Aristotle's account of virtue is secondary to that of a social role, while Benjamin Franklin's is secondary to that of utility.[23] Along the same lines, the question for my approach is this: What is an excellent or perfected relationality with God, self, others, and creation?

Following the theocentric turn, I argue that a "good relation" is determined in reference to God. Here, a brief excursus into Aquinas's treatise on charity is helpful, because it contains the Christian tradition's most lucid argument for a relational, theocentric virtue ethics. There, Aquinas explains the interconnection of the love of God and neighbor in relational terms:

> Friendship extends to a person in two ways: first in respect of himself, and in this way friendship never extends but to one's friends; secondly, it extends to someone in respect of another, as, when a man has friendship for a certain person, for his sake he loves all belonging to him, be they children, servants, or connected with him in any way. Indeed, so much do we love our friends, that for their sake we love all who belong to them, even if they hurt or hate us; so that, in this way, the friendship of charity extends even to our enemies, whom we love out of charity in relation to God, to Whom the friendship of charity is chiefly directed.[24]

Aquinas takes it for granted that one should love the friends of one's friend. For example, for someone to love me, they must also love my sons and my wife because I love my sons and wife. They must relate to my family by accounting for the ways in which I relate to my family. If a friend harms or hates my family, my relationship with that friend will be damaged. Similarly, Christians are called to relate to all creatures in relation to how their friend, God, relates to all creatures. Because God loves all persons, so too should the one who loves God love all persons. One should care for nonhuman creatures because God loves nonhuman creatures. Further, this is the reason why Christians should exercise a preferential option for the poor. The God revealed by Jesus Christ is a partial God, a God who opts for the poor. The Christians who follow this God should opt for the poor because God does.[25] In sum, the relationship with God should form the moral priorities, character, actions, and relations of the believer.

A good relation, therefore, involves relating to others as God relates to them. That is to say that a good relation involves charity. Charity is the unique form of love in which the believer loves God and loves the neighbor for the sake of God who loves the neighbor. As an infused virtue, Gustavo Gutiérrez described charity as "God's love in us."[26] As a form of love, charity is unitive.[27] It culminates in the union of the person and God. Drawing on Aquinas, Anthony Flood noted that "divine friendship requires melting on the part of the human person—a readiness and willingness to allow the ecstasy and mutual indwelling of love to occur."[28] Charity is also active. As Pope Benedict XVI put it, "To love someone is to desire that person's good and to take effective steps to secure it."[29] This statement is true but lacks specificity. What, exactly, is a person's good?

Again, Aquinas provides a helpful account. This account is found in his question on natural law.[30] For Aquinas, the natural law provides instruction regarding the human good. There, he describes the three generic natural human inclinations. Each natural inclination has as its object a generic human good. In the end, natural law provides a set of human goods that are worthy of human moral pursuit. This theory stipulates that there are three overarching kinds goods: the goods of life and health (self-preservation); the goods of the life, health, and education of one's family and others (preservation of species); and friendship with God and neighbor. These levels are ordered hierarchically. Life is a great good but is not lived for its own sake. People should live for the sake of promoting the well-being of others and, finally, love of God and neighbor. The summit of the human good is found in friendship and union with God and God's beloved. This is the integral human good that Pope Paul VI referred to in *Populorum progressio*. Paul argues that the world should be structured such that persons could pursue their physical, educational, social, and spiritual good.[31] Thus, the human good involves promoting the integral well-being of oneself and others and moving toward a loving friendship and union with God and others. Of course, only the grace of God enables the human person to attain this integral good.

Love as Union

Unitive friendship is the goal of the Christian life. Union is achieved through love—that passion that apprehends the good in another, desires to be united with the other, and rests in the other. As Bernard Brady wrote, love always involves an emotional component: "No moral theologian would define love primarily as an emotion; yet to miss emotion in love is to miss a necessary element."[32] The lover is emotionally moved by the goodness of the beloved and desires to promote that good and to be in union with the beloved. For example, when a wife loves her husband, she desires and wills the good for him and counts his friendship with her to be constitutive of the husband's well-being. The goal and effect of this impassioned loving are indwelling, a sharing in the life of the other. Her husband's well-being is not merely that he is healthy, loves his child, his friends, and God; his good is also found in the friendship that unites him with his wife.

As this account suggests, there is a movement from the passion of love that desires union to the real union that love ultimately effects. Aquinas recognizes this in his distinction between real and affective unions of persons: "There is real union, consisting in the conjunction of one with the other.... There is also an affective union, consisting in an aptitude or proportion, insofar as one thing, from the very fact of its having an aptitude for and an inclination to another, partakes of it: and love betokens such a union. This [affective] union precedes the movement of desire."[33] In short, the affective union that a person is inclined to have with another person is the first movement toward a real, actual union of persons. Commenting on this passage, Livio Melina argues that an "affective union... is that first, intentional union experienced as an original promise of fulfillment that precedes and provokes every movement tending toward achieving a true union with the beloved."[34] The affective union that a lover has with another is an indication that the lover sees the other as transcendently valuable and desires to promote the good and be in union with the other. Such desires are not realized as of yet; but the lover is disposed to promote the good of the other and enter into friendship with the other if the opportunity arises. Such a person is open to, cultivates the conditions for, and attempts to move toward friendship and union with the beloved. All love begins with an affective union—a disposition to be in union with the beloved.

The twofold union Aquinas describes may appear, at first glance, to be of little ethical consequence. However, this first, affective union is ethically crucial for Christians living in a world where they are in relation with distant others. The affective union that a consumer has with the worker who sewed her clothing constitutes recognition and affirmation of the value of the worker. This union "provokes" the consumer to consider the well-being of the garment worker when the consumer discerns her clothing purchases.

The centrality of union and friendship suggests that the human good is always, to a degree, a common good. Friendship is a good that is realized by an individual only when others share and participate in it. One, of course, cannot be friends by oneself. This kind of good is what David Hollenbach has called an intrinsic common good.[35] An intrinsic common good is "the good of being a community at all—the good realized in the mutual relationships in and through which human beings achieve their well-being."[36]

However, the Catholic social encyclical tradition has tended to emphasize the second meaning of the common good—its instrumental nature. Certain goods are instrumentally valuable for people because people are needy. People need the goods of society to be distributed in such a way that persons have "easy and ready access" to the goods needed to live a dignified and happy life.[37] Again, individuals need the world to be structured such that they have access to the goods needed for their well-being. Aquinas captures this aspect of the common good when he writes that "the individual good is impossible without the common good of the family, state, or kingdom."[38] Both aspects of the common good are necessary. However, as David Cloutier has argued, and this subsection on union has suggested, the common good is primarily about personal relationships (the intrinsic common good) and is only secondarily materialistic (the instrumental common good).[39]

Virtue Defined

A virtue is an operative habit that enables a person to consistently, easily, and joyfully relate well to God, herself, other persons, and the created world.[40] Here, virtue is about the quality of the person's relationality. Further, it concerns how the whole person relates to others. The movements internal to the person—such as her intellect, intentions, motives, and emotions—are constitutive of her character, as are her external actions. A person's character emerges from all these personal realities and cannot be reduced to any one of them. Virtues and vices are distinguished by their capacity to promote good, right, and loving relations or their opposites. Such relations necessarily will be "reasonable," but their "reasonableness" does not drive the analysis; the quality of the person's relationality does. This account of virtue is thick, or content-full. The good for a person is the good of loving God, self, neighbor, and creation.

Given what has been established above, a theocentric personalist virtue theory consists in those traits that enable the person to

- Recognize and promote the value and well-being of the other. That value is found in the object's/subject's relation with God.
- Be open to, cultivate the conditions for, and move toward love and union with God and God's beloved. In particular, the believer is called to exercise a special love and care for the poor, sick, and forgotten.[40]

There is a lexical ordering of the two parts of virtue. That is, one must recognize the value and dignity of the other and promote her well-being in order to be open to a loving union with the other.

This is a theocentric account because, first, God is recognized as the Good and the source of all created goods. Second, it is God's relationship with one's neighbor and creation that determines how the agent should relate to these realities. As Stephen Pope has written, "God is the primary object of charity, and through it one loves all that God loves."[41] A theocentric virtue theory begins with the love of God and then moves out toward whom and what God loves. It is a personalist account because values, virtues, and right actions are relationally determined. Here, the subject of a virtue is a human relation. We become our moral selves through how we relate to God, self, neighbor, and creation.

The virtues, in their fullness, are infused by God. The infused virtues are those that God pours forth into the habits of the person, directing those habits to God. Charity, as the architectonic virtue, directs all the virtues—faith, hope, and the moral virtues—to its own end of union with God.[42] As I show below, the infused virtues must be accepted by the agent in order to be possessed. With the theological virtues, God infuses the other virtues so that the person can properly enact the theological virtues throughout the whole of her life.[43] Jean Porter has written that "charity is oriented toward a distinctive kind of action, in this case, a distinctive kind of love of God. In order to work effectively in other spheres of life, it needs to work through other virtues, which are immediately oriented toward other, moral particular kinds of goods."[44] Although charity is the form and summit of all the virtues, many other infused traits—such as prudence, justice, temperance, mercy, and solidarity—are required so that an agent can actively and effectively love God, self, neighbor, and creation. In their acquired states these virtues are directed toward human flourishing and the common good, not union with God.[45]

A Relational, Prudential, Nonconsequentialist Account

Because the virtues are about the quality of one's relationality, this account is decidedly nonconsequentialist. The virtues enable persons to ever more lovingly relate to others. As I argued above, this will involve working for the well-being of others, because active benevolence is at the core of what it means to love. As a result, the virtuous person needs to possess and exercise prudence in order to know, here and now, what comports with the well-being of another. The virtuous person understands the circumstances of the situation, recognizes and desires to promote the dignity and well-being of others, and acts in a way that authentically promotes their good.

The necessity of prudence has been evident during the COVID-19 pandemic. Due to the highly contagious nature of the virus, a prudent adult child knows that she should not visit a parent in a nursing home because the COVID-19 virus poses a high risk for morbidity and mortality for the elderly. In these circumstances, the child lovingly promotes the well-being of the parent by maintaining social distance. Here we find that the virtue of love can be rightly practiced only in tandem with prudence. A person must discern what will promote the good of the other if her action is to be loving.

However, the consequences of an agent's active benevolence are not determinative of virtuous action. As Aquinas writes, "Although the goodness of an action is not caused by the goodness of its effect, yet an action is said to be good from the fact that it can produce a good effect."[46] Virtuous agents aim at good outcomes, but their virtue is not indexed to the quality of the outcomes the person actually produces. In a broken world, one should aim to enhance the integral well-being of others but cannot guarantee it. Further, though a moral agent should attempt to produce a good effect, the successful production of such an effect is insufficient for virtue. Instead, the quality of the relations that the agent has with others is determinative of her moral character.

Contrast this approach with two contemporary accounts of virtue. Michael Slote has argued that good motivation alone is sufficient for virtue. Here, the virtues are agent-based, as they are entirely reduced to the inner moral sentiments of the person.[47] The external effects of one's actions in this account lack moral standing. Conversely, trait consequentialists maintain that "a virtue is a character trait that, generally speaking, produces good consequences for others."[48] Although it is generally true that the virtues do produce good consequences, there is no necessary connection between love and good consequences, whatever the latter may mean. Consider Julia Driver's now-famous example of the Mutors. The Mutors are an alien people whose children enjoy a 50 percent increase in life expectancy if they are beaten at exactly 5.57 years of age. Their children are upset by the beating, which is carried out by a unique class of Mutors, who revel in beating small children. These Mutors do not beat the children for the sake of the longevity of the children but, rather, for the perverse pleasure that these Mutors experience when they do this. According to Driver's account, the trait that gives rise to this sadistic behavior is a virtue, because "it is valuable in that it actually does produce good and a significant social benefit."[49] Driver's trait consequentialism renders an agent's intentionality, her commitment to the good, and the quality of her relations morally irrelevant. A personalist account of virtue views all these internal movements as relevant and thus would hold that the Mutors who beat children are vicious because they fail to recognize or intentionally promote the good of the children. Further, these Mutors are not cultivating the conditions for, or moving toward, a loving relationship with the children they beat—quite the opposite.

THE FORMATION AND CULTIVATION OF VIRTUE

A helpful way to understand moral character is by way of an analogy with nonmoral skills, such as guitar playing or book writing. Following Aristotle, Julia Annas has argued that virtues are like skills because they are also acquired through habituation. Further, she notes that the result of a virtue, like a skill, is not routine but the kind of actively and intelligently engaged mastery that is found in experts, such as athletes or pianists.[50] Drawing on the thought of Bernard Lonergan, Jeremey Wilkins has also argued that virtues are skill-like. Wilkins argues that a skill is a flexible circle of schemes of recurrence.[51] In order to keep a toy top spinning, a skillful spinner will recurrently lash the top in a variety of ways—sometimes quickly, sometimes slowly, and sometimes to correct an imbalance in the top. The skillful spinner knows the circumstances in which to employ each of these techniques in order to achieve the goal. Similarly, a virtuous person has the qualities of character that enable her to act in a morally skilled or prudent manner given the circumstances. She is a moral expert.

Skills are not moral virtues, however. The acquisition of a technical skill, such as carpentry, does not affect a person's moral character. A carpenter who recently completed an apprenticeship has undoubtedly grown in her carpentry skills but is not necessarily more just or merciful than she was before training. Carpentry is a nonmoral skill because it does not directly pertain to human relationality.

Habits and Dispositions

The notion that the virtues are habits is often misunderstood in the current context. The colloquial view is that a trait is a habit if it produces action in a "seemingly automatic fashion."[52] In this account, habitual action is executed without reflection, akin to a compulsion or a routine. Consider, for example, one's commute.[53] Driving to work is a mindless activity for many commuters. This routine allows one to arrive at work with no explicit or intentional thought. In fact, sometimes one finds oneself absentmindedly driving to work on a day off. In such an instance, one's action (driving) has bypassed explicit decision-making. Here, driving to work "happens to" the person, in a sense. If virtue is like a routine, then it indeed would be subrational and automatic.

The Thomistic tradition of virtue offers a different view of habits. For Aquinas, habits are strong dispositions to certain kinds of actions and emotions.[54] Thomas repeatedly distinguished between mere dispositions and strong dispositions, only the latter of which can properly be called habits. The difference between the former and the latter is that the latter "impress" order into the person's character. This happens over time, much in the same way that "many drops hollow the stone."[55]

Once a habit has been impressed on the person's character, it functions as a second nature. This is the case because habits produce an inclination, or strong disposition, similar to a natural one.[56] A person's acquired or infused second nature gives her new principles of motion and rest. Specifically, an acquired virtuous habit contains rational principles of action and inaction. Although acquired habits guide the person to do the good, reasonable action, the action arising from a habit is freely chosen. For Aquinas, good acquired habits are suffused with reason and are not mere routine. Habits infused by God also constitute a second nature but are not directed toward the natural good. Instead, such habits are principles of motion and rest regarding one's relationship with God. Infused habits orient the person to the supernatural good of participating in God's life.

Furthermore, a habit has causal power. Once acquired, habits are metaphysically prior to and causally contribute to action. The human act is an emergent reality but emerges from within a variety of causes: strong dispositions, rational reflection, psychological states, social pressures, and so on. Although the virtuous person's action is free, there is also ease in acting in predisposed ways. For instance, a person who has temperance will have an easier time passing on the second piece of cake and would find it difficult to indulge. Here, her strong disposition has played a causal role in passing on the cake.

Second, habits do not despotically cause actions. Instead, they guide, incline, enable, and facilitate agents to act in certain ways.[57] Habits incline agents to certain moral species of actions (e.g., acts of courage), not certain material acts (pulling people out of burning cars). An agent chooses specific acts through prudential reasoning. Thus, dispositions do not subvert prudence or deliberation; they simply orient the agent to choose certain kinds of acts and not others. Put differently, dispositions underdetermine action.[58] They do not blindly, and without reflection, cause a person to act in such-and-such a manner. The just person acts justly because she is both disposed to just actions and has prudentially discerned what ought to be done. Again, her disposition guides her to do what is just and to figure out, here and now, what is just in this situation. Good habits enable a person to act with less effort but not with less reason.[59] Annas has argued that good moral habits sharpen one's response to new situations: "The virtuous person responding to a situation is thus like the skilled athlete or craftsperson who understands immediately what to do in a situation without explicitly having to apply rules."[60]

Mindless activities, such as routines, cannot deliver prudent, situationally sensitive, intelligent, and morally imaginative responses to new circumstances. For example, if you have shopped in the same grocery store for years, you probably have developed a routinized way around the store. You seamlessly and easily move from the produce to the deli to the dairy, and finally, the boxed goods. What happens when the store is renovated or you shop elsewhere? Grocery shopping becomes significantly more time consuming and difficult. Why? Because in the latter instance, your routine has been upset. At this moment, you realize that you lack the character trait of "shopping well" and instead have mastered a routine that is specific to a single store. For most people, grocery shopping is nontransferable because it is a routine. Contrast this example with a virtuous trait, such as the virtue of care. A change in scenery does not stymie caring persons. Such people can be caring for different kinds of people, whether it be their children, their siblings, their students, or their colleagues. The virtue of care is not a routine, because no routine enables a person to respond in creative and imaginative ways.[61]

Third, habits are sensitive to stimulus events. Consider the example of a person seeing an attractive woman or man.[62] Dispositions related to sexual relationships are activated in such situations. Those who have a lustful disposition will typically respond differently to those stimuli than those who possess a chaste disposition. This example shows that though every situation that a person encounters is unique, there are generic kinds of situations that betray habits which are cross-situational. That is, good moral habits such as generosity are realized in a wide variety of situations and contexts. The generous person is generous with her money by giving to charity, or with her time by volunteering. All this is to say that dispositions integrate the person's response in all the areas of life in which a disposition is relevant.[63]

Finally, habits are durable. Aquinas argued that a habit implies a character trait's "lastingness"[64] and that it is removed only with difficulty.[65] Most people have an intuitive grasp of the durability of a habit. We respond with shock and surprise when a usually temperate aunt becomes intoxicated at a family party, or a typically honest friend tells a lie, because such actions are "out of character." Virtues help people to "stay in character," much like an actor during a performance. However, this is not to claim that habits are static. Habits are continually being reinforced or diminished. However, crucially for this study, habits grow, change, and are lost slowly. Once established, agents tend to maintain their established habits through the actions that regularly arise from that habit. Habits are hard to change because they stably and consistently produce the kinds of actions that reinforce themselves. Habits essentially create feedback loops that tend to ingrain their presence in a person's moral character.

The Emergence of Habits

Aristotle's adage that "Like acts cause like habits" goes only so far.[66] It is true that repeated actions form natural, or acquired, habits. Aquinas adds nuance to this claim when he writes that habits increase when the person performs "the action more intensely, more perfectly, . . . not simple repetition."[67] The performance of an activity is only one aspect of the formation of a habit. How and why one acts matters as well. Robert Adams and Julia Annas have emphasized the latter point in their work. The virtuous, they argue, are committed to the good.[68] There is, then, more that must be said regarding how persons acquire habits and how the acquisition of virtue differs from the acquisition of vice. However, the central truth of Aristotle's claim is that it recognizes the historicity of the moral life.

Aquinas takes a similar approach to the acquisition of virtue: "That a habit is engendered little by little, is due, not to one part being engendered after another, but to the fact that the subject does not acquire all at once a firm and difficultly changeable disposition; and also to the fact that it begins by being imperfectly in the subject, and is gradually perfected. The same applies to other qualities."[69] Human beings are not creatures who can, with a single movement of their will, acquire the habits they desire. This fact is more obviously recognized as it regards what Aquinas calls "other qualities," such as athletic skills. For instance, one day of batting practice will not make one a significantly better hitter. Instead, it will take years of regular practice to perfect the quality of one's hitting.

Skills, like virtues, take time to develop because they involve many aspects of human existence. Both skills and virtues are emergent realities. Recall Christian Smith's definition of emergence, presented in chapter 3. Emergence is "the process of constituting a new entity with its own particular characteristics through the interactive combination of other, different entities that are necessary to create the new entity but that do not contain the characteristics of the new entity."[70] This is "strong" or "ontological" emergence because it maintains that genuinely new realities come to exist that cannot be predicted or reduced to the sum of their parts.[71] For instance, the chair in which I am sitting has emerged from the relation of wood, screws, glue, cushioning, and fabric. The chair cannot be reduced to any of these elements and is not merely the aggregate of its parts. The reality of the chair emerges only when all its parts are rightly related.

Athletic skills emerge from many aspects of an athlete's life. The ability to consistently hit a baseball is not only a by-product of the frequency and intensity of one's batting practice. In addition to taking batting practice, a ballplayer will also lift weights, do hand-eye coordination exercises, eat a nutritious diet, and rest when needed. Thus, a player's hitting ability emerges from the relation of these activities with each other. In fact, a player's hitting ability will be diminished if one of the activities is done poorly or not at all. A ballplayer who fails to get enough sleep or who drinks alcohol to excess diminishes her ability to hit a baseball.

In chapter 3, I drew on Elder-Vass's argument that human action emerges from conscious decision-making, "stored decisions," and social structures. He argued that the human act was irreducible to any one of these and that each played a causal role in shaping the act. A personalist approach to the moral act also finds that the human act is an emergent reality. Actions cannot be reduced to any of the parts that compose it. The act is not fully explained by the intended end, the chosen object of the act, or any of the external aspects related to the act, such as local or structural circumstances. The full moral act emerges from the relation of all these parts with each other.

Similarly, a personalist approach to virtue must be emergentist. It is the whole person—her actions, intentions, values, emotions, reasoning, and even bodily movements—that interrelate to form how she relates to God, others, self, and creation. Moral character is real, but it is substantially different from, for example, the reality of an action or intention. Because character endures in a way that discrete acts and intentions do not, it exists on a different level of reality from these. Character emerges from within acts and intentions, but it cannot be reduced to them. Just as the ability to hit a baseball cannot be reduced to the number of hours spent in the batting cage, the acquisition of virtue cannot be reduced to actions or intentions alone.

Conversely, physicalist, voluntarist, and intellectualist approaches reduce moral character to a dominant aspect of personal being.[72] In these accounts, traits become the mere accumulation of one's physical acts, one's intentions, or one's practical reasoning. These reductionist accounts offer a simpler and possibly more satisfying explanation than the complex emergentist portrait offered here. However, such accounts do not withstand testing.

Consider the virtue of temperance. Almost no one intends to become a glutton, but many people acquire this trait. Why? Temperance is about habituated action, not the will alone. Habit is shaped by intentional actions—even actions executed with a divided will. Saint Paul recognized his own divided will when he wrote that "the willing is ready at hand, but the doing is not. For I do not do the good I want, but I do the evil I do not want" (Romans 7:18–19). Likewise, Saint Augustine's torturous conversion narrative in *Confessions* captures the experience of possessing a divided will. When Saint Augustine did the "evil that he did not want," he became an intemperate man.[73] So though a person cannot become virtuous unless she genuinely wants to do the good for herself and others, wanting to do the good is only a necessary and not a sufficient condition of virtue. Conversely, desiring to do the good can coexist with vice. Persons with substance use disorder often desire to be freed of their afflictions, but such desire is constrained by their habits, neurochemistry, and psychology.

The point is this: We do not only become what we do, what we want to do, or what we think we should do. Character emerges from the relation of a multiplicity of aspects of the person. Moral character is then irreducible to "lower-level" realities—such as actions, intentions, and emotions—and is instead a reality that emerges, over time, from within the relation of all these. Of course, all the virtues will be similar in certain ways. Robert Adams rightly has emphasized that the agent must be committed to do the good and be able to reason practically.[74] Again, though goodwill and the capacity to rightly exercise practical reason are necessary for virtue, neither is sufficient. The virtues, then, emerge from a complex web of personal moral realities.

Moreover, just as the parts of a chair must be rightly related in order for the chair to exhibit its emergent reality and properties, so too must the various aspects of the person be rightly related in order for virtue to emerge. Aquinas offers something of an emergentist notion of virtue insofar as he located the fullness of virtue in the right and reasonable integration of the person's intellect, will, and passions. All these powers must relate well to the others for a single virtue to develop. For example, Aquinas holds that in order for temperance to take root in a person, the concupiscible appetite needs to be complacent about the choice of prudential reason,[75] and the person's acts of temperance needed to be freely willed. Further, Aquinas famously argues that each virtue emerged from within its relation with other virtues. Interrelated virtues thus grow like the fingers on a hand.[76] That is, each virtue grows in relation with the other virtues. A virtue's relation with other traits enables or constrains the virtue's growth. Justice develops only if other virtues, such as temperance, develop as well. This interconnected notion of virtue views each virtue as a complex trait that emerges from within the whole of the person, not simply from an abstracted aspect of the person.

The Generation and Growth of Infused Habits

The infused virtues are also emergent realities. Here we can distinguish between the offer of the infusion of the virtues, the acceptance of the virtues, and the growth or destruction of the virtues. The offer of the infused virtues is entirely due to the action of God. The offer of charity "depends, not on any natural virtue but also on the sole grace of the Holy Ghost Who infuses charity."[77] In short, those with the acquired virtues do not merit the divine offer of faith, hope, and charity. However, though Aquinas maintains that "infused virtue is caused in us by God without any action on our part," he also noted that this is "not without our consent."[78] On this point, Nicholas Austin has noted that "virtue's infusion is not coercive."[79] Graced habits generated by God can only be accepted or rejected by the agent, not acquired ex nihilo. Here, the agent must be open to and accepting of the outpouring of God's grace, which is the source of the infused virtues.[80] This acceptance is itself graced, as God enables the person to accept the divine gift.[81] The infused virtues, then, emerge from within the relationship of God's offer of grace and the agent's acceptance of it.

Aquinas contends that the sacraments, derived from Christ, instrumentally cause the infusion of grace.[82] The sacraments confer the infused virtues and dispose a person to accept them. For instance, a person "receives grace and virtue in Baptism," Penance restores all the infused virtues, and the habit and practice of charity is "kindled" by the Eucharist.[83] For Aquinas, the Eucharist is the supreme sign and cause of charity. He writes that "because it is a special feature of friendship to live together with friends. . . . He promises us His bodily presence as a reward."[84] The Eucharist is a sacrament in which Christ, as a friend, lives with us through his body and blood. Reflecting on this account, Mark Jordan argues that the sacraments are embodied teaching events that make the virtues livable.[85] His book *Teaching Bodies* emphasizes that the sacraments offer the most effective way for God's grace to reshape a person's moral character.

Next, Aquinas offers that an agent's acts of charity can play a causal role in increasing the intensity of her charity. One must be careful here, because acts of charity do not directly cause an increase in charity. In this way, the growth of charity differs from the growth of acquired justice. For the acquired virtues, like acts directly cause like habits to be formed or increase. Recurrent just acts, for example, cause a just person to become more just. But the same is not true for the growth of the infused virtues. Austin argues that, for Aquinas, "acts of infused virtue prepare us to receive an increase of them from their divine source, but they do not directly cause the virtue to increase."[86] So acts of charity do not cause the increase; they only "dispose man to receive the infusion of charity."[87] The growth of charity remains a divine gift that a person's actions prepares her to receive.

Acts of charity, though capacitated through the gratuitous gift of habitual grace, emerge from the free will of the agent. The person with the infused virtues is not an automaton of charity. She is not hydraulically moved by grace to love God and neighbor. Rather, she is a person who is *empowered* to love God and neighbor and is someone who then *freely decides* to do so. Although she is strengthened by grace, her free moral subjectivity remains operative.

Thus, though agents do not acquire or generate the infused virtues, they do accept and play a causal role in developing and intensifying them. Aquinas suggests that charity does not increase in the absence of acts of charity. The person must cooperate with God's grace in order for it to grow. The various degrees, or stages, of charity—the beginner, the proficient, and the perfect—develop in relation to how the agent performs acts that dispose herself to an increase in charity.[88] Perhaps, then, it is not inaccurate to claim that agents cultivate, in some way, the growth of the infused virtues.[89] Although the initial infusion of charity is always a divine gift, those who already possess the infused virtues can prepare themselves to be the "good soil" in which God's gracious gifts may bear fruit. Therefore, for the remainder of this book, when I write about the cultivation or development of virtue, I take this to mean that the performance of acts of charity *disposes* a person to receive an increase in the virtue of charity through God's gracious infusion. The offer and infusion of the virtues remain wholly the work of the Holy Spirit.

The relationship of moral agency and the infused virtues raises another question: How do those who already possess the infused virtues know what acts of virtue to perform? Recall that the infused virtues do not hydraulically move the agent to perform certain actions. Graced habits need to be actualized in particular circumstances and should be enacted in a prudent manner. Although the moral reasoning process is strengthened by the infused virtues, it is not subverted by them. Like the acquired virtues, the infused virtues underdetermine concrete action. Aquinas writes that charity is principally about the end of "cleaving to God," whereas exterior acts of charity "are a means to the end, and so have to be measured both according to charity and according to reason."[90] Clarifying this point, Paul Waddell has written that "even charity is not enough for the virtuous life. It is essential, but not sufficient. Charity needs to be guided by prudence."[91] In fact, the necessity of prudence for the performance of acts of charity is suffused throughout questions about beneficence, giving alms, and fraternal correction in the *Summa theologiae*.[92]

Throughout this book, I assume that virtues and vices both can be acquired by agents and that some agents accept and then practice the infused virtues. In order to practice the infused virtues, the agent needs to reflect on what she ought to do given the particular circumstances. This deliberation involves infused prudence that reflects both on the circumstances and on other moral guides—such as norms, practices, exemplars, and the virtues themselves. To ascend from beginner to proficient to perfect, the agent will need not only the grace of God but also these formational modalities to focus her moral deliberation.

In short, I am arguing that the person with the infused virtues still needs the action guidance provided by norms, practices, exemplars, and the virtues. The infused virtues render knowing and doing the virtuous action *easier* but not necessarily *easy*. Although those who perfectly possess charity may know and do acts of charity with ease, this is not necessarily the case for the beginner and the proficient. The first concern of those who are beginning a life of charity is "avoiding sin and resisting his concupiscences."[93] Here norms, commands, and laws all guide the beginner away from vicious and sinful actions that may destroy her charity. Even the proficient will still be significantly guided to acts of charity (and thereby disposed to receive an increase in charity) through the practice of the Christian life, the emulation of exemplars such as the saints, and reflection on the virtues. And though the infused virtues cannot be acquired, their development is, as argued above, in relation to the freely willed and prudentially discerned actions of the agent.

The Modes of Virtue Acquisition and Cultivation

Thus far, I have maintained that character is about relationality with God, self, neighbor, and creation and that it emerges from persons-in-the-whole. I have yet to present how character is shaped in community. The contemporary consensus among those working on the virtues, according to Christopher Vogt, is that the virtues are formed from within practices, communal traditions, and narratives.[94] This reflects MacIntyre's tripartite approach to character formation. Although I find much insight in this approach, I propose a more specific set of formational modalities.

First, I agree that practices, as MacIntyre defines them, form character. Second, tradition is important as well, but MacIntyre's definition of tradition needs to be amended to be useful for Catholic ethics. Tradition, according to MacIntyre, is a "historically extended, socially embodied argument, and an argument precisely in part about the goods which constitute the tradition."[95] Although this account of tradition functions well in a philosophical system of ethics, it fails to capture the fullness of tradition in the Catholic sense.[96] This is due, first of all, to the revelatory nature of the Christian tradition. The Catholic moral tradition is not only historically extended and socially embodied but also contains all that has been handed down through the guidance of the Holy Spirit, including a notion of the human good, virtues, norms, and moral exemplars. Here tradition exists at a level above virtues, practices, and narratives, all of which, in part, compose the tradition. For Catholic ethics, it is essential to note that the tradition forms the character of the faithful in a remote sense, though moral norms, exemplars, and practices are formative in a proximate sense.

My second correction involves the role of narrative. Narratives are essential insofar as they provide a sense of unity in one's moral life.[97] In addition, narratives certainly impart a thickness to the virtues that academic definitions lack. The virtue of mercy, for example, is in many ways grasped in light of Gospel parables, such as that of the Good Samaritan. However, though narrative plays an essential role in understanding the virtues, I argue that the value of narratives to form and shape the character of persons is derived, to a substantial degree, from the fact that narratives contain moral lessons in the form of norms, present portraits of exemplary characters, and provide thick descriptions of the virtues. Narrative informs and illumines other formational modalities.

In addition to practices, norms, and exemplars, the virtues themselves guide agents to acquire and cultivate the virtues. The virtues are action guides. When used as such the virtues causally contribute to the acquisition of the virtues or dispose the agent to the reception of the graced virtues. This appears to be tautological, but as I show below, it is not. There are, then, four primary ways in which character is formed: through moral practices, the following of norms, the emulation of exemplars, and by reflecting on virtues themselves. None of the three is architectonic, and none is an aspect of any other. They are all equally fundamental and morally formative in their own right. Finally, though each is related to the others (there is a dialectic between exemplars and norms, as I show below), each is a distinct mode of moral formation and cultivation.

Practices

The introduction of the concept of a "practice" in the field of virtue theory is due to the work of Alasdair MacIntyre. Let us start with his technical definition of the concept and then move to examples.[98] MacIntyre defines a practice as "any coherent and complex form of socially established cooperative human activity through which goods internal to that form of activity are realized in the course of trying to achieve those standards of excellence which are appropriate to, and partially definitive of, that form of activity, with the result that human powers to achieve excellence, and human conceptions of the ends and goods involved, are systematically extended."[99]

MacIntyre argues that there are moral practices as well as practices in the fields of arts, science, politics, and games. In all these arenas, practices are not mere acts, such as "throwing a football or punishing a child, but rather human activities, like the game of football and raising a family."[100] MacIntyre's most famous example is about chess, which he argues is a practice, whereas tic-tac-toe is not. Why? Because chess is complex and socially established, and the goods available to the chess player are found only in playing chess. That is, one plays chess for its own sake, not for the sake of something else. The good of playing chess can be realized only by playing chess. Further, what it means to "play chess well" can grow over time. New strategies can be created and executed, which eventually redefine what excellent chess playing is. Tic-tac-toe, conversely, is not complex. Although it is socially established, one wonders how far one could "extend" excellence in tic-tac-toe.

Within his discussion of chess, MacIntyre offers an important illustration. He imagines teaching a bright, but uninterested, seven-year-old how to play the game. Using candy, he bribes the child into playing. Here, the child plays for an external good: candy. Eventually, MacIntyre surmises, the child could begin to acquire a genuine interest in the game and play for the sake of the goods internal to the game—"analytical skill, strategic imagination, and competitive intensity."[101] It is only when the child plays for these internal goods that chess becomes a practice for her.

To be precise, for MacIntyre, practices are fields or arenas of social life. For instance, medicine is a practice, consisting of many different subpractices, such as making diagnoses and performing surgery. Moreover, the Christian life as a whole is a practice, through which Christians are enabled to progressively grow in love and union with God and neighbor. The sacraments and the works of mercy are important subpractices of Christianity.[102] Throughout the remainder of the book, I focus on the subpractices that help individuals cultivate the virtues. Following the custom of contemporary theological ethicists who simply write of practices, I do not make the practice/subpractice distinction.

Action is only one aspect of a practice. One must also have the proper intention for the habituated action to truly become a practice. Imagine a situation in which a young person volunteered at a soup kitchen, outwardly practicing the work of mercy of feeding the hungry. However, she engaged in this subpractice in order to make a good impression on a love interest. We intuitively know that this young person would not become merciful, which is one of the goods internal to the practice of the works of mercy. In this scenario, the person is not practicing for the sake of mercy but with an ulterior motive. Here, feeding the hungry becomes a technique to a different, and much more selfish, end.[103]

All is not lost for this young person, however. Because virtue is an embodied reality, the bodily practice of feeding the hungry can be the beginning of the cultivation of the moral virtue of mercy, much in the same way that a child learns chess through candy bribes. If she comes to practice for the sake of the suffering, then the works of mercy can cultivate a merciful disposition in the practitioner. Feeding the hungry is an authentic practice of mercy only when the person suffers with the hungry and treats the hungry as transcendently valuable and loved by God in thought, emotion, and action. This distinguishes the merciful practice of feeding the hungry from the practice of community service. In community service, the person feeds the hungry because they have needs, and to better her community, but she lacks the sorrowful heart and the orientation to God that are at the core of mercy.

Further, practices often require some explicit coaching. A baseball player practices batting by keeping his eye on the ball, taking a short stride, and maintaining balance as he swings. This is called "deliberate practice," which is different from ordinary practice.[104] In deliberate practice, the batter's coaches consistently critique his swing, correct his deficiencies, and require him to continue to practice the swing until it "becomes him." Nondeliberate practice involves taking round after round of batting practice without attending to technique or receiving coaching. The promise of deliberate practice is that, eventually, the ballplayer will have the correct swing, which will enable him to hit well in games.

Moral practices function in a similar fashion. Candidates for the sacrament of confirmation often receive a certain level of deliberate practice of the works of mercy. They serve in soup kitchens and are prepared for such work by their religious education teachers, sponsors, or family members so that they serve in a way that recognizes the dignity of those they serve. They are told to make eye contact with the hungry person, to engage them in conversation, to be open to the sadness of their stories, and to be vulnerable themselves. Their teachers of religious education often direct the candidates to recognize that God has a special love for those who are hungry, to pray for them, and to implore God to deliver them from their suffering. The candidates are also invited to group reflections on their experiences, in which they are given an opportunity to express their sorrow at the situation of those they served. In this way, the candidates are deliberately practicing the fullness of a work of mercy.

All moral practices are ultimately about relationality. The works of mercy are about entering into the suffering of others and thus serve as a primary way in which the faithful express their love of the God who also loves the poor and suffering. In order to grow progressively in their relationships with God and others, persons need to engage in practices such as the works of mercy and centering prayer. But such practices are not habits. They are prescribed, complex, socially established activities that eventually form how the practitioner relates to others. Authentic moral practices form habits and dispositions. They create a second nature that over time "becomes the person," or opens the agent to the further inpouring of God's grace.

Norms

Like practices, norms are primarily heuristic. They exist to educate and form persons in the virtuous life.[105] The personalist virtue theory developed in this chapter maintains that norms are codified moral wisdom regarding how to relate to God, self, neighbor, and creation. The category of "norm" includes both rules and commandments. Norms are thinner than practices. A norm prescribes or proscribes specific actions. One might, for instance, instruct a religious novice to practice centering prayer. The novice will, most likely, need coaching from an expert to learn the practice. In this example, the action guide, "practice centering prayer," serves only to direct the action of the other person; it does not show the person how to execute the practice. Only explicit coaching enables the practitioner to "practice" well.

Turning to the tradition, we find that norms played an essential role in Aquinas's ethics. He argues that without these "rules of thumb," those lacking virtue would have little guidance in the performance of the good. Using the analogy of training a person in science, Aquinas argues that moral training should begin with concrete moral guidance: "Just as we instruct a man in some science, we begin by putting before him certain general maxims even so the Law, which forms man to virtue by instructing him in the precepts of the Decalogue, which are the first of all precepts, gave expression, by prohibition or command, to those things which are of most common occurrence in the course of human life."[106]

Echoing Aquinas, William Frankena maintains that virtues without norms are blind.[107] By this he means that virtues fail to guide right action and only serve to direct motives. Although I disagree with the fullness of his claim, it contains a kernel of truth. The young and the vicious require explicit action guidance. These groups, lacking internal (virtue) guidance to the good, are mostly incapable of envisioning and achieving the good. The student in the moral life requires the concrete guidance in the good that is primarily communicated in norms. In short, the student in the moral life often begins by following norms. Alasdair MacIntyre has argued that we learn virtues, such as courage, by understanding that certain types of action are always wrong.[108] Virtues are not blind, but the vision provided by the virtues takes time to develop. However, once acquired, the virtues enable the person to discover and do the good with ease and joy. The virtuous person is guided to more easily discover and execute right action precisely because she has the virtues.

There is, however, a certain asymmetry in the depth of guidance that norms provide. They are more effective in guiding persons away from vice than they are in teaching virtue. Think of the Seventh Commandment, "You shalt not steal." If a woman follows this commandment, and never unjustly takes material goods from others, she has likely avoided becoming an unjust person. However, the mere avoidance of vice does not equate to the virtue of justice. The simple fact that this woman has never stolen anything does not guarantee that she will possess justice. First, she could be unjust in any number of other ways. Second, the Seventh Commandment says nothing of what a just person should do. Further, even prescriptive commandments provide limited guidance. For example, the Fourth Commandment, "Honor your father and your mother," guides a person to treat her parents justly. And yet it is much less useful in guiding the agent than the prohibition against stealing. This is the case because it is possible to honor one's parents in action (by taking care of them in their old age) but fail to truly honor them in one's heart (while resenting having to do so). In this case, the person has failed to grow in justice because the norm has only guided her external action and not the entirety of her moral act.

We understand the value and meaning of norms by scrutinizing their generation. There is a dialectical relationship between norms and virtues. Although norms play an instructive role in the character development of the human person, they also reveal and clarify who the good person is. Consider a contemporary example. Recently developed moral norms concerning the treatment of the environment have served to define the virtue of environmental responsibility. Only after the articulation of these norms, such as the norm prescribing the recycling of paper, did a sense of the virtue of environmental responsibility emerge. Furthermore, this virtue emerged precisely in response to the norms that had already begun to guide the proper treatment of the Earth's resources. Environmental moral norms were originally sporadically articulated. Out of those norms arose the notion of a type of life whereby persons responsibly related to the environment. The virtue of environmental responsibility followed from a reflection on the norms regulating how persons used or misused the resources of the world. "Going green" is now understood to be a lifestyle consisting, implicitly, of the virtue of environmental responsibility. Although going green has mostly supplanted talk of individual norms regulating an agent's use of environmental resources, those individual norms were epistemologically prior to the virtue.

Conversely, the discovery of moral norms often emerges from a reflection on the virtues. The emergence of the smartphone provides a helpful example. As with any new technology, there are few established norms regarding how to rightly use a smartphone. Is it, for instance, permissible to text while talking to a friend or to use a phone while in a public restroom, or to carry on a phone conversation while on a crowded elevator? At the time of the writing of this book, norms regarding these and other questions pertaining to smartphones have yet to be established. In the absence of established norms, people of goodwill often turn to exemplars of virtue for insight. The virtues and the virtuous generate norms. This point is developed in greater depth below.

The application of norms is also rightly understood only in relation to the virtues. Let us return to the Seventh Commandment. The commandment prohibits stealing but does not define what stealing is. Is stealing taking another's goods without permission? What if one's family is starving? Does that count as stealing? Second, when does such a commandment apply? Is all stealing wrong? What if I were to take my neighbor's shotgun from her if I knew that she was suicidal? These questions show the insufficiency of norms and the need for the virtue of prudence in discerning if and how a norm should guide action. Novices, who lack settled dispositions to the good, will follow norms to the letter, often with comical results. Consider the four-year-old child who recently was taught that she should not talk to strangers. When asked her name by the clerk of the local supermarket, the child did not respond. This child, after all, was told not to talk to strangers, and the clerk is a stranger. However, here the child invokes the wrong norm. The norm "Do not talk to strangers" is useful only in situations where talking to strangers poses a danger to the child. The circumstances, in this case, dictate that no such danger is present. The capability to understand the situations where a given norm applies is a function of the virtue of prudence.[109]

One finds that the life of virtue is far more dynamic and rich than a life of following rules. Norms open up the possibility of acquiring the virtues insofar as they can guide the agent away from vicious acts and toward virtuous ones. However, as the case of the child and the clerk demonstrates, norms alone are insufficient to cause right and good action. The child needs to discern which norm is relevant and needs a semblance of prudence in order to rightly apply the norm and to rightly relate to the clerk. Frankena is again helpful, with his insight that norms without virtues are impotent.[110] Norms cannot consistently deliver good and right actions unless accompanied by good character traits. Thus, the virtues serve as the hermeneutical context for moral norms.[111] Because no norm is self-interpreting, all interpretation of norms occurs within the context of the virtues. Norms do not function in their own sphere, isolated from the kind of life that a person should live and the relations that a person ought to foster.

In a personalist virtue framework, norms provide codified moral wisdom regarding how to relate well to God, neighbor, self, and creation. The cultivation of good relations, especially in its earliest stages, will be characterized by the following of norms. However, the following of norms is insufficient for a good life. The human end consists in the person's friendship with God. Actions mediate this return but do not compose it. Therefore, norms are prudently applied for the sake of cultivating and sustaining loving relations with God, self, others, and creation. Furthermore, norms recede in importance upon the acquisition of virtues. Eventually, the values and insights carried by norms become internally possessed by the virtuous person. Because the meaning of the norm has been internalized in the person of virtue, she knows what values the norm protects and promotes. This agent understands the primacy of the spirit of the norm and not the letter. She is a person of complex moral reasoning, and this kind of reasoning cannot be communicated through norms. To construct a comprehensive set of moral norms is an impossible task, given the importance of context and circumstances in right human action. A comprehensive set of virtues is a more achievable and beneficial undertaking.

Exemplars

In addition to practices and norms, exemplars guide an agent's acquisition and growth in virtue. Mark Jordan argues that human beings require exemplars because embodied teaching is the best moral pedagogy.[112] The most influential advocate for an exemplarist approach is the philosopher Linda Zagzebski.[113] For Zagzebski, the virtues are grounded in the actually existing persons who embody them. Although she has admitted that her approach is foundationalist, insofar as the virtues have a foundation in exemplars, she has argued that it is nonconceptual. That is, the virtues are known by "direct reference" to the exemplars of moral goodness. She has written that "good persons are persons *like that*, just like gold is stuff *like that*."[114] Identifying exemplars can fix the reference of the term "good person" without the use of descriptive concepts.[115] Zagzebski's exemplarism does not rely on anthropological claims and is not bound to the claims of a communal tradition.

How do we know who is an exemplar for Zagzebski? We admire them. Our admiration arises when we encounter morally attractive and imitable persons. Essentially, exemplars elicit an emotional response of admiration in us. Our admiration is aroused when we view news footage of Martin Luther King Jr. marching for voting rights in Selma or of frontline health workers risking their lives by caring for patients during the COVID-19 pandemic. These are morally attractive persons. We desire to possess the traits of such people.

Zagzebski argues that the characteristics that exemplars possess, such as courage, count as virtues. The virtues are simply the traits of an admirable person. For example, King's traits, such as courage and justice, qualify as virtues for those who admire him. King is not admired because he was courageous and just. Rather, he is admired because of the fullness of his person. His admirers count his traits as virtues because they are his traits. *He* is admirable, and therefore *his traits* are admirable. The virtues are derived from admirable persons, not the other way around.

Why should we trust the emotional responses on which exemplarism relies? Zagzebski argues that "it is rational to trust [our emotions] when they survive conscientious self-reflection."[116] In particular, she argues that admiration is a more trustworthy emotion than romantic love, anger, and fear.[117] These latter emotions frequently do not survive critical reflection, whereas admiration, compassion, and indignation often do. She maintains that though not every person will have the capacity to identify truly admirable exemplars, a community will discover what traits are virtuous as long as some people in the community can identify moral models.[118]

It is certainly true that one can derive virtues from exemplars. For instance, Saint Francis, in his great witness to Christ, showed the Christian tradition that ecological justice is a true virtue. However, Zagzebski seems to conflate the discovery of virtues with the identification of virtuous persons.

The Christian discovery of the virtue of ecological justice is not entirely pre-conceptual. Instead, the very recognition of the virtue is partly based on a latent theology of creation, which Francis helped the Church to more fully recognize.

Zagzebski's account, as important as it is for contemporary virtue theory, contains a number of problems. First, her approach is ahistorical. She argues that an advantage of exemplarism is that one does not have to articulate what qualities "make a person good at the outset."[119] However, even if it were desirable to investigate virtue without any knowledge of the good life, this kind of reasoning would be impossible. There is never an "outset." All moral reasoning begins from a time and a place and is mediated by concepts that are communally generated. There is no moment of pure emotional admiration that is unadulterated by preexisting concepts of the good and of virtue.

Although Zagzebski seems to have rejected any other way of recognizing virtue, the theologian Patrick Clark has taken a more moderate approach. He argues that Catholic virtue ethics has the seeds of, and can profit from, a more in-depth focus on exemplarism in virtue ethics.[120] He identifies a strand of exemplarist thinking in the virtue theory of Aquinas and in the moral theology of John Paul II in *Veritatis splendor*. For example, John Paul writes that "Jesus' way of acting and his words, his deeds and his precepts constitute the moral rule of Christian life."[121] Jesus's words, deeds, and even precepts were of charity and mercy. Importantly, Clark's study of the tradition leads him to advocate for assigning exemplars a more significant role in shaping the moral agency of Christians. Exemplars provide "individual embodiments of human goodness in the world," which the embodied followers of Jesus need if they are to become christomorphic.[122] In a more recent article, Clark argues that the saints are exemplars because of their relationship with God. What is admirable is the saint's participation in God's love.[123]

Exemplars help to cultivate virtue in three ways. First, they serve as inspirational models. As Zagzebski argues, they attract us to the point that we desire to emulate their ways. Kenneth Himes argues that Catholics should turn to exemplars for moral motivation. Exemplars move us emotionally by instilling a love of goodness, thereby helping us to want to do and become good.[124] Second, once we are drawn to emulate a person, these persons provide concrete examples of what a virtuous person would do in certain situations. When slighted by a peer, we may recall an exemplar of patience, perhaps one's mother, and think, "How would she respond to a slight?" One would then model our response on her response. In this way, exemplars are most useful when norms do not exist or a person is unaware of relevant norms. Finally, exemplars continue to inspire persons to the heights of virtue. There is no moment of self-satisfaction in a virtue ethics in which exemplars consistently relate to God, others, and creation far more lovingly than most persons. Jesus Christ and the saints play unique roles in Catholic virtue ethics because they are recognized as the moral exemplars whose ways should be imitated but will never be equaled.

Consider the example of César Chávez, who led the United Farm Workers union from the 1960s to the 1990s. He lived in solidarity with the farm workers by living a life of voluntary poverty. He earned a salary of $5,000 a year, and at his death he did not own a house or a car.[125] He "chose to live as a poor person, not for the sake of poverty, but for the sake of resisting injustice and for the sake of working with the poor to liberate themselves for their unjust suffering."[126] Here, simplicity is oriented to a certain kind of relationship with the poor—a relationship of solidarity. Chávez's life attracts and inspires us to be like him. We can imagine how he would live if he were in our shoes, and his example challenges us to do and be better.

As Clark has suggested, and as Chavez embodied, a personalist approach to virtue finds that exemplars are such because of the quality of their relationality. It is precisely because they love God, the poor, their families, and creation that we admire and turn to them as moral models. The Christian notion of the good—namely, that the greatest good is love of God and neighbor—informs who counts as an exemplar.

The Virtues

Finally, the virtues themselves guide their own acquisition and development. They do so because of the action-guiding capacities of the virtues, which were discussed at the beginning of this chapter. However, that virtue ethics provides action guidance is a contested claim. During the infancy of contemporary virtue ethics, Robert Louden argued that "people always expected ethical theory to tell them something about what they ought to do, and it seems to me that virtue ethics is structurally unable to say much of anything about this issue."[127] I contend that Louden is wrong on two counts. First, an ethical theory should not *tell* people what to do, because theories are incapable of this. Theories *guide* the agent in the discernment of what is good, right, and virtuous. Ethical theories are at the service of moral discernment and should neither replace nor subvert it.

Second, virtue has much to contribute to discernment of the moral act and the subsequent acquisition and development of virtue. On this issue, many virtue ethicists have followed the work of Rosiland Hursthouse, who has argued that the virtues guide action by being converted to virtue-rules, or "v-rules."

She maintains that "not only does each virtue generate a prescription—do what is honest, charitable, generous—but each vice a prohibition—do not do what is dishonest, uncharitable, mean."[128] Although Hursthouse has done much to convince ethicists of the usefulness of the virtues, I see no reason why the virtues must be translated into rules in order to guide agents in their moral decision-making. The virtues are fundamentally unlike rules, which typically stipulate only moral minimums. The virtues orient the agent to moral excellence and supererogation. Instead of translating the virtues into rules, the virtues themselves directly guide moral discernment. Here, the direction of analysis is from the virtues to virtuous action. Virtuous action is discovered through reflection on the virtues in light of concrete circumstances. And though practices and norms play a heuristic role in the acquisition of the virtues, they are not capable of guiding the acquisition of virtue in every ethical situation. There is no exhaustive master list of practices and norms. In order to become virtuous, therefore, the person also will need to reflect on the virtues and use them to guide her action.

Virtue ethics contains its own distinct "normative pattern of recurrent and related operations yielding cumulative and progressive results."[129] A virtue approach directs the agent to recurrently ask, "What is the virtuous action given these circumstances?" More specifically, the agent asks, "What is the merciful thing to do?" Here, the virtues are the tools with which the agent morally discerns and discovers the virtuous action in a given set of circumstances. This kind of reasoning relies on a thick account of the virtues. Such an account is supplied through an understanding of the virtue's object, through recalling narratives that illustrate the virtue as well as exemplars of the virtue. This method takes counsel from the virtues; it discerns with the virtues. In this way, virtue ethics does not propose a decision procedure but, rather, a method of discernment.[130] This method yields "cumulative and progressive results" as the agent either acquires the virtues or cultivates the infused virtues through her virtuous actions.

Two scenarios demonstrate how the virtues guide action. First, imagine you are already late to an important meeting.[131] As you briskly walk, you come upon a man on the sidewalk suffering from homelessness who appears to be unconscious. You pause for a moment and begin to deliberate on what you ought to do. In such a moment you may recall exemplars of mercy (the Good Samaritan or an especially merciful friend) and query what they would do if similarly situated. You may also ask yourself, What would a loving, kind, and merciful person do in these circumstances? Additionally, what kind of person would walk away from such a person? These questions provide content-full action guidance. The merciful person, you discern, would stop and care for the man. Here, we discover not only that caring for the man is right but also why such an action is right. It is right because it is merciful. What kind of a person would fail to care for the man?—an unmerciful, callous person. Such a response is wrong because it fails to enact mercy in a situation where a work of mercy is the virtuous response, and instead embodies the vice of callousness. So you gently shake the man to see if he is conscious and take his pulse and assess his breathing when he fails to rouse. Finally, you call for an ambulance when his vital signs show a slowed heart rate and shallow breathing. In this case, you have used the virtues to guide your action and have executed a loving and merciful action.

Again, the advantage of a virtue ethics is that it pertains not only to dilemmas, such as the situation discussed above, but also to more mundane ethical matters. So second, consider a case in which a tired mother, María, is rubbing the back of her sick child as the child fitfully falls asleep. Here María appeals not to a principle or a duty, because none exists for such a scenario. Instead, she appeals to the virtue of care. She reasons that in this situation the caring action is to comfort her sick child, even when doing so is tiresome and monotonous.

SUMMARY

This chapter has attempted to synthesize some of the most critical and insightful developments of post–Vatican II theological ethics. The theocentric, personalist virtue theory that I have developed moves contemporary Catholic virtue beyond the powers-based approach, which has lost explanatory capacity. Individual virtues are not anchored to a single power but emerge from the fullness of the person.

Human relationality, in all its forms, is the matrix for the development of character. Persons become who they are in relation to self, others, creation, and God. However, though character formation is about relations, it happens through engaging in practices, following norms, imitating exemplars, and reflecting on the virtues themselves. That ethics should be organized around the virtues does not mean that ethics should be reduced to the virtues. Unlike Zagzebski's exemplarist approach, a personalist approach to virtue is noncompetitive. It does not compete with, but rather is based on, a prior notion of the good, and it is refined and aided by practices, norms, laws, and exemplars. It is multimodal. Practices, norms, and exemplars aid in acquiring, accepting, and living the virtues.

The project now has a "best account" of virtue theory. As noted at the outset of the chapter, such an account is needed to understand how social structures shape virtue and vice and how structures themselves are virtue-like and vice-like.

NOTES

1. Aquinas, *Summa theologiae*, prologue to the *Secunda secundae partis*.
2. Nicholas Austin disagrees with such an assessment in the introduction to his *Aquinas on Virtue*, xvi. He appears to hold a definition of virtue ethics derived from the philosopher Rosiland Hursthouse. In her account, virtue ethics provides an alternative to deontology and utilitarianism, the two influential ethical methodologies of the twentieth century. For Hursthouse, and other philosophers, virtue ethics must be "pure" in order to be a true virtue ethics. For example, Christine Swanton has argued that virtue ethics typically rejects a notion of the good that names the good entirely independent of the virtues; see Swanton, "Definition." Most Christian virtue ethicists do not ascribe to such a limiting definition of virtue ethics, and neither do I. A virtue ethics can be based on a prior notion of the good, as found in the Scriptures and theological tradition, and function within a framework of commandments, Beatitudes, and the like.
3. Austin, "Normative Virtue Theory."
4. Salzman and Lawler, *Virtue*, 77.
5. Turri, Alfano, and Grecco, "Virtue Epistemology."
6. See Annas, "Learning Virtue Rules"; and Austin, "Normative Virtue Theory."
7. Anscombe, "Modern Moral Philosophy."
8. Aquinas, *Summa theologiae*, I-II, 111.2.
9. Snow, "Models," 259.
10. Herdt, *Putting on Virtue*, 344.
11. Vogt, "Virtue," 188.
12. See Hauerwas, *Community*; MacIntyre, *After Virtue*; Slote, *Morals*; and Zagzebski, *Exemplarist Moral Theory*.
13. Porter, "Virtue Ethics."
14. In the *Nicomachean Ethics*, Aristotle wrote more on friendship than any other virtue, and Aquinas's hierarchy of virtues is topped with the relational virtues of justice and charity.
15. Spohn, "Return."
16. Waddell, *Friendship*, 142.
17. Keenan, "Proposing Cardinal Virtues," 718.
18. Curran, *Catholic Moral Tradition*, 113.
19. Unlike Keenan, Curran's primary methodology is the relationality-responsibility model. For Curran the virtues aid in living out such a life. See Curran, *Development*, 260.
20. Porpora, "Four Concepts," 14.
21. Rubio, *Hope*, 45.
22. MacIntyre, *After Virtue*, 186; Hauerwas, *Community*, 117.
23. MacIntyre, *After Virtue*, 186.
24. Aquinas, *Summa theologiae*, II-II, 23.1 ad 2.
25. Gutiérrez, "Option," 319.
26. Gutiérrez, *Theology*, 113.
27. Aquinas, *Summa theologiae*, II-II, 23.1.

28. Flood, *Metaphysical Foundations*, 165.
29. Benedict XVI, *Caritas*, 7.
30. Aquinas, *Summa theologiae*, I-II, 94.2.
31. Paul VI, *Populorum progressio*, 14–22.
32. Brady, "Love," 151.
33. Aquinas, *Summa theologiae*, I-II, 25.2 ad 2.
34. Melina, *Epiphany*, 12
35. Hollenbach, *Common Good*, 81.
36. Hollenbach, 82.
37. Second Vatican Council, *Gaudium et spes*, 26.
38. Aquinas, *Summa theologiae*, II-II, 47.10 ad 2.
39. Cloutier, "What Can Social Science Teach," 176.
40. If one omits the word "God" from the sentence, one has a secular or natural notion of virtue, which I believe can and does exist. The fullness of virtue, however, is found in relation to God through the infusion and acceptance of charity. Mark Jordan suggests that Aquinas is principally concerned with the infused virtues, then "specifies acquired virtue by a kind of subtraction." See Jordan, *Teaching Bodies*, 141.
41. Pope, "Overview," 39.
42. Aquinas, *Summa theologiae*, II-II, 23.8.
43. Aquinas, I-II, 65.3.
44. Porter, "Moral Virtues," 52.
45. I ascribe to the transformation theory of infused moral virtues, which stipulates that with the infusion of charity all the prior existing habits, such as the acquired cardinal virtues, are wholly transformed into infused cardinal virtues. The acquired cardinal virtues do not exist on a parallel track in the person transformed by grace. See Jean Porter.
46. Aquinas, *Summa theologiae*, I-II, 18.2 ad 3.
47. Slote, *Morals*.
48. Driver, *Uneasy Virtue*, 60. G. E. Moore was the first modern ethicist to espouse virtue consequentialism, in his influential *Principia Ethica*.
49. Driver, *Uneasy Virtue*, 55.
50. Annas, *Intelligent Virtue*, 14.
51. Wilkins, "Grace," 735.
52. Magundayao, "Dispositions," 103.
53. I borrow this example from Annas, *Intelligent Virtue*, 13.
54. See Aquinas, *Summa theologiae*, I-II, 49.
55. Aquinas, *Disputed Questions*, q. 9 ad 11.
56. Aquinas, *Summa theologiae*, I-II, 58.1.
57. Cates, *Choosing to Feel*, chap. 1.
58. Reichberg, "Intellectual Virtues," 132.
59. Aquinas, *Disputed Questions*, 9 ad 19.
60. Annas, "Applying Virtue to Ethics," 8.
61. Annas, *Intelligent Virtue*, chap. 2, esp. 15.
62. Miller and Knobel, "Some Foundational Questions."
63. In the background of this point is the situationist critique, which maintains that moral character is fragmented, highly local, and specific to certain situations. Thus, situational variables influence a person's action more than her character traits. For a critique of situationism, see Magundayao, "Dispositions."

64. Aquinas, *Summa theologiae*, I-II, 49.2.
65. Aquinas, I-II, 53.1 ad 1.
66. Aquinas, I-II, 52.3.
67. Aquinas, I-II, 52.2.
68. Annas, *Intelligent Virtue*, 102. See also Adams, *Theory*, 48; there, he defines virtue "as persisting excellence in being for the good, and particular virtues as traits whose excellence can be part of the excellence of virtue."
69. Aquinas, *Summa theologiae*, I-II, 54.4 ad 1.
70. Smith, *What Is a Person?* 26.
71. Clayton, "Conceptual Foundations," 8–10.
72. Kotva, *Christian Case*, 26–27.
73. Augustine, *Confessions*, book 8, ix–x.
74. Adams, *Theory*, chap. 2.
75. Aquinas, *Summa theologiae*, II-II, 141.1 ad 2.
76. Kim, "Progress," 167.
77. Aquinas, *Summa theologiae*, II-II, 24.3.
78. Aquinas, I-II, 55.6.
79. Austin, *Aquinas on Virtue*, 173.
80. Aquinas, *Summa theologiae*, 110.3 ad 3.
81. Aquinas, I-II, 113.3.
82. Aquinas, I-II, 112.2 ad 2.
83. See Aquinas, III, 69.4, on Baptism; III, 79.4, on Penance; and III, 89.1, on the Eucharist.
84. Aquinas, III, 75.1.
85. Jordan, *Teaching Bodies*.
86. Austin, *Aquinas on Virtue*, 174.
87. Aquinas, *Summa theologiae*, II-II, 24.2 ad 3. Austin referred to this as "dispositive causality"; Austin, *Aquinas on Virtue*, 174.
88. Aquinas, *Summa theologiae*, II-II, 24.9.
89. Austin made a similar point in an analogy between the infused virtues and the begetting of children. Parents acknowledge that their child is both "their child and a gift from God." Austin suggested that the causal relationship of the parents' action to the child's existence stretches our understanding of causality. The increase of infused virtue seems to present a similar causal quandary due to the fact that it appears to emerge from both God's grace and human agency: "In this way it may be possible to assign a greater causal role to human action in the attainment of infused virtue without undermining its giftedness"; Austin, *Aquinas on Virtue*, 201.
90. Aquinas, *Summa theologiae*, II-II, 27.6.
91. Waddell, *Primacy*, 131.
92. See, esp., Aquinas, *Summa theologiae*, II-II, 31.2, 31.3 ad 1, 32.5, 33.1 ad 1, 33.2.
93. Aquinas, I-II, 24.9.
94. Vogt, "Virtue," 188.
95. MacIntyre, *After Virtue*, 222.
96. Second Vatican Council, *Dei verbum*, 7–10.
97. MacIntyre, *After Virtue*, 218–21.
98. See MacIntyre, 186; there, he admits that his definition of practice does not comport with ordinary usage of the term.
99. MacIntyre, 187.

100. Cloutier, *Vice*, 85.
101. MacIntyre, *After Virtue*, 187.
102. Kallenberg, "Master Argument," 38.
103. Spohn, *Go and Do Likewise*, 42. In the Catholic tradition, virtue is self-effacing. The acquisition of virtue is a secondary goal of the virtuous person. Her primary goal is to do the good, to love God, neighbor, self, and creation. See Aquinas, *Summa theologiae*, II-II, 24.9 ad 3: "Even the perfect make progress in charity: yet this is not their chief care, but their aim is principally directed towards union with God."
104. Stichter, "Virtue."
105. Daly, "Relationship." I am grateful to the *Heythrop Journal* for allowing me to use material from this article.
106. Aquinas, *Summa theologiae*, II-II, 122.3 ad 4.
107. Frankena famously articulated this insight in his *Ethics*, 3.
108. MacIntyre, "Plain Persons," 10.
109. Aquinas, *Summa theologiae*, II-II, 47.3.
110. Frankena, *Ethics*, 53.
111. Daly, "Relationship."
112. Jordan, *Teaching Bodies*, 37.
113. See Zagzebski, *Exemplarist Moral Theory*; and Zagzebski, "Exemplarist Virtue Theory."
114. Zagzebski, "Exemplarist Virtue Theory," 50.
115. Zagzebski, 51.
116. Zagzebski, "Exemplarism and Admiration," 260.
117. Zagzebski, 261.
118. Zagzebski.
119. Zagzebski, "Exemplarist Virtue Theory," 53.
120. Clark, "Case."
121. John Paul II, *Veritatis splendor*, 20.
122. Clark, "Case," 70, 79.
123. Clark, "Particularity," 124.
124. Himes, "Formation," 174.
125. Dalton, *Moral Vision*, 100–101.
126. Dalton.
127. Louden, "On Some Vices."
128. Hursthouse, *On Virtue Ethics*, 35–36.
129. This is Bernard Lonergan's definition of a method, in *Method*, 13–14.
130. Hursthouse disagrees, and argues instead that v-rules contain a decision procedure. The v-rules render virtue ethics strongly codifiable, which is a necessary condition of a decision procedure. See Hursthouse, *On Virtue Ethics*, chaps. 1 and 2.
131. This case draws on Singer's case of the drowning child in his widely cited article, "Famine," and Annas's article, "Applying Virtue to Ethics."

CHAPTER 6

Structures of Virtue and Vice

This book opened by diagnosing a problem in contemporary Catholic ethics. A highly structured world needs to transcend an interactional mode of ethical analysis. As the Rana Plaza case showed, contemporary modes of analysis and the theoethical vocabulary fail to adequately account for moral reality. Instead, what is needed is an ethics that accounts for all realities that produce human outcomes and affect personal actions and character.

Chapter 2 went further and argued that the moral tradition contains two additional problems: the tradition inadequately understands structural realities, and it lacks a coherent account of how structures relate to human well-being and agency. The chapter then recapitulated the development of the concept of the structures of sin. Although the Church came to see the importance of social structures in terms of what structures did to the poor, and how they shaped personal moral character, the chapter argued that the Church's approach remains inconsistent and, worse, incoherent. The structure-agency problem has been recognized in Church teaching, but its solution is sociologically unsophisticated. And though some Catholic theologians have begun to make progress in this area, their work is only in its infancy. The chapter closed with a call to produce a better account of what structures are and how structures and agency relate. The relationship of structure and agency should be a growth area of the tradition, just as Christian theology grew in its use of the natural sciences in the twentieth century.

With the problems diagnosed, chapter 3 marshaled resources capable of offering solutions. The chapter argued that critical realist social theory comports with Catholic control beliefs and was the "best account" of structural, cultural, and agential realities. Further, it argued that critical realism has five propositions that are pertinent to this study. First, structures are real, complex, and irreducible to any other reality. Unlike methodological individualism, critical realism argues that structures cannot be reduced to the aggregate of individual human actions. Second, structures are a collection of relations among social positions. Structures are made of relations, which consist of differentiated social positions (e.g., student–teacher). Relations emerge when many persons assume specified social positions and when cultural realities support those positions. Third, a single structure is composed of a web of relations. For instance, an established social relation is among students and teachers. The student–teacher relation does not, by itself, compose the American educational structure. There are other relations—such as between principals and students, principals and teachers, and teachers and departments of education—that interrelate to compose a structure. Fourth, structures shape, but do not determine, human agency and moral action. Once one enters a position, there are practices and activities prescribed therein, which the occupant is expected to perform. These practices and activities effectively enable and constrain the activities of the person who inhabits the position. Finally, in the words of Elder-Vass, there are two major kinds of structures: normative social institutions and organizations.[1] Normative social institutions are arrangements involving large numbers of people whose behavior is guided by norms and roles. An organization is a normative social institution that contains well-defined positions of authority.

Chapter 4 continued to marshal resources. It argued that three theological trends constitute the best of the post–Vatican II tradition: theocentrism, personalism, and the retrieval of virtue ethics. Since the council, Catholic ethics has developed a more theocentric vision. The Magisterium and theological ethicists increasingly understand that all value derives from an object's relationship with God. The theocentric move has been coupled with a move to a more personalist approach, which turns from anthropologies that abstract aspects of the person, toward an integral and relational understanding of the person. When one views the whole person in relation to God, one finds that she is substance-in-relation—at once a substantial self (an embodied soul) in relation to God, self, others, and creation. Her transcendent value emerges from her relation to God. The chapter then argued that recent popes increasingly have turned to the virtues in their moral theology and social ethics.

With resources identified, chapter 5 aimed at a synthesis. There, I developed what I called a theocentric, personalist virtue theory. I argued that the virtues are operative habits that enable an agent to love God and who and what God loves. The virtues enable a person to recognize the value of the other and consistently move the agent toward union with the other. Conversely, a vice prevents the formation of good relations and often fails to recognize the value of the other. Vices alienate their possessor from loving relations with God, self, neighbor, and creation. As these definitions suggest, virtues and vices are habitual and dispositional aspects of the person's relationality. The chapter then addressed the formation and cultivation of the virtues. The acquired virtues emerge from recurrent "like acts." For example, just acts make a person just. In this way a person acquires a second nature that enables, but does not determine, human action. Although good or bad character is about relationality, it is formed through habituated action, which is often directed by participating in practices, by following norms, and by modeling oneself on exemplars. The infused virtues cannot be acquired, and instead are received as gifts from God. The increase of the summit of the virtues, charity, transpires through repeated acts of charity, which dispose the agent to receive a greater infusion of the virtue. I also argued that it is appropriate to claim that the infused virtues can be cultivated by an agent so long as one acknowledges that this cultivation merely prepares the person for the reception of the graced habits.

The current chapter continues the synthetic move begun in the previous chapter. Specifically, it integrates critical realist social theory within a theocentric personalist virtue theory. The goal of the chapter is to articulate concepts that are capable of ethically scrutinizing the situations that have been presented throughout the book. The chapter accomplishes this by defining the structures of virtue and vice and then demonstrating the explanatory capacity of these concepts. It demonstrates how structures causally contribute to a person's acquisition of moral character as well as how structures causally contribute to or detract from the well-being of persons and communities.

STRUCTURES AND MORAL CHARACTER

We are now equipped to articulate the best moral account of how structures contribute to the formation of moral character and how structures influence the well-being—or lack thereof—of groups and individuals. Let us turn to a rather blunt historical example, which will serve to show that it is possible to scrutinize the moral quality of relations and positions.

Chattel slavery in the United States was a normative social institution that centrally consisted of a relation between slave owners and enslaved persons. Material and cultural realities supported it. Social materials—such as slave ships, slave auction houses, and slave sleeping quarters—were constructed to enable slaveholding. Cultural beliefs, such as the widely held notions that Black persons were less valuable and intellectually inferior to whites, also supported slave-owning structures. Finally, slavery was viewed not only as morally permissible but also, as Senator John Calhoun infamously proclaimed, a "positive good" for enslaved persons.[2]

That slavery was and remains a terrible moral evil hardly needs defense. Without question, slave owners violated the normative dignity of the persons they enslaved. This violation was systemic, as it was written into the structure of slavery. The master–slave relation was the center of the institution of slavery. Was such a relation morally neutral? Was the evil of slavery only related to the activities of the slaver owner, or might one be able to make a moral claim about the quality of the master–slave relation itself? I argue that the relations that composed the structure were morally vicious. There is something profoundly and intrinsically vicious about a social structure that *enables* a person to own other persons. A fortiori, there is something evil about a structure that treats persons as less than human and radically *constrains* the agency of persons, to the point that they cannot make meaningful life decisions for themselves. However, the evil of slavery was not limited to one relation, that of master and enslaved person. A web of relations, positions, institutions, associations, and cultural beliefs supported slavery. For instance, many slaveholders took out policies to protect against "losses." New York Life, which is currently the largest mutual life insurance company in the United States, wrote 336 of its first 1,000 policies to insure the lives of enslaved persons.[3] What this suggests was that moral evil existed on multiple levels relative to slavery and was not only within the individual character of the slave owner.

The same is true regarding the example that I offered at the beginning of the book. The plight of sweatshop workers, such as those 1,127 people killed at Rana Plaza in 2013, invites essential questions. We can again ask, Is the structure that was a causal factor in their deaths morally neutral? Is Sohel Rana, the owner of the factory who ordered workers back into the dilapidated building, the only one to blame? A culpability approach would suggest just such a moral answer. Such an approach suggests that it was Rana alone who directly and freely played a causal role in the death of the workers. However, as this study has shown, Rana's position as factory owner and manufacturer is a social position that stands in relation to many other social positions. Rana's actions constituted a regularized practice in the garment industry. Clothing brands typically contract with manufacturers that provide product at the lowest cost to the brand. In order to produce clothing as inexpensively as possible for the brand (in this case, the Children's Place, among others), factory owners often fail to maintain the physical structure of the factory and demand that workers sew clothing in unsafe conditions.[4] Rana's relation to the Children's Place, for instance, likely nudged him toward certain unjust practices.

And there is more. American consumers exist in relation to factory owners as well. Retailers like the Children's Place capitalize on the buying priorities and habits of Americans and contract with manufacturers that can deliver an inexpensive piece of clothing, as opposed to one that was made under dignified working conditions. As a result, there is "reciprocal action" between the consumer and the garment worker. The consumer buys what the factory owner has produced through his workers. There is no relationship between the consumer and the factory owner, but there is a real, morally relevant relation between these parties. We find that the actions and habits of American consumers are related to the actions and practices of Sohel Rana. Because this relation is part of a web of relations in which poor persons are harmed, it is morally problematic and deserves greater scrutiny.

STRUCTURES AS CIRCUMSTANCES

I argue that the examples described above show that the relations, positions, and practices that enable and constrain action do tell part of the contemporary moral story. But which part of the story? In the traditional language of moral theology, structures and positions are aspects of the circumstances of the moral act. It may seem odd at first to claim that structures have a moral character and then to add that structures are circumstances. Traditionally, circumstances were seen as neither good nor evil; rather, human action should reasonably promote the good within the given circumstances. However, as I show below, social structures are a unique species of circumstances because of their ability to enable or constrain action. Before I make a case for this, let us recall what circumstances are and how they function in ethics.

The Catholic tradition has consistently maintained that circumstances should be considered in moral deliberation.[5] For Aquinas, the consideration of circumstances is essential in moral analysis because "acts are made proportionate to an end by means of a certain commensurateness, which results from the due circumstances." John Paul II echoes Aquinas in *Veritatis splendor* when he writes that "what must be done in any given situation depends on the circumstances."[6] Aquinas defines them as extrinsic to the substance of the moral act, but as "touching" the act.[7] Circumstances are the conditions surrounding the person when she acts. Aquinas, citing Cicero, argues that one must consider these circumstances when determining the rightness of an action: "who, what, where, by what aids, why, how, and when?"[8] For our purposes, "who" stands out as especially morally significant. The "who," in many cases, is a person who acts from within her social relations. For example, a family acquaintance may not be morally responsible for correcting a child's lack of politeness, but due to his relation to the child, a father is. In this case, the "who" matters.

The question for this study is: Are structures a species of circumstance? Recall that structures are webs of relations among social positions. Each position is value-laden, containing norms and practices that both enable and constrain the activities of those who inhabit that position. It seems, then, that structures are extrinsic to the moral act but also touch the act. As the examples given above show, people act from within their relations and positions. The professor–student relation directs the former to return graded work promptly and to refrain from taking a phone call during an exam. The professor–student relation is external to the professor's action, but it "touches" her action. When a person acts as a professor, her relation to students serves as an important condition surrounding her action.

This means that the positions and relations that compose structures affect the circumstance of "who." When people enter a social relation, they are assuming a "who" in relation to other persons, and this "who" affects the activities of the position holder. For example, when a person suffers cardiac arrest on a plane, it is the nurse or doctor who first is obligated to attend to the person, not the professor of theology. The fact that a woman is a doctor is not part of the substance of the moral act; it is a condition surrounding the moral act. However, it is a crucial aspect of the act. If she fails to treat the arresting person, one will judge her to have acted wrongly.

As this example shows, structures are not merely the "conditions surrounding the action"; they are conditions *facilitating* or *impeding* action.[9] By virtue of her socially established relation to the sick, the physician is enabled to care for the arresting patient. If a person identifies herself as a physician, other passengers will allow the physician to treat the patient. Further, by virtue of her position, the physician is constrained from inactivity. If the arresting patient died, and the airline later found that a physician was aboard, they may report such behavior to the physician's place of employment. This physician could face disciplinary action for failing in the "duty to rescue."[10] Even if the physician wanted to ignore the arresting patient, she would be constrained by social norms and practices from doing so. Because of her relation with those who inhabit the social position of "the sick," she would be compelled to treat the patient.

The fact that structures facilitate and impede certain activities deserves further exploration. Take, for instance, the case of US Federal District judge Mark Bennett and defendant Mark Weller. Federal judges like Bennett are the inheritors of legislation that emerged during the War on Drugs, which was declared by President Richard Nixon in the early 1970s. This "war" produced what many consider to be unjust sentencing laws. Implicated within these laws is a particular relation among federal judges and drug offenders.

Judges relate to offenders through the laws that guide sentencing. Judges such as Bennett inhabit a position in which they are compelled to disproportionately punish the petty drug crimes of mostly poor, mostly nonwhite, Americans. When confronted with a case in which Mark Weller had been arrested with 233 grams of methamphetamine, Judge Bennett was required to enforce the mandatory minimum: ten years imprisonment. Bennett told Weller as he sentenced him, "My hands are tied on your sentence. I'm sorry. This isn't up to me."[11] Bennett later said that Weller should have received a year of drug rehabilitation. However, US district judges are not empowered to sentence based on their best judgment. Judges are appointed to enforce the legal guidelines and norms that have been established, however unjustly, by the legislative branch. Weller was a victim of poor legislation and, more than that, of an immoral and unjust structure. Bennett was the agent of the structure, which constrained his action. To paraphrase Elder-Vass, due to judicial structures, Bennett acted differently than he would normally have done.[12] The unjust structure was only enacted when Bennett, in his position, handed down the sentence that was in accordance with customary judicial practice.[13]

In this case, the sentencing laws were more than ordinary circumstances. This example shows that there is a qualitative difference between circumstances that "touch" an action and those that enable and constrain action. For this reason, I argue that "structural circumstances" are a unique species of the broader category of circumstances. There are then two kinds of circumstances: discrete and structural. Discrete circumstances are local and unique. They are circumstances in the traditional sense. For example, imagine two assailants, one of whom attacks a person with a soup spoon and the other of whom attacks a person with a meat cleaver. In these examples, the weapon used is morally significant but is a discrete circumstance. It is local and unique. Further, these circumstances do not constrain or enable the action of the one attacked. Although the meat cleaver does not prevent the victim from running away any more than the spoon does, it does make running more urgent.

Structural circumstances are different. Judge Bennett was not forced to render the ten-year sentence, but he was enabled to do so and was constrained from acting otherwise. Here the legal structure does not merely "touch" Bennett's action; it facilitates specific actions and penalizes others. Because structures punish action that conflicts with accepted practice, they are circumstances and as such must be accounted for in moral analysis. However, as circumstances, they typically have been ignored. The moral tradition has invited ethicists to focus more on the local, discrete, and personal circumstances and less on the social structural conditions that enable and constrain action. Accounting for structural circumstances adds value to a contemporary theological ethics that has difficulty scrutinizing the structures that renders it so easy to do evil and so hard to do good (and vice versa). The added value is a more accurate account of what structures are and how they regularly play causal roles in human action. Again, we would do well to recall Elder-Vass's adage that structures often cause "individuals to act differently than they would do otherwise."[14]

Just as the sixteenth century gave rise to casuistry, and its conceptual bundle, so too does a highly structured world need the capacity to evaluate new realities with a new conceptual framework. What is needed is a moral nomenclature that corresponds to moral reality. The new conceptual framework should emerge from the best current insights of the theological and sociological fields. That, I have argued, includes a theocentric, personalist virtue theory that calls Christians to attend especially to the suffering, poor, and marginalized. Such a framework should also be informed by a sociologically rigorous account of a social structure. Critical realism offers just such an account.

An adequate moral understanding of social reality should also recognize the twofold manner in which structures are morally relevant. First, structures shape the actions and character of those persons who inhabit the structure's social positions. Slave owners became certain kinds of persons based on the socially established relation of slaveholder and enslaved person and the practices that were embedded in the former position. Second, structures affect human outcomes and well-being. The structure of slavery devastated the lives of the many Africans enslaved. Structures shape both personal character and social and individual well-being.

THE STRUCTURES OF VIRTUE AND VICE DEFINED

The structures of virtue and vice have a twofold definition. First, virtuous structures contain social relations that enable and facilitate a person's performance of virtuous actions and subsequent acquisition and cultivation of the virtues. Such structures engender habits that dispose the agent to recognize and promote human dignity and human well-being, especially that of the vulnerable. These are structures that contain positions that consistently function to enable or facilitate the further cultivation of a person's loving and merciful relation with God, self, others, and creation. In addition, these relations constrain vicious behavior and the cultivation of vicious character. They are relations that often play a causal role in the acquisition of good moral character.

Second, virtuous structures are those webs of relations that consistently promote the normative human dignity and well-being of all affected by those relations, especially the vulnerable. These are structures that encourage decisions that contribute to social justice, and its fruit, the common good. This aspect of the structures of virtue concerns the effects that structures have on those affected by them. These structures are composed of relations in which the persons who participate in those relations are enabled to perceive and promote the normative dignity and well-being of those with whom they share a relation.

Vicious structures contain social relations that enable and facilitate the acquisition of vicious traits by those who participate in the structure. Vicious structures include positions in which persons are constrained in their ability to recognize and promote the dignity of others, especially the poor and marginalized. Such structures are relations in which friendship and love of God, others, and creation are rendered more difficult. In the words of Gustavo Gutiérrez, such structures are characterized by the breach of friendship between the person and God and neighbor.[15] Further, structures of vice are webs of relations that consistently harm normative personal dignity, human well-being, and happiness, especially that of the vulnerable. Also, vicious structures promote social injustice and undermine the common good. There is a duality in personal and structural character. The structures that enable the acquisition of virtuous character are the same ones that promote the dignity of others.

Structures are only metaphorically virtuous or vicious. Only persons have moral agency and are capable of acquiring moral character. Structures do not act; instead, they exist in and through the actions of persons. However, structures have a moral character because of how they enable and constrain personal agency. Slavery is an unjust structure because it enables persons to own each other and harms the life, health, education, and relationships of the enslaved. The structure of slavery played a causal role in the abuse of others. Because the social structure of slavery lacks moral agency, it is metaphorically, not literally, vicious.

Slavery provides an example of a wholly evil structure. It has no redeeming qualities. However, for most structures, the binary distinction of "virtuous" and "vicious" needs to be massaged a bit. Because structures emerge from the relations of many social positions, they are morally complicated. Like individual people, structures often possess both virtuous and vicious aspects. Because of this, it is more important to name those virtuous and vicious elements of a person or a structure than it is to make a single sweeping judgment about moral character. The example of Martin Luther King Jr. is instructive. He was a socially just, but, at times, he was an intemperate man.[16] Broad claims about individual people, like MLK, are only partially insightful. The full moral picture is more complicated than claiming that MLK was a man of justice. Although this is true, we understand the character of the man better if we acknowledge both his virtues and vices. The same holds for structures of virtue and vice. There will be aspects of structures that are vicious, while other parts we may find to be virtuous. A structure may, in some ways, promote the common good and benefit the poor and, in other ways, undermine the former and harm the latter. Similarly, a social position may cultivate a person's virtue in certain relations while cultivating vice in other relations.

HOW STRUCTURES SHAPE PERSONAL MORAL CHARACTER

The first way in which structures are virtuous or vicious is in how they shape the actions and character of agents. Both Christian ethics and critical realist social theory maintain that structures can shape, but do not "hydraulically" determine, the actions and character of individuals. For this, and other reasons, I make no global claims about the individual persons who inhabit certain positions within a social structure. There is no simple correspondence between a "vicious" relation or position and the character of the individual who inhabits that position. My claims are about what kinds of actions and character traits structures constrain and enable. I am only claiming that the position itself is characteristically "virtuous" or "vicious." Another way of envisioning this is to imagine a person following all the norms, practices, and exemplars prescribed within the social position they inhabit. What kind of person would this person become?

Let us consider two cases to illustrate this point. The first case briefly describes how the agency of an assistant professor is constrained by his position. This case is analyzed in greater depth in chapter 7 but is presented at this point to show how a social position constrains agency. The second case is extensively developed to show how personal moral development transpires through participation in social structures.

Case: The Carbon-Consuming Assistant Professor

Imagine that there is an environmentally conscious, tenure-track professor, John Doe. Doe is an assistant professor of ecological ethics. Professor Doe bikes to the college from his micro-apartment, which is powered by renewable energy; eats an organic vegan diet; shops at second-hand stores; and rides a stationary bike to power his office computer. He vacations locally and travels by air only if it is morally necessary—that is, for the sake of his relationships with family or friends. Doe has a low carbon footprint and a low-waste footprint, all while living a life in contemporary consumer society. Such a life is not easy, but he does so because he values the created world and is concerned about the effects of global warming on the ice caps, polar bears, and the Great Barrier Reef.

However, Professor Doe is a tenure-track assistant professor, which means that he will need to be present (and hopefully present papers) at least two times a year at peer-reviewed academic conferences and other smaller conferences and meetings. He will fly at least three other times to serve on a national environmental ethics board, to deliver an invited lecture at a university, and to meet with colleagues regarding his contribution to an edited volume of essays. This gives him a minimum total of five professionally related airplane flights a year. Why does he do this? His position requires participation in these professional activities and thus requires air travel. This presents a moral problem for Doe because he understands that, according to climate scientists, if one takes five long flights a year, this typically accounts for three-quarters of one's annual warming effect.[17] So, if Doe wants to secure tenure, he cannot maintain a low carbon footprint.

Case: The Little-Leaguer

Imagine a child who is joining a Little League baseball team for the first time. As he assumes the position of "teammate" and enters into a relation with his fellows, he immediately meets certain constraints and enablements.[18] He realizes that, for instance, he must wait in line to take batting practice. He also realizes that he must wait in a certain way: patiently. He should not demand to move up in line or complain that the line is taking too long. His coaches and fellow teammates will punish such selfish behavior. He will also learn deeper values, which specific practices will help to ingrain. Explicitly and implicitly, he will learn that he is expected to support his teammates. The regularized practice of exchanging high fives will mark the successes of his teammates. His lack of participation in such practices will be met with disdain from his teammates. When a teammate fails at something, he will follow the example of those who give out words of encouragement to the suffering teammate. If, instead, he lashes out at those who fail, he will be chastised by his team. He will also hear his coaches and teammates preach the importance of working toward a collective team goal and the importance of sacrificing individual success and accolades for the sake of the team. Such sacrifice will be enthusiastically congratulated by his team. Self-serving play will be roundly criticized and will often result in the loss of playing time.

The structure of Little League baseball is an organization (or, an organized normative social institution) that comprises smaller organizations, such as local leagues and teams. Within this structure is the position of "teammate," which this child has assumed. In many ways, the enablements and constraints baked into the position facilitate his performance of virtuous actions. The child will likely perform a recurring set of actions that will, over time, facilitate his acquisition of the virtues of patience (waiting well in relation to others), mercy (suffering with others in order to heal them), and solidarity (effective commitment to the common good). He may resist the performance of these actions (and thus fail to acquire these traits) either by failing to practice what is prescribed above or because he practiced it begrudgingly and without any interior motivation. However, it will be hard for this child to be a teammate in the future if he rejects these practices and the values for which they stand. A child who resisted the prescribed practices and norms of the position of teammate would likely stop participating in team sports altogether.

There are three ways in which this structure plays a causal role in this child's character development. These three ways reflect the definition of structures of virtue and vice, which claims that structures enable persons to acquire habits in which they recognize the value of the other, promote the normative dignity of the other, and enter into loving and merciful relations with others.

First, in his position he is enabled to recognize the value of his fellow teammates. Recall that practices are, in the word of Christian Smith, "motivated in part by normative and moral valuations and guides."[19] The position of teammate and the practices that compose the position are value-laden. The child who consoles his teammate who struck out may eventually do so, not out of a sense of obligation to do so but rather out of a true concern for his teammate's well-being. Over time, the child will transform his values. Again, if he fails to value the well-being of his teammates, then he will most likely remove himself from this social relation.

Second, the child in this example is enabled to promote the normative dignity and well-being of his teammates and is constrained from acting against these goods. He has regular opportunities to do objectively good actions—that is, acts of virtue. We can assume that waiting for one's turn, comforting the suffering, and acting for the sake of the good of others are objectively good actions for this child in these circumstances. Although these acts lack the fullness of virtue, they are the building blocks of virtue. Like the child who learns the practice of chess, this child may, over time, learn that there are goods internal to the practices associated with being a teammate. An embodied, personalist virtue ethics recognizes there are formative aspects to a person simply saying "you'll get 'em next time" to a teammate who has failed.

Human actions, irrespective of motive, matter. The sacramental theologian Bruce Morrill has claimed that ritualistic actions—such as receiving ashes on Ash Wednesday or, in the example above, "high-fiving" teammates—shape moral character. Rituals, such as the sacraments, create, sustain, and "gradually morph the identity and agency of the members (of the social body) *by their very participation therein*" (emphasis in the original).[20] Morrill continues by emphasizing that such an embodied approach to communal and personal formation "is to resist the modern temptation to prioritize thought over action, mind over body, supposedly autonomous individuals over social institutions."[21] Morrill makes two critical points here. First, he argues that the acquisition of character is embodied—it is not idealist. Bodily performance plays a role in the virtuous becoming virtuous, and the vicious becoming vicious. Moral character is an emergent reality, as argued in chapter 5. The whole person is the subject of her virtues and vices. It is through the relation of a person's intention, rational deliberation, and bodily performance that her character emerges. Second, Morrill rejects the modern individualist explanation of moral agency and instead argues in favor of a model that gives space to the causality of social institutions. (More on the second point below.)

Because bodily performance matters, and can play a causal role in the character development of the person, vice is often cultivated in an agent even when she does not wish the harm on the other person. For instance, Judge Bennett's actions in the Weller case were unjust and therefore vitiated him. In pronouncing an unjust sentence, Bennett became an agent of injustice. Now, Bennett publicly has acknowledged the injustice, lamented his role in it, and called for a change in the laws that required him to act unjustly toward Weller. It is clear that he remains opposed to what he did to Weller. All this speaks to the fact that he continues to possess of the virtue of justice, even if that trait was weakened through the sentence that he handed down. However, one can imagine that if Bennett regularly sentenced drug offenders unjustly, his character would begin to reflect this. Further, such actions would likely dull the edge of his conscience, and he likely would both cease to speak out against such sentencing and weaken his opposition to the laws that mandate such sentences.

Judge Bennett is not alone in lamenting the harm that he has produced in the lives of the marginalized. Returning to the issue of sweatshop labor, most American consumers would choose not to have a harmful relation with the people who sew their clothes. A 2013 National Consumer League poll found that 94 percent of American consumers said how garment workers are treated is "important" to them. Supermajorities of shoppers reported that they would be willing to pay between $1 and $5 more for garments made under more just working conditions.[22] However, the position of American consumer contains bargain hunting practices, which in turn often result in the purchase of sweatshop-made clothing. The harm that garment workers suffers is real but is not intended by American consumers. Benefiting from such types of harm may vitiate the agent because it signifies that the agent has failed to account for and promote the dignity of those who suffer from the relation. Practices that alienate and harm others are unloving. Such practices are vicious if the effects of one's relation to others are known or can be known through reasonable effort.

Conversely, other social relations constrain vicious behavior, such as hate speech. The social constraints on hate speech constrain (but do not prevent) the acquisition of the vice of racism.[23] Those who commit racist, sexist, and homophobic actions and speech are regularly punished by those who hold positions of authority. As a result, the racist physician who privately harbors her racism will be less racist than she otherwise would if she could publicly espouse her racist views. This may seem like a small moral improvement, and it is. This physician is *still* racist and most likely shares her racist beliefs with like-minded persons. However, because some of their actions are constrained (namely, their public actions), her character is *less* vicious than it would be otherwise. In the end, the social structure constrains actions that harm others, and thus it constrains the further development of the vicious trait.

Returning to the example of the Little Leaguer, we find that the preexisting social relation between teammates enables this child to form merciful and just relations with his peers. The relation among teammates is usually one of mutual respect, in which each teammate recognizes the intrinsic value of the other. Although some teammates will be better players than others, members of a team typically value all members of the team. Disrespectful behavior toward a teammate for reasons such as performance, race, ethnicity, or education level is typically, but not always, punished by other teammates. Sexual orientation remains an outlier in this regard but is improving in the early twenty-first century. On the whole, the position of teammate provides a structure that promotes friendship among teammates.

Like nearly all positions, the position of teammate cultivates vice in certain areas of relationality. Although teams provide a structure within which friendship is enabled intrateam, the same is not true interteam. The structure of team sports can contain a culture of vilification and hatred of the opponent.

For example, Nick Saban, the legendary University of Alabama head football coach, was once asked after a victory against Louisiana State University how his team limited the performance of one of the other team's players. He said, "We have some pretty hateful guys that play defense around here who are pretty good competitors."[24] The "hate" that his players had was for the Louisiana State University players. This was corroborated by an Alabama player, who quite bluntly said of his team, "Mostly, we're all hateful guys. We hate everybody on the other team. Everybody that's lined up across from us, we hate you; we're trying to kill you."[25] Those in team sports often celebrate such a perspective. Hating one's competitor is often embedded in the culture of a team or a sport and is often endorsed and enforced as a positive value and practice. Exemplars of hate, such as Chicago Bears defensive lineman Dick Butkus, are held in esteem. Butkus reportedly said, "When I played pro football, I never set out to hurt anyone deliberately—unless it was, you know, important, like a league game or something."[26] More recently, the New Orleans Saints of 2009–11 instituted a "bounty" for players who injured opposing players. Players received $1,000 for causing an opponent to be carted off the field, while ending an opponent's game garnered $1,500 from a pot created by coaches and players. These are extreme examples. However, they are indicative of an attitude that often exists within team sports, such that one can reasonably claim that the position of teammate can at times constrain the possibility of friendship with one's opponents. In sum, the relation between teammates enables virtue in specific ways and constrains it in others. Importantly, this is a socially constructed relation between positions. The position of teammate can be transformed to eliminate any vicious norms, practices, and exemplars that are sewn into it.

The cases of Professor Doe and the Little Leaguer show that all social positions contain norms, practices, and exemplars that are value laden, regularly benefit or harm others, and facilitate friendship or render it more difficult. Consider the relation of a Benedictine monk with his brothers and abbot. In the prologue to his *Rule*, Saint Benedict states his intentions in founding monasteries: "We intend to establish a school for the Lord's service.... The good of all concerned, however, may prompt us to a little strictness in order to amend faults and to safeguard love." In order to root out "faults" or vices and instill "love," or virtues, Benedict establishes norms, practices, and exemplars for the monks. In order to cultivate good works, and ultimately the love of God, monks should follow norms such as "refrain from too much eating and sleeping, and from laziness. Do not grumble or speak ill of others" (4.36–40). Humility, he determined, should be cultivated through twelve practices, such as confessing all the sinful thoughts that one has (7.44) and by silence

(7.56). Once one mastered the twelve "steps" to humility, he would "arrive at the perfect love of God," which he "will now begin to observe without effort, as though naturally, from habit, no longer out of fear of hell, but out of love for Christ, good habit, and delight in virtue" (7.67–69). Finally, Benedict designed the position of abbot as the exemplar for the other monks. He noted that "anyone who receives the name of abbot is to lead his disciples by a twofold teaching: he must point out to them all that is good and holy more by example than by words" (2.11).

Benedict's *Rule* reflects an insight that is implicit in Bhaskar's position-practice system: social positions shape actions and moral character. Because monasteries were cloistered and had limited and plain food, monks lacked opportunities to acquire lust and gluttony. Even the most lustful and gluttonous person would likely experience a decrease in these vices if he lived in a monastery for an extended period. Vices, such as lust and gluttony, require "practice," just as do the virtues of chastity and temperance. Further, the man who assumed the position of monk would have his character shaped by the three formational modalities that I identified in chapter 5. Benedict intentionally created the position of monk with these norms, practices, and exemplars to enable and facilitate the monk's growth in loving friendship with God and neighbor. In short, Benedict made it easier for his monks to be good.

However, he fully acknowledged the position of monk could only guide the monk to a certain point of moral development. At the end of the *Rule*, Benedict noted that it is "for beginners. After that, you can set out for the loftier summits of the teaching and virtues we mentioned above, and under God's protection you will reach them" (73.9). The position of monk facilitated the acquisition of virtue, but like any position, it did not hydraulically move a person to virtue or enable persons to reach the highest limits of virtue. The path to the summit of virtue is, as Benedict noted, dependent on the grace of God.

From Structures to Personal Character

The previous subsection showed that structures can enable and constrain action. However, recall that the simple fact of entering a social relation did not automatically determine one's character. Although one's relation with other positions enables and constrains activity, Elder-Vass has emphasized that agents retain flexibility in how to perform their roles.[27] People can and do resist the practices and prescribed relations of their position.

Archer's notion of the "internal conversation" helps to explain the interplay of structures and agency. Chapter 3 outlined Margaret Archer's account of how people deliberate about what to do in the face of social structures. Recall that the internal conversation is the internal dialogue whereby agents reflexively deliberate on the social circumstances that confront them.[28] Armed with her life projects and values, the moral agent searches for positions that enable her to realize her projects and live her values. Then, after "reflexive deliberations," she chooses a social position from among the social positions available to her. Once she has assumed a social position, such as associate professor, she then reflexively deliberates regarding how to practice the position given her values and goals and the objective structural enablements and constraints that confront her.

Interestingly, Archer's internal conversation corresponds, to a degree, with what theological ethicists call moral deliberation or prudential reasoning. Let us compare Archer's notion of the internal conversation with Aquinas's treatment of the inner workings of moral deliberation.[29] Questions 6 through 17 in *Prima secundae* of the *Summa theologiae* contain a descriptive treatment of moral deliberation and the moral act. After distinguishing between voluntary and involuntary actions, Aquinas turns to an acknowledgment of the circumstances (Archer: preexistent structural world) within which persons act (q. 7). Aquinas then moves to the will (qs. 8 and 9), which intends to attain human goods (Archer: values and life projects). Once the person has ordered her goods, she must, according to Aquinas, create a chain of ends (Archer: practical projects) that will ultimately attain the overall good desired, which is also to say that she must begin to choose the means (q. 13) to the ends that she desires. The right choice of means emerges through counsel (Archer: internal conversation), for Aquinas (q. 13). Counsel has both individual and interpersonal aspects. Internally, one draws on past experiences, uses norms, and reflects on her circumstances to arrive at the good means to the end.[30] Counsel also involves "sitting together" with others so that the agent accounts for all the relevant circumstances of a situation.[31]

Aquinas does not stop at a descriptive account of moral deliberation; he then moves to explicate how to ethically reason well. This is the role of the virtue of prudence. For Aquinas, prudence finds the right means to the ostensibly good end. He repeatedly emphasizes that the goal of the agent's action preexists the means to the goal.[32] Prudence is the virtue that enables the person to find the right means easily.[33] Prudential reasoning should lead to virtuous actions, which subsequently form virtuous moral character.

Archer's work on the internal conversation shows that people reflexively deliberate about which positions to assume and how to practice those positions based on their values. When read in light of Aquinas, Archer's work reveals that and how an individual's moral character emerges through her decisions and activities within the positions she assumes throughout her lifetime.

The notion that social structures offer opportunities for character formation is not novel. Alasdair MacIntyre has written that "we discover our character in tension with what our society and our roles ask of us."[34] MacIntyre's claim can be deepened with an account of the inner workings of how roles "ask" actions of people. The structures of virtue and vice offer just such an account. Character is not merely "discovered." Social structures are causal factors in the acquisition and cultivation of virtue or vice.

If we return to the similarities between Aquinas and Archer, we find that there are three moments when character is shaped in relation to structures and social positions. First, both Aquinas and Archer begin with personal values. Every person has some "notion of the good" and has goals and life projects that are congruent with this notion. I take it for granted that not all notions of the good are equal, nor are all goals and life projects. A person who values wealth or pleasure as an ultimate good will be less virtuous than one who values the common good and friendship in this way. Thus, the selection of one set of goods or life projects may be more virtuous than another. Second, Thomas and Archer both then turn to how the person intends to live out her values and achieve her goals or life projects. This often involves the selection of positions that will help her attain her goals and life projects. The selection of social positions is critical for moral formation because in choosing, the person typically knows the activities, practices, and goals of the position. Just as not all goods are equally morally valuable, not all positions are equally virtuous. There is a real moral distinction between a person who chooses to support a family through construction work and one who does so through loan-sharking. Third, a person's moral deliberation or internal conversation does not terminate at the choice of social positions but continues when one practices a position. At this stage the norms, practices, and exemplars of the position confront the agent and require her to deliberate about if and how to act given all her structured relations.

Recall the example presented in chapter 3 of Sally, a saleswoman at Speaker City. First, Sally pursues employment in order to pay for her college tuition. This is a reasonable and good motive and is better than desiring a job for the sake of buying illicit drugs or a luxury watch. Second, in her quest to pay for her education, she is confronted with preexisting social structures, which contain certain social positions that are available to her. Let us assume that given her education and work experience, the best jobs that are available to her are as a barista at a local coffee shop and as a saleswoman at Speaker City. In the interview process, she learns of the norms and practices of the positions as well as their wages and benefits. She learns that baristas should be friendly and should take a genuine interest in the lives of the regulars who frequent the shop. Baristas earn $14 an hour, with tips typically netting them $16 an hour. At Speaker City, Sally learns that the store recommends and rewards salespeople who "upsell" customers on more expensive speakers. The store encourages sales staff to "befriend" customers in order to use "friendship" to pressure customers into purchasing on the spot. Speaker City pays $15 an hour and offers a 5 percent commission on each set of speakers sold. Salespeople who use the prescribed upselling tactics typically net $25 an hour.

Due to the values that have emerged from her Catholic faith, Sally believes that lying is wrong and that she should conduct herself with honesty in dealing with others. As a result, she is morally uncomfortable with Speaker City's selling strategies. However, she is attracted to the earning potential at Speaker City. This is formative moment number two. The position she chooses will shape whom she becomes. Is she willing to assume a position in which she knows that her religiously based commitment to honesty is likely to be compromised? Finally, once in the position of saleswoman, how does she relate to customers and her supervisors? Does she model herself on the most successful salesperson in the store and follow the norms and practices of the position? Alternatively, does she push against them and thereby risk not only a lower income but also disciplinary action from her manager?

This example shows how organizational structure shapes Sally's character. Social structures offer Sally limited employment options, and if she is to attend college, she must choose among them. She will, in part, become her moral self in and through her choice to be either a barista or saleswoman. Because structural powers incentivize a recurring set of actions and punish another set of actions, Sally's character will develop through the practice of her position. She will freely choose among her options; but again, these options are limited and will require certain practices of her.

The point here is that structures shape personal character in two ways. First, they prescribe specific actions and modes of relation, which, over time, can become new habits. As argued above, people become, in part, what they intentionally do, even if the resulting character trait is undesired. For instance, no one aims to acquire alcohol use disorder; rather, one desires to experience the pleasures of drinking. Insidiously, the disorder emerges when one consistently drinks to excess. Here, the change in character happens obliquely. In this way, character change often is unintentional. However, the *actions* that change character are entirely intentional. Only intentional action can change one's character, even if one cannot predict where one's character will end up. This is how social positions shape one's character. Although the position holder does not desire to acquire the traits woven into the position, she does intentionally practice the activities that give rise to those very traits. We become what we do, not whom we want to become.

Second, there is a dialectical spiral between a person's values and the structured relations in which she participates. As Archer has shown, people choose positions based on their preexisting values. However, once one inhabits a position, the person's set of values can be shaped by that position. Structures often shape the values of position holders. This change in values then alters the positions that one desires to hold. For example, a person whose social position renders her more comfortable lying to clients will eventually become a liar and will then be more prone to select social positions in which lying is permitted or valued. This reminds us that positions are value-laden—they carry a particular notion of good within them. On this point, Elder-Vass has argued that social positions influence not only the actions and dispositions of people but also their beliefs about what is real and good.[35]

Character as Emergent, Revisited

There are other reasons, in addition to the existence of free will, why participation in a given structure does not automatically lead to the acquisition of the moral traits prescribed in the structure. First, and most obviously, individuals simultaneously participate in multiple structures. Some of these positions will be cross-cutting; one will enable and encourage honesty, while another may constrain such a trait. Second, structures do not hydraulically create moral character because, as argued in chapter 5, character is an emergent reality. Moral character, which is a higher-level reality, cannot be explained solely in terms of lower-level realities, such as a person's actions, intentions, emotions, bodily movements, and structures in which the person participates. Instead, one's habits of relationality to God, self, neighbor, and creation are acquired and cultivated from within the relation of a person's actions, to her conscious reasoning, intentions, emotions, and bodily movements. All these shape who she becomes. Moral character is complex and is irreducible to any one dominant aspect of human existence.

Because character does not admit of a reductionistic explanation, the best account of character formation should name *all* its causes. This chapter has shown how social structures causally contribute to human action and character. Through prescribed relations and social positions, structures enable and constrain a person's relationality with others. Structures affect one's ability to recognize the intrinsic dignity of the other, to promote the normative dignity of the other, and to move toward friendship with the other. Structures play a different formative role than, say, intentions, which are about aspects internal to the person. However, the fact remains that all of the above factors—actions, reasoning, intentions, emotions, and bodily movements—are deeply affected by social structures. Structures do not hydraulically cause the person to act, reason, will, feel, or move in specific ways, but they do make certain acts more easily executed and sustained and make others more difficult.

This is a crucial point. Structures are ontologically distinct from the will, reason, and emotions of the person. All character formation and cultivation will emerge from the person's freely chosen actions. However, this study has shown that the structural circumstances in which a person makes a free choice privilege some choices and penalize others. Also, this study has shown that no choice is entirely free. Only God has complete freedom. Human persons are constrained by the physical realities of existence, along with social realities. The nature of these constraints can be different; a person can never choose to time-travel but can choose to flout accepted social practices such as "upselling." As the example of Professor Doe shows, people can choose to live a low-carbon lifestyle. However, such a life would prevent Doe from achieving many of the goods that he valued. Structures constrain agency and cause persons to act in specific ways because they impose penalties on certain ways of acting and reward others. The takeaway is this: structures are ontologically distinct from personal agency, action, and character but can causally influence each of these personal realities.

What we find is that moral character has multiple causes.[36] Moral character emerges from one's moral values, actions, intentions, and emotions as well from within the relations and social positions that one has assumed. The story of character must include the latter realities if the story is to be complete. The result of this approach is a more social and relational notion of moral character. This comports with Bruce Morrill's argument that we should "resist the temptation to prioritize ... individual autonomy over social institutions."[37] Agents exercise their autonomy through and within social institutions. Such institutions are distinct but not separable from moral agency.

HOW STRUCTURES SHAPE OUTCOMES

The second way in which structures are virtuous or vicious is in their capacity to affect the well-being of people and groups. Structures can either systematically promote or undercut the well-being of persons. In order to determine the character of a structure, one should ask, first, how does the position affect the well-being of the vulnerable, the poor, and the socially marginalized? Is the dignity of the poor routinely recognized and promoted, or ignored and thwarted? The preferential option for the poor serves as the fundamental test of a structure's character. This is a distinctively theocentric test of a structure, as it attends first to the weakest members affected by a structure because those are the ones for whom God first opts.

Second, does the structure promote or thwart the common good? More specifically, how does the structure affect the instrumental aspects of the common good? Recall that the previous chapter argued that the common good is instrumentally valuable for people; people are needy. The instrumental common good exists if goods are distributed in such a way that persons have "easy and ready access" to the goods needed to live a dignified and happy life. Does the structure promote this kind of access to the goods that all need for a dignified existence? For example, does it enable all persons to access healthy food, high-quality primary education, basic medical care, and regular periods of rest and leisure?

Examples of Structural Character

As noted above, this account of structural character finds that there is no perfectly virtuous structure. It is more accurate to write of structures that are more or less virtuous and those that are growing in virtue. Further, we should identify the virtuous and vicious aspects—that is, the virtuous and vicious relations among positions—of a given social structure. In this subsection, I consider three contemporary examples of structural character. The first example, the structured practice of police brutality to African Americans, is covered in depth. The two others, the garment industry and the guild of obstetric and gynecology physicians, further illustrate how structures have moral character.

Before turning to the first example, I acknowledge that the structural character of organizations is easier to identify than that of "basic" normative social institutions. Recall that, in general, a normative social institution is a social structure composed of relations among social positions that endorse and enforce the beliefs and norms of a group. Some normative social institutions are organizations, such as the New York City Police Department, and others are "basic" normative social institutions, such as queuing or "lining up." Organizations contain highly structured positions, some of which wield authority over others. For example, by virtue of her position, the chairwoman of an academic department is empowered to require other members to attend scheduled department meetings. In addition, organizations often have clearly articulated norms and rules for members to follow. Many academic departments follow *Robert's Rules of Order* during department meetings. Notice that the relations among social positions and the norms governing these relations are clear. The clarity of organizational structures renders them more easily ethically evaluated than the relations in basic normative social institutions. Basic normative social institutions neither contain positions of authority nor written norms. However, although there is no organization endorsing and enforcing lining up, as a normative social institution, Elder-Vass argues that it *still* influences the actions of individuals. Individuals who wish to "cut" the line are constrained from doing so, in part, because of the penalties—the dirty looks and the chastisement of those persons who are members of the normative social institution of lining up—they are likely to suffer if they choose to flout queuing norms.

Mindful of these distinctions, I am prepared to identify structures of virtue and structures of vice in the field of law enforcement. Because of their social positions, police officers are enabled and are required to, for example, protect individuals from domestic abusers.[38] This constitutes a virtuous relation among social positions insofar as the structure is designed to promote the well-being of abuse survivors. However, there are vicious relations embedded in the social structure of law enforcement. The repeated killings of unarmed African Americans at the hands of on-duty police officers requires people of conscience to investigate the agential and social factors that give rise to this systemic social injustice. The data are startling. The *Washington Post* found that "an unarmed black man is about four times more likely to be killed by police than an unarmed white man."[39] Minneapolis police have used physical force against African American persons at seven times the rate that they have used force against white persons.[40] George Floyd, an African American man, was murdered in May 2020 when a Minneapolis police officer pressed his knee into Floyd's neck for almost 9 minutes.

We are confronted with an effect and must search for its causes. Certainly, the disproportionate use of physical force against African Americans is caused, in part, by individual white police officers who hold and are motivated by explicitly white supremacist/antiblackness ideology. However, though the use of excessive force by police officers against African Americans is woefully understudied, there are indications that social structures also play causal roles.[41] What follows is an attempt to understand the sociostructural causes of police violence against African Americans.

Policing practices are guided both by written, organizational norms and by unwritten norms contained within a basic normative social institution that exists among police officers. When individuals assume the social position of police officer, they simultaneously assume an organizational position, such as patrol officer of the New York City Police Department, and they also join a second organization, a police union, that is distinct from their department, and thus become members of the larger police guild: the normative social institution made up of police officers. When a person joins the New York City Police Department, she is required to follow the norms that are endorsed and enforced by the organization, which are contained in the department's *Patrol Guide*. The *Patrol Guide* states that "race, color, ethnicity, or national origin may not be used as a motivating factor for initiating police enforcement action," and that "EXCESSIVE FORCE WILL NOT BE TOLERATED" (emphasis in the original).[42] Violation of these norms could result in the punishment of a patrol officer by commanding officers in the department. These norms are pertinent to the murder of Eric Garner, a forty-four-year-old African American man, who was choked to death by officer Daniel Pantaleo in 2014. The officer who unjustly killed Garner cannot reasonably claim that the organizational norms of the New York City Police Department influenced his decision to use excessive force on Garner. As the *Patrol Guide* states, the organization explicitly prohibits, and may punish, the use of excessive force that is motivated by race.[43]

However, Pantaleo's union defended his use of physical force against Garner.[44] In general, police unions are organizations in which positions of authority, such as union president, contain norms and practices that direct the individuals who hold these positions to defend, not punish, union members who abuse African Americans.[45] The message to the members of the union is clear: the union will defend police officers who brutalize Black persons.

There is more. For police officers, as members of a basic normative social institution, or guild, there are unwritten norms guiding the practice of policing that go beyond and often conflict with the written norms of an officer's department. Officers learn these structured relations and norms through informal occupational socialization.[46] The long-standing use of physical and deadly force against African Americans suggests that there is an unwritten norm within the guild that permits, enables, and proscribes punishment for police officers who resort to physical force against this group of people. A structured relation ("a police officer" and "an African American suspected of criminal activity") and norms ("officers can justifiably use excessive force against African Americans") may emerge from notions of "black dangerousness" and "black inferiority" that are deeply embedded in the dominant white American culture.[47] Because African Americans are perceived as dangerous, officers may believe they need to employ more physical force on African American suspects than they do with white suspects. Because they are perceived as less inherently valuable than whites, the use of more violent means against African Americans are considered by some as justified. If the social relation is between "a police officer" and "a white person suspected of criminal activity," the person inhabiting the former position is constrained, due to the valuing of white lives and the threat of punishment, from employing violent means against the individual who inhabits the latter position.

Here we find two structures of vice, and their interrelation renders it easier for police officers to brutalize and murder African Americans like George Floyd and Eric Garner. In keeping with the definition of a structure of vice offered above, police unions contain a vicious relation because one position holder (the police officer) is enabled to violate the normative dignity and well-being of another position holder (the African American suspect). When individuals enter the preexisting social position of "police union member," they encounter the norms and practices of an organization that consistently fails to constrain and punish its members for the excessive use of force against African Americans.

A second vicious structure, in the form of a basic normative social institution, justifies and fails to constrain the use of excessive and deadly force against Black persons. The social relations and norms of the police guild, like those regarding standing in a line, are unwritten and real, and they causally influence action. A probable cause of police brutality against African Americans is the social relation that exists between officers and this racial group. It is a relation in which officers are socialized to devalue Black lives and to follow norms that justify the use of physical and often deadly force against Black individuals. This is a vicious structure insofar as it directs officers to ignore the inherent dignity, and to violate the normative dignity, of a race of people.

We are, then, mistaken if we reduce structures to organizations. Even if one concedes, for the sake of argument, that no *organizational norm* authorizes police brutality against African Americans, this does not mean that no such *structural norm* exists. Normative social institutions, even highly diffuse ones, are structural realties that prescribe, enable, and reward certain relations, actions, and practices and proscribe, constrain, and punish others. In this instance, the norms of a normative social institution appear to cross-cut the department-based organizational norms that direct officers to treat persons of all races without discrimination.

I do not argue that all white police officers are "racists" and espouse an antiblack ideology. Nor do I argue that officers are free of moral culpability for unwarranted physical force against African Americans. I do, however, suggest that police officers often belong to two social structures—a union and a guild—that together enable them to use more brutal and deadly force on African American suspects than on white ones. Institutionalized racism exists, and it is a structure of vice.

We also find vicious relations in the garment industry. The web of relations between the positions that comprise the structure (CEO–consumer; CEO–shareholders; factory owners–CEO; factory owners–laborers) produces a situation where laborers are systematically harmed by their working conditions and their remuneration. In this structure, the well-being of the poorest members of the structure, laborers, is neither considered nor promoted. The garment workers do not count as persons in this structure; their inherent dignity is unrecognized and their normative dignity is violated. Although the structures of the garment industry enable many persons around the globe to access suitable clothing, such a benefit does not justify the working conditions in which the clothing was produced.

Another structure that has both virtuous and vicious aspects is the contemporary practice of obstetrics and gynecology. Physicians of obstetrics and gynecology compose a normative social institution, in which the members of the norm circle or guild endorse and enforce norms and practices in their treatment of women and girls. These same physicians are members of smaller organizations—such as hospitals, clinics, and private practices—in which there is a hierarchy of positions of authority. The web of relations between girls and women, obstetricians and gynecologists (OB/GYNs), and the unborn often promotes the well-being and dignity of girls, women, and the unborn. It is a structure in which poor women increasingly have benefited from medical care concerning reproductive issues. The Affordable Care Act has enabled more poor women and girls to enter the position of "patient" relative to the OB/GYNs' position of "medical provider." This is a virtuous aspect of this social institution. However, OB/GYNs, because of their social relation with the unborn, are enabled to terminate new human life. Here, the OB/GYN, in her position as "medical provider," is enabled to intentionally kill a weak, vulnerable, and transcendently valuable being. OB/GYNs hold a position in which they are enabled to violate the normative dignity and well-being of the unborn. Any structure that enables position holders to ignore human dignity and intentionally terminate innocent life is, in this way, profoundly vicious.

On the Emergence of Virtuous and Vicious Structures

Structural virtues and vices develop asymmetrically. Take, for instance, the emergence of vicious structures. Gregory Baum has argued that not all sinful social structures have been created with evil intent.[48] He claims that even the best of intentions often produce hidden contradictions implicit in the institutional structure.⁴⁹ This is the case because structures are emergent realities. Many aspects of social life combine to develop a structure, and the results are not predictable. There are often vicious effects of structures that were created for ostensibly good or neutral ends. Global warming provides a timely example of this. The structures that compose modern industrial society were not designed to pollute the oceans or warm the globe. These vicious aspects were unintended by-products of the industrial age. However, at a certain point in history, the adverse effects of a structure become clear. It is at this point that those who benefit from a harmful structure often intentionally perpetuate it with full knowledge of its harmful effects on the poor, the vulnerable, and creation. People are now well aware (or should be aware) of the destructive environmental effects of burning fossil fuels. Still, people and institutions continue to choose the less environmentally friendly options.

Also, many consumers are well aware that many of the clothing products that they purchase are unjustly manufactured. Still, people continue to prioritize price over working conditions through practices of "bargain hunting." The point is that vicious structures often emerge and are sustained in situations where those who participate in the structure fail to account for the well-being of the vulnerable. Such structures often exercise a functional preferential option for the rich. The good of the powerful is primarily and, at times, exclusively sought. Thus, though Baum is correct that some structures are not created with evil intent, such a point should not be overplayed. Vicious structures often are perpetuated through a failure to account for the well-being of all who are affected by the structure.

Conversely, virtuous structures rarely emerge haphazardly. Their emergence is more typically the result of coordinated social action. For instance, the normative social institution of racism began to change only through an intentional, concerted effort on the part of African American activists, government officials, individuals and groups, and institutions. These groups explicitly endeavored not only to change how African Americans were valued but also to alter the norms and practices informing African American–white relations. Likewise, the transformation of environmental structures will happen only through intentional action on a global scale. This points to the importance of social movements in the transformation of social structures.

As we learned in chapter 3, the reformation of social structures transpires on multiple levels of social reality. Thus, the most effective way for a group to change structures is through a coordinated effort in which a society's relational categories, concepts, material goods, normative beliefs, social sanctions for noncompliance, modes of communication, and bodily practices are altered. Change in all these areas is, without question, beyond the reach of any single social group or organization.

THE VALUE ADDED IN STRUCTURES OF VIRTUE AND VICE

Chapter 1 quoted Albino Barrera, who claims that, in the ethical evaluation of sociostructural issues, "In the absence of an alternative method, the principle of double effect is by far one of the most useful conceptual tools we have in sorting through moral dilemmas in economic life. We just have to use the principle with appropriate caution and safeguards."[50]

Here, Barrera implies that an "alternative method" of scrutinizing sociostructural problems is needed, and it is just such an alternative method that this chapter has sought to provide. It is a method developed from the main currents of postconciliar theology and ethics: theocentrism, personalism, and virtue. Also, it is a method designed to facilitate the ethical analysis of the moral problems—problems of structures and agency—that Barrera and others have attempted to address.

The concepts of the structures of virtue and vice benefit contemporary theological ethics in three ways. First, these concepts recognize that structures have a discernible moral character and do not merely produce discrete effects. Structures are durable and consistently play a causal role in generating social outcomes. Because of the regularized and consistent effects of social structures, the language of virtue and vice is a more fitting description of structures than "sinfulness." A sin is an isolated action, whereas a vice captures the regularity of structural outcomes and the causal influence that structures have to create those outcomes. Just as virtues and vices causally influence a person's actions, so too do structures of virtue or vice causally contribute to human actions and outcomes. Second, the claim that structures have a moral character is morally neutral. This claim does not assume or imply that structures are all vicious or evil. As shown above, there are structures that are more or less virtuous. The Catholic Church, for one, has viewed institutions and structures as indispensable for building up the common good. However, the tradition lacks a developed notion of what constitutes a good or virtuous structure. Third, this notion of structural character uses a social-scientifically established notion of "structure." As chapter 2 argued, the Catholic Church's definition of a social structure is incoherent and sociologically unsophisticated. This book has argued that just as good medical ethics relies on good medical science, good social ethics relies on good social science.

Further, the notion that structures have a moral character helps to provide a more accurate account of what, exactly, social justice is. In *Economic Justice for All*, the US Conference of Catholic Bishops notes that the term "social justice" has been used in a variety of ways in the Church's social tradition.[51] For instance, the *Catechism of the Catholic Church* emphasizes the distributive aspects of social justice, which holds that "society ensures social justice when it provides the conditions that allow associations or individuals to obtain what is their due, according to their nature and their vocation. Social justice is linked to the common good and the exercise of authority."[52] The US Conference of Catholic Bishops adds and emphasizes the contributive component to the definition when it writes that social justice implies "that persons have an obligation to be active and productive participants in the life of society and that society has a duty to enable them to participate in this way."[53] Both *Populorum progressio* and *Caritas in veritate* envision social justice as rightly ordered relations among nations and persons.[54]

To these definitions, I add that social justice is mainly a product of what I have termed "virtuous structural character." Structural character concerns how structures influence human actions, which then affect the well-being of others. The entire question of social justice concerns how the relations between social positions affect the well-being of people and communities. Social justice emerges in a society of virtuous structures where preexisting social relations enable persons to recognize the inherent dignity and promote the well-being of all with whom they relate. To this end, a socially just society constrains practices that exploit and harm vulnerable persons. More needs to be said regarding this relation, but this will suffice for the moment.

CONCLUSION

In his book *The Vice of Luxury*, David Cloutier writes that what we need is an ethics of virtue that can form us into virtuous actors. Thomas Aquinas reminds us that individuals do not become virtuous on their own. Virtue is best formed in schools for moral education.[55] An ethics of virtue will, to a certain degree, need to be written into the structures—the institutions and organizations—of society. We will need to create and develop social relations which reward virtuous ways of being and discourage vicious ways. The notion that a person can cultivate her character on her own, over and against social structures, reflects an individualist view of the person that is anathema in Catholic ethics. Moral agents need organizational and institutional supports to foster the acquired virtues and to accept, cultivate, and sustain the infused virtues.

As I noted above, virtuous structures typically do not emerge organically but rather must be intentionally created to promote authentic goods. As Saint Benedict well knew, the good community only emerged in a situation in which social relations and positions were *designed* to make straight the paths to union with God and the emergence of the common good. Thus, organizations, institutions, and social groups must recognize that both building a socially just world and shaping the character of their members requires that they do more than inspire their members to "be better." Pious appeals miss the fact that the person, as substance-in-relation, needs society to offer preexisting relations that facilitate the growth of a person's virtue. Thus, like-minded groups will need to coordinate and co-design a response to both the social injustices that harm the vulnerable and the socially enabled vices which malform the young and impressionable. Although some groups may have the capacity to try to revision a society's normative beliefs (e.g., the US Conference of Catholic Bishops), other groups may be able to engage in disruptive bodily practices (e.g., the Black Lives Matter movement).

Second, individual persons need to be more aware of the social positions that they hold and how those positions shape their moral character. We need to ask, Do I belong to institutions and organizations that are, in Saint Benedict's words, schools for the Lord's service? Do I engage in practices, such as the sacraments and works of mercy, that dispose me to receive the divine assistance that I need to live a life of charity? Further, we need to be critical of the institutions and organizations to which we already belong. Who am I becoming in and through the social positions that I have assumed? What would a person of high moral character do if she held this position?

Third, I have repeatedly argued that structural change is the work of groups and institutions. Unlike methodological individualism, this portrait of social reality reveals that individual action is insufficient to change social structures. Individual action may be prophetic and thus may play a role in the cultural changes required to alter a structure. However, a critical realist approach to social structures shows that positive social change develops only through communal and social action. No prophet changes a structure alone. This fact renders membership in groups that work toward building a world of love, justice, and mercy a moral imperative for Christians of the twenty-first century. To quote Benedict XVI, this is the "institutional path of charity."[56]

Finally, my approach shows that the barriers between so-called personal ethics and social ethics are misplaced. People are formed by the social structures in which they participate, and which influence their well-being and that of others. The social structures that enable or constrain personal virtue or vice are the same ones that harm or benefit the material well-being of people and creation.

NOTES

1. Elder-Vass, *Causal Power*, 195.
2. Calhoun, "Positive Good," 600. Calhoun stated, "I hold [slavery] to be a good, as it has thus far proved itself to be to both, and will continue to prove so if not disturbed by the fell spirit of abolition. I appeal to facts. Never before has the black race of Central Africa, from the dawn of history to the present day, attained a condition so civilized and so improved, not only physically, but morally and intellectually."
3. Cox, "Insurance Companies."
4. Ross, *Slaves to Fashion*.
5. See Aquinas, *Summa theologiae*, I-II, 7.1–7.4, 18.3 ad 2, 18.4. In 7.2 Aquinas writes that "circumstances come under the consideration of the theologian, for a threefold reason. First, because the theologian considers human acts, inasmuch as man is thereby directed to Happiness. Now, everything that is directed to an end should be proportionate to that end. But acts are made proportionate to an end by means of a certain commensurateness, which results from the due circumstances. Hence the theologian has to consider the circumstances. Secondly, because the theologian considers human acts according as they are found to be good or evil, better or worse: and this diversity depends on circumstances, as we shall see further on. Thirdly, because the theologian considers human acts under the aspect of merit and demerit, which is proper to human acts; and for this it is requisite that they be voluntary. Now a human act is deemed to be voluntary or involuntary, according to knowledge or ignorance of circumstances, as stated above (question 6, article 8). Therefore the theologian has to consider circumstances." See also John Paul II's *Veritatis splendor*, 52, where he writes, "Furthermore, what must be done in any given situation depends on the circumstances, not all of which can be foreseen; on the other hand there are kinds of behaviour which can never, in any situation, be a proper response—a response which is in conformity with the dignity of the person."
6. John Paul II, *Veritatis splendor*, 52.
7. Aquinas, *Summa theologiae*, I-II, 7.
8. Aquinas, I-II, 7.3.
9. Aquinas, I-II, 7.1.
10. Beauchamp and Childress, *Principles*, 206–9.
11. Saslow, "Against His Better Judgment."
12. Elder-Vass, *Causal Power*, 124.
13. It is instructive to note that Bennett implemented the law even though he is, according to the Constitution, an Article III judge. Such judges are appointed for life and can be removed only by impeachment in the House of Representatives. He faced a low probability of hard sanctions if he chose to ignore the law. Nevertheless, he carried out the norms associated with his position.
14. Elder-Vass, *Causal Power*, 124.
15. Gutiérrez, *Theology*, 100–101.
16. Jean Porter makes this argument in "Virtue and Sin."

17. Gutowski et al., "Environmental Life Style Analysis."
18. As this example shows, being a good teammate is not a skill; it is a moral virtue because it is principally about relationality. Playing baseball is a skill. A child's ability to hit a baseball says nothing of her moral character. However, to say that someone is a good teammate does say something of the kind of person that she is.
19. Smith, *What Is a Person?* 326.
20. Morrill, "Sacramental Liturgy," 16.
21. Morrill.
22. Blumgart, "Sweatshops."
23. Scholars categorize racism in a number of different ways. In *White Fragility*, Robin DiAngelo defines it as a social structure. In *Racial Justice and the Catholic Church*, Brian Massingale argues that racism is a cultural reality. In a colloquial sense, people often use the concept to describe a vicious character trait of a person.
24. Casagrande, "What Nick Saban Said."
25. Zenor, "No. 1 Alabama's Defense."
26. Gitlin, *One Hundred Greatest American Athletes*, 212.
27. Elder-Vass, *Causal Power*, 160.
28. Archer, *Structure*, chap. 4.
29. See Aquinas, *Summa theologiae*, I-II, 7–17.
30. Aquinas, II-II, 49.1.
31. Aquinas, I-II, 14.3.
32. See, esp., Aquinas, II-II, 47.6.
33. Aquinas, II-II, 47.1 ad 2.
34. MacIntyre, "Social Structures."
35. Elder-Vass, *Causal Power*, 125.
36. This is a repurposing of Elder-Vass's claim that human action may be affected by social causes without being determined by them. See Elder-Vass, 87.
37. Morrill, "Sacramental Liturgy," 16.
38. E.g., like many states, New York State has a "mandatory arrest" law that requires police officers to "make an arrest when they have reasonable cause to believe that a person has committed specific crimes against members of their family or household." See New York State Office for the Prevention of Domestic Violence, "What Is 'Mandatory Arrest?'"
39. Since 2015, the *Washington Post* has collected data on all fatal shootings by on-duty police officers in the United States. See Blanco et al., "What We've Learned."
40. Oppel and Gamio, "Minneapolis Police Use Force."
41. Alpert et al., "Bird's Eye View," 310–11.
42. On racial targeting, see New York City Police Department, *Patrol Guide*, procedure 200-02. On the use of excessive force see, New York City Police Department, procedure 203-11.
43. Daniel Pantaleo, the officer whose chokehold caused Eric Garner's death, was fired by the New York City Police Department in August 2019. He was not charged with a crime for his actions.
44. Police Benevolent Association of the City of New York, "PBA President."
45. See Friedersdorf, "How Police Unions and Arbitrators Keep Abusive Cops on the Street"; and Davis and Hartmann, "Police Unions Must Police."
46. Smith, "Structural and Organizational Predictors," 550–51. Smith's data analysis shows that a "racial threat," defined as the proportion of African American residents in a city,

is "positively correlated with total police killings and killings of black citizens." Smith surmises that organizational norms may have little effect on the use of force by police: "Training and screening may have little impact on the culture of policing, which is passed on through the process of occupational socialization.... Furthermore, field training may encourage the informal socialization process by enhancing contact with experienced officers who are not only responsible for training, but who socialize with new police officers informally." Smith notes that this field training may encourage the use of deadly force. I surmise that it may also encourage the use of deadly force against African Americans. As Smith and others note, more research is needed in this area.

47. In fact, such cultural beliefs influence *all* guilds in the United States, including academia. See Bennett and Plaut, "Looking Criminal." See also a study that suggests that Americans continue to associate Black persons and apes: Goff et al., "Not Yet Human."
48. Baum, "Structures," 114.
49. Baum.
50. Barrera, *Market Complicity*, 18.
51. US Conference of Catholic Bishops, *Economic Justice*, n. 27.
52. *Catechism*, 1928. John XXIII, *Mater et magistra*, 40: "The second point which We consider basic in the encyclical is his teaching that man's aim must be to achieve in social justice a national and international juridical order, with its network of public and private institutions, in which all economic activity can be conducted not merely for private gain but also in the interests of the common good." In paragraph 71 of *Economic Justice for All*, the US Conference of Catholic Bishops writes that "justice also has implications for the way the larger social, economic, and political institutions of society are organized. This form of justice can also be called 'contributive,' for it stresses the duty of all who are able to help create the goods, services, and other nonmaterial or spiritual values necessary for the welfare of the whole community."
53. US Conference of Catholic Bishops, *Economic Justice*, 71.
54. Paul VI, *Populorum progressio*, 44, 61; Benedict XVI, *Caritas*, 35.
55. Jordan makes this argument in *Teaching Bodies*, 161. He argues that Aquinas concludes the *Secunda pars* of the *Summa theologiae* with a treatment of the "states of life" because it is only through adopting "a way of life that is a school for charity" that a person will "learn how to enact the coherent human life described in the *Secunda pars*."
56. Benedict XVI, *Caritas*, 7.

CHAPTER 7

The Output Power of the Structures of Virtue and Vice

Conceptual developments in theological ethics aim, in part, to enable more accurate normative outputs regarding how to live the Gospel in the current age. This chapter endeavors to do just that—to show how an understanding of structural virtue and vice provides the best account of how persons should respond to contemporary structural evils.

The book opened by arguing that ethicists are currently staring into something of a normative abyss. The incapacity of Christian ethics to address the moral problems of the age cries out for a Grotian moment, for a time when ethicists question the tools of ethical analysis, jettison those inadequate to the task, and fashion new ones from the tradition. Chapter 6 offered the structures of virtue and vice as a tool with which to understand and analyze the moral problems generated by contemporary social structures.

I have insisted that ethical responses to social problems should reflect an accurate understanding of their structural causes. It is only with such an understanding that persons and communities will be enabled to cure social pathologies. An analogy with medical ethics is instructive. From the third to the twentieth centuries, many in the medical community believed illness was caused by imbalances in the "humors" of the body.[1] Bloodletting was reputed to restore balance to the humors and thus was prescribed by physicians for well over one thousand years. It was not until the mid–nineteenth century that Pierre Charles Alexandre Louis's statistical studies disproved the efficacy of bloodletting.[2] Until then, ignorance of disease's cause produced an inappropriate, unproven, and ultimately counterproductive "therapy."

Catholic social ethics remains in an "age of bloodletting." It is an age when the causes of, and effective treatment for, social pathologies are at times prescientific. This book has proposed a scientific understanding of what constitutes a social structure. Such an understanding is necessary to identify effective remedies for vicious structures. Only then will Catholic social ethics become an exercise in social analysis and not a sermon.[3]

The previous chapter demonstrated the explanatory capacity of the structures of virtue and vice. There, I showed that these concepts provide an insightful explanation of moral reality. Social structures play a causal role both in the development of personal character and in shaping human outcomes. This chapter puts the concepts to work and demonstrates the output power of structural virtue and vice. As I noted in chapter 1, a concept's output power is its ability to produce sound moral claims regarding what constitutes a virtuous action and a virtuous structure.

There are two generic kinds of outputs that a structural ethical analysis produces, both of which this chapter demonstrates. First, a structural ethical analysis enables a person to morally categorize social structures in a way that manualist principles cannot. By using the structures of virtue and vice, a person can identify which relations among social positions undermine and threaten the well-being of persons. This puts much more content on the claim that structures are "sinful." Structures are sinful—or better yet, vicious—because the persons who inhabit certain social positions (e.g., the CEO of clothing brand) are enabled to play a causal role in harming persons who inhabit other positions (e.g., a garment worker).

Second, a structural ethical analysis aids in the prudential discernment of how to virtuously respond to a vicious structure. Such analysis produces sharp new normative claims about how a person should act in relation to vicious structures. With knowledge of structural vice in hand, a virtuous person is then capacitated to respond virtuously. However, like Pope Francis, I do not profess to provide a "recipe" for the solution to social problems, only suggestions regarding the shape of virtuously living the Gospel today.[4]

After a brief account of how the virtues guide action, the chapter scrutinizes the John Doe and Rana Plaza cases, using a "structural ethical analysis." A structural ethical analysis should be employed when social structures have an impact on important moral decisions, as in these two cases. A structural ethical analysis uses the lens of the structures of virtue and vice to generate normative claims. This approach is opposed to employing a "manualist ethical analysis," which typically uses the principles of double effect and cooperation. The chapter then teases out essential implications from these structural ethical analyses for Christian theological ethics.

THE VIRTUES AND ACTION GUIDANCE

Before proceeding to the case analyses, we should recall how the virtues guide action. As argued in chapter 5, in virtue ethics the "direction of analysis" is from the virtues to good and right actions. When confronted with an ethical question, one would ask, "What would a loving, or merciful, or patient person do in this situation?" or "What kind of a person would I become if I did X?" Here, the virtues guide moral discernment; they do not "tell people what to do."[5] Morally discerning with the virtues (as opposed to with principles or rules) opens up creative and imaginative ways of doing the good in relation to God, self, neighbor, and creation. Also, the virtues guide a person to act with moral excellence: with an abundance of charity, mercy, and solidarity.

The virtues are especially helpful when confronting situations where principles are inept and rules nonexistent. Chapter 1 argued that manualist principles could not account for the moral complexity of a highly structured world. A way forward for Christians and all people of goodwill is found through turning to the virtues.

This chapter is an exercise in virtue action guidance. I use the language of action guidance as opposed to applied virtue ethics because the latter implies a deductive use of the virtues in case ethics. The language of action guidance avoids this problem. A virtue perspective guides and illumines what a person should do; it does not deductively generate answers to moral questions.

As suggested in chapter 5, the virtues produce far richer moral outputs than principles. The principles of double effect and cooperation determine whether an action is morally licit or illicit—permitted or prohibited. A virtue approach determines if an action is just or unjust, loving or hateful, merciful or callous. Although the former is content-thin, the latter is content-thick. Further, a virtue approach also enables one to discuss moral gradations. There is a meaningful distinction between actions that are virtuous in an exemplary manner, those that are ordinarily virtuous, and those that are minimally virtuous. The binaries of licit/illicit do not admit of such moral gradations and offer a considerably narrower account of the moral act than a virtue approach provides.

ANALYSIS OF THE CARBON-CONSUMING ASSISTANT PROFESSOR

The last chapter presented the case of John Doe, an assistant professor of ecological ethics. Professor Doe lives a low-carbon lifestyle, except for the airplane flights he takes for professional purposes. These flights render him a high carbon user. Again, his position (assistant professor) and its practices (delivering papers and lectures throughout the country) enables his large carbon footprint.

Doe, like all assistant professors, is constrained from having a low carbon footprint. By his position and the travel needed to maintain it, it appears that Doe is enmeshed in a structure of vice—a structure that, as I argued in chapter 6, enables and facilitates the acquisition of vicious traits and that consistently harms the well-being of the vulnerable. Through his position, Doe faces restrictions and opportunities that lead him to harm creation consistently. Let us investigate the relations, positions, and practices that compose an important aspect of this structure.

American higher education is composed of a web of relations that enables assistant professors to consume exorbitant amounts of carbon while constraining their ability to produce a low carbon footprint. Specifically, Doe's relations with the dean, his chairperson, and the tenure committee each play a causal role in Doe's carbon consumption. It is his membership in this social structure and his relations with these position holders that influence his decision to "act differently than [he] would do otherwise."[6] Deans, chairpersons, and members of tenure committees enable and reward assistant professors who deliver papers throughout the nation and around the globe. The position of assistant professor contains norms, practices, and exemplars that other position holders (deans, chairs, and tenure committee members) endorse and enforce.

Those who inhabit these university positions (of dean, chairperson, and tenure committee member) are themselves expected to follow the norms, practices, and exemplars of their own positions. A dean, for example, is constrained from granting tenure to those who fail to present conference papers. Imagine that Doe's academic dean, Dean Jane, supported his tenure candidacy even though Doe refused to travel to present papers. It is likely that the university president would punish Dean Jane for her failure to execute her position well. Why? Well, the position of dean contains an established norm that candidates should (almost always) be denied tenure if they fail to present conference papers. It is the relation of assistant professor (inhabited by Doe) to the position of dean (inhabited by Jane) that incentivizes or discourages the actions of both parties. We find, then, that all members of a social structure experience the enablements and constraints of their social positions. Further, this example explains the precise social mechanisms—the relations, the positions, and the practices and norms—that render this an ecologically problematic structure.

However, the structure of vice in which Doe participates and benefits from exists at a level above higher education. Universities and colleges did not construct the carbon-based energy economy. Thus, if professors are to travel for academic reasons, they must enter the social position of "airline passenger." At the time of the writing of this book, there is no low-carbon way to travel long distances quickly. Thus, there is no alternative social position that Doe can assume if he is to pursue the goods of academic exchange and securing tenure. Notice that Doe's agency is free but constrained. More accurately, then, air travel contains a structurally vicious component in which academia participates, which it exacerbates, and from which it benefits. Although it is true that American higher education is *itself* constrained by the structures that enable travel over long distances, this fact does not acquit it. In this particular way, American higher education contains a structure of vice. It is a structure that enables and facilitates environmentally damaging actions by those who assume positions in its structure. In this way, academia renders it more difficult for persons to be good and easier for them to be bad. This structure consistently harms the well-being of a vulnerable creation through the practices, norms, and exemplars it prescribes and admires. In short, American higher education contains a vicious structure.[7]

The next question is, What should Doe do? He could lower his carbon footprint significantly if he refused to attend conferences that required air travel. In doing so, he would save over twenty tons of carbon for each year in which he refused to fly. Additionally, he could petition his academic societies in writing to change the format of the conference in order to reduce the carbon output of the attendees and the conference overall.

However, there are significant risks to such an approach. First, he can make the argument for going green more effectively in person than in writing alone. Conference attendance enables Professor Doe to fully engage in dialogue and debate regarding the merits of meeting every other year, or in regional meetings, as opposed to national ones. One can reasonably expect that he will have a more significant influence over the direction of an academic society's ecological culture by attending.

Next, his refusal to attend the meetings of academic societies will likely produce unintended types of harm. His failure to present academic papers at learned societies will harm his research as well as the research of others. Ideas must be exchanged and critically engaged by academics for the sake of the creation of new knowledge. Also, his lack of conference presentations will be reflected in his tenure file and will harm his chances of garnering an affirmative tenure vote. The choice to forgo the conference circuit may then lead to the loss of his academic position. Because holding an academic position remains an essential tool for receiving a public hearing of one's ideas, the loss of his position will likely curtail his cultural influence regarding ecological ethics. He will suffer a diminished capacity to shape the conceptual and normative beliefs of students and the society-at-large through his teaching, writings, public lectures, media appearances, and consultation services. Nonprofessional goods also would be threatened through his refusal to fly. He may lose income, a healthy sense of self-respect, and a sense of purpose that marked his vocation as an environmental ethicist. A moral dilemma confronts Doe. Either he flies and retains all these goods or he dramatically lowers his carbon footprint and threatens them.

As I argued in chapter 5, moral problems should be analyzed according to a theocentric, personalist virtue ethics. Recall that the virtues are those traits enabling a person to recognize and promote the value and well-being of the other and move toward a loving union with God, self, others, and creation. The chapter also emphasized that prudence is required in order for one to promote the good of the other and to move toward union with the other. There, I emphasized that "although the goodness of an action is not caused by the goodness of its effect, yet an action is said to be good from the fact that it can produce a good effect."[8] The virtuous person must discern what will actually promote the good of others if her action is to be virtuous. Such prudential discernment relies on an understanding of all the relevant circumstances of the situation. Recall that chapter 6 argued that social structures should be accounted for as a special kind of circumstance and, thus, should be accounted for in any prudential discernment.

An important circumstance, in this case, is the overdetermination of global warming. Doe's decision to fly or not fly will not alter the warming of the globe because the result will be determined by the structures of energy generation and usage. A counterfactual account proves this. Even if Doe saved 20 tons of carbon each year due to his refusal to fly, the globe would still warm between 1.6° to 4.3° C by 2100.[9] Doe's actions will not cause the actual figure to change.

The only way for Doe to play a causal role in decreasing the amount of carbon in the atmosphere is to work to transform the structures that encourage the use of carbon fuels and constrain clean energy options. Doe's commitment to combating global warming must be met, then, with an attempt at changing these structures. How, then, are social structures transformed? This is a technical, sociological question requiring a technical, sociological answer. The broad outlines of such an answer were suggested in chapter 3 in discussing the work of Christian Smith. Smith argues that seven areas of social life are implicated in structural change.[10] Four of these areas are pertinent to Doe and his desire to change the structures of energy production and usage.

First, Smith notes that conceptual developments play a causal role in the transformation of social structures. As an academic, Doe is uniquely positioned to contribute to the idea that global warming is caused primarily by human activity and that it can be slowed through the transformation to a renewable energy economy. Second, cultural changes in normative beliefs often contribute to structural changes. As an ecological ethicist, Doe can argue that current carbon usage is unethical and can show the virtues of moving to a renewable energy economy. As noted above, Doe can contribute to a cultural, conceptual, and normative consensus through teaching, writing, media appearances, and the influence that he exerts on students and on political and industrial leaders. Academics such as Doe exert outsize influence in these cultural spheres and have the capacity to create the "new [ecological] culture" that Francis called for in *Laudato si'*.[11]

Third, Doe could contribute to legislative changes that would punish those who fail to comply with the reduction of carbon usage and encourage the adoption of clean alternatives. Academics and intellectuals often play important roles in advocating for the passage of legislation that subsidizes and requires renewable energy usage by states and industries. Fourth, Smith's account maintains that disruptive bodily practices contribute to the emergence of altered structures. Again, Doe's position enables him to play an influential role in organizing and participating in marches, rallies, and other public demonstrations on behalf of the environment. For example, the environmentalist and eco-justice exemplar Bill McKibben has been a national leader on issues pertaining to global warming through his disruptive bodily practices.

Each of these four practices requires carbon usage. These are nonideal solutions to the problem. However, ideal, non-carbon-emitting solutions do not exist. McKibben, for one, has argued that some of the means employed to fight the climate crisis (e.g., using fossil fuels to drive or fly to events) are morally justified. Speaking as a leader in the environmental movement, he argued, "We're not going to be forced into a monkish retreat from society—we need to engage this fight with all the tools of the moment."[12] As a result, McKibben has admitted to spending much of the 2000s "in frenetic travel, much of it on airplanes."[13] He has justified such travel because of the nature of the crisis. In an article titled "The Question I Get Asked the Most," McKibben argues against individualist solutions to global warming. In answering the question "What can I do?" McKibben argues that "one's Prius is a gesture. A lovely gesture and one that everyone should emulate, but a gesture. Ditto riding the bike or whatever one's particular point of pride. North Americans are very used to thinking of themselves as individuals, but as individuals, we are powerless to alter the trajectory of climate change in a meaningful manner."[14]

McKibben has understood that global warming is a structural problem that requires structural, not merely individual, solutions. Unlike "personal ethics" and social ethics, the discipline of medical ethics has a long history of prescribing tragic but prudential actions. Limbs will need to be amputated to save patients because it is only through attacking the cause of the disease that the patient can be cured. In dealing with structural vice, Christians and people of goodwill should expect to habituate nonideal, but prudentially effective, actions, such as expending massive amounts of carbon for the sake of dismantling the carbon economy.

In the final analysis, Doe should remain a high carbon user for the sake of reducing the global carbon output. The healing that the planet needs may be accomplished, in part, through his engagement in structural transformation. Ironically, it is not in the planet's best interest for Doe to stop flying. Instead, his love of creation, which is nothing more than actively willing the planet's well-being, needs his influence and engagement with organizations and corporations to change structures. Like those who walked away from Omelas, a "retreat from society" will change nothing. Also, Doe should continue to live in his micro-apartment, bike to work, and forgo eating beef. These are more than "lovely gestures," as McKibben puts it. Such actions are characteristic of a person who attempts to love creation as God loves creation. Biking to work, for instance, is indicative of Doe's affirmation of the goodness of creation and of his desire to form a fraternal relation with the nonhuman world. The life of virtue concerns the whole of a person's life—not just one's contributions to the creation of virtuous structures. The eco-just person strives to recognize and promote the well-being of creation in as many ways as possible. Such a person "stays in character" whether she is renting an apartment, considering her commuting options, or organizing a rally in support of the Paris Climate Accords.

Notice that by using the structures of virtue and vice, one arrives at different moral outputs than manualist principles would suggest. The genuinely virtuous action, for Doe, is discovered only with a structural ethical analysis. Such an analysis turns away from a focus on individual moral purity and toward living in a way that effectively promotes the good.

ANALYSIS OF THE CONSUMER AND SWEATSHOP LABOR

Chapter 1 opened with the case of the collapse of the Rana Plaza sweatshops, in which 1,127 garment workers perished. The chapter asked how Christian ethicists ought to analyze not only the actions of Sohel Rana but also the consumers who purchased garments produced under unjust and exploitative working conditions. Again, we begin by asking if the garment industry contains vicious structures—that is, structures that constrain virtuous activity and play a causal role in human suffering.

Unsurprisingly, the garment industry contains a structure of vice. At the risk of simplifying a complex structure, let us investigate the web of relations among the positions of garment worker, factory owner, apparel corporation CEO, and board members. In this explanation, Sohel Rana represents a typical owner of a garment factory, while Jane T. Elfers, the CEO of the Children's Place at the time of the building's collapse, represents a typical CEO.

Corporate boards hire and reward CEOs such as Elfers primarily based on total shareholder return (TSR).[15] TSR consists of the entire financial return—stock value plus dividends—from a corporation to its shareholders. The board–CEO relation determines the practices and the norms of the position of CEO. The position of CEO contains practices and norms designed to produce "sustainable sales, profit, and total shareholder return."[16] Although boards account for "soft" factors—such as the public interest, the environment, and worker well-being—such boards overwhelmingly prioritize TSR in the assessment of a CEO. Consider the example of the Commonwealth Bank, which recommended that CEO compensation be indexed to the following metrics: "TSR, 50%; customer satisfaction, 25%; and people and community, 25%." However, indexing 50 percent to nonfinancial data "proved to be a step too far for some shareholders, precipitating their revolt in November 2016."[17] Today, TSR remains the standard metric by which corporate executives are assessed.

It is important to note that both elected board members and CEOs encounter enablements and constraints in their positions. Shareholders can remove board members, and board members can fire CEOs. This web of relations incentivizes CEOs like Elfers to consistently focus on manufacturing garments at the lowest cost that will produce the highest profit margin. Elfers could undoubtedly choose to prioritize the well-being of garment workers over TSR, but such a decision would likely threaten her position as CEO. Thus, CEOs like Elfers will incentivize the managerial class of the corporation to source garments from factory owners like Sohel Rana. As a point of fact, Rana's capacity to produce inexpensive garments in his ramshackle factory was enabled and rewarded through his relation with the Children's Place and its CEO, Jane Elfers.

Thus, the relation of Elfers with Sohel Rana played a causal role in Rana's decision to order workers to return to the building that was to become their killer. Although Rana freely willed his decision to order the workers into the building, he was enabled and incentivized to make this decision given his relation with Elfers. The corporation, through the freely willed direction of Elfers, rewarded Rana for a consistent stream of inexpensive clothing, without regard or account for the conditions under which the clothing was produced. There was, then, a harmful web of relations that extended from Elfers to Rana to the garment workers who died in the collapse.

In addition to unsafe working conditions, the garment workers suffered from substandard wages. In 2013, the year of the collapse at Rana Plaza, the minimum wage for garment workers in Bangladesh was $0.18 per hour. The minimum monthly wage for these workers was less than $40. In 2013 studies showed that a single individual required $133 per month for a decent standard of living in Bangladesh.[18] Such a standard supported the material needs of the individual regarding food, housing, clothing, medical care, remittances to family members, and a small amount for recreation. Minimum wage garment workers earned about $100 per month less than what constituted a decent wage. These workers were significantly constrained in their ability to promote all three generic human goods set forth by Aquinas: life and health, the well-being and education of family members, and relationships with the neighbor and the divine.

The multiple types of harm suffered by these garment workers were in part structurally caused. They were the result of the moral quality of the web of relations among the positions that compose the structure. Although individual moral agents, such as Sohel Rana, actualized the structure through his actions, this example shows that a previously established social structure facilitated and rewarded his decisions. We can conclude that the garment industry harbors a structure of vice because it contains a web of relations among social positions that are causal factors in the regularized types of harm that vulnerable garment workers suffer. Although some garment workers die premature and preventable deaths, the lucky ones often earn wages that fail to support the foundational human good of health.

In this vicious structure, some individuals have causal power and moral culpability. The CEO (Elfers), executives, the agents who source the garments, factory owners (e.g., Rana), and factory managers all have a causal moral responsibility for the unjust wages and working conditions that afflict garment workers. They have all freely committed actions that harm these workers. Others, such as the corporate accountants and attorneys, cooperate in the evil actions of the other parties. Importantly, consumers fit into neither category. Consumers neither cause nor aid in these labor abuses. Instead, they exist in a web of social relations whereby they benefit from a vicious social structure.

As I argued in chapter 3, causality is not primarily a relation among events.[19] That is, the deaths of the workers at Rana Plaza were not merely the result of a chain of discrete decisions made by Elfers, corporate sourcing agents, and Rana. Critical realism teaches that causal power resides in both human actions *and* the relations among certain social positions. There is a social reality—a social structure—that exists at a level above Elfers and Rana and that influences their deliberations and actions. More specifically, the preexisting, socially established relation between an apparel brand CEO and factory owner was a causal factor in the deaths and diminished the lives of the garment workers. The actual decisions made by Elfers and Rana were influenced, in large part, by the preexisting social structure in which they participated. For instance, the policies that Elfers implemented and enforced were incentivized by her relation to board members, just as those same policies causally influenced Rana's decisions. As I have argued, structures exert their causal power by constraining and enabling the freely willed decisions of agents who act from within their social positions.

But what of the consumer? What is the moral status of buying sweat-made clothing? First, the consumer finds that she is enabled and financially rewarded by purchasing inexpensive sweat-made clothing and is structurally constrained from purchasing fair trade clothing. Few companies produce fair trade clothes, and they skew toward high-end brands such as Patagonia and prAna. Consumers of goodwill quickly find their will is constrained by a structural circumstance: the dearth and expense of fair trade clothing.

Given that a structure of vice confronts consumers, what is the consumer of goodwill to do? First, consumers will find little guidance in the traditional category of moral culpability. Recall that moral culpability pertains to situations where an agent has causal responsibility for the harm and has freely willed the action. Although the purchase of sweat-made clothing is freely willed, it did not cause harm to accrue to the garment workers. Again, a counterfactual account proves this. If a given consumer does not buy a sweat-made garment from the Children's Place, do the workers still die in the collapse? Sadly, they still do. Further, does the sweatshop industry still exist if this consumer never purchases sweat-made clothing? Again, yes. The moral issue for the consumer is not one of moral culpability for the harm suffered by the garment workers. Questions of responsibility and culpability are often misplaced regarding structures of vice.[20] Instead, consumers must raise a question of character. What kind of person regularly benefits from a web of relations that systematically causes poor garment workers to live diminished lives and suffer a premature death?

I argue that only an "indifferent" person (to use Pope Francis's language) consistently would benefit from the suffering of others. Chapter 4 showed that Francis has repeatedly cited "indifference" to suffering as a contemporary vice. The vice of indifference involves closing one's "heart to the needs of others."[21] It is, in many ways, the vice of sloth in a contemporary idiom. Sloth is a vice opposed to charity insofar as the slothful person sees the good of loving God and neighbor as "toilsome, or troublesome, or as a hindrance to the body's pleasure."[22] This is precisely the acquired disposition of those who consistently purchase garments without regard to the conditions under which the garments were manufactured. In benefiting from the suffering of garment workers, the consumer fails to consider the well-being of the poor and instead focuses on adorning her own body. To return to the definition of virtue offered in chapter 5, such a person fails to recognize the inherent dignity of the other. Instead, the garment worker becomes a machine through which the consumer lives a life of pleasure and material comfort. In addition, there can be no desire for union with a devalued, distant neighbor. An exploitative relation lacks the affective union that Melina defines as "that first, intentional union experienced as an original promise of fulfillment that precedes and provokes every movement tending toward achieving a true union with the beloved."[23] Here, there is no first intentional union, only indifference.

Further, such a person lacks solidarity with the poor. Solidarity is the virtue whereby a person enters into the suffering of a group of people, shares in their plight, and works with the suffering for their liberation. John Paul argued that "togetherness" and "interdependence" are the foundations of solidarity. Those who regularly benefit from the exploitation of garment workers certainly neither share in the plight of the workers, nor do they actively promote their good. Instead of sharing in the plight of the garment worker, the consumer benefits from it. By benefiting from their labor, the consumer lives as if the plight of the suffering is separate from her own life. There is no "togetherness" here. Only an indifferent person regularly benefits from exploited labor. Again, I refer to consumers for whom purchasing alternatives to sweat-made garments is a financial possibility—those who lack such capacity do not act viciously when they purchase sweat-made garments.

As with the Doe case, a fully virtuous moral response requires the consumer to be actively engaged in transforming the structures that are causal factors in the existence of sweatshops. An individualist account of how garment workers are harmed may lead the consumer to believe that her primary or only response to sweatshop labor is to refrain from purchasing sweat-made clothing. However, an individual boycott will not affect the structurally caused vicious outcome. Garment workers will still be exploited. A structural ethical analysis of this situation invites the consumer to address the factors that contribute to the structure itself. Those who acknowledge that structural mechanisms cause the suffering of garment workers find that the scope of what it means to act virtuously is enlarged. The virtuous consumer understands that she should address one or more of the areas of social life that are causal factors in the emergence of exploited labor.

Again, recall that according to Smith, structures emerge from the interplay among conceptual developments, normative developments, social punishments or the lack thereof, and disruptive bodily practices, to name but four of the seven. Consumers can play a role in each of these, depending on their social situation. The first two—conceptual and normative developments—are aspects of culture, as they pertain to socially endorsed beliefs. As I argued in chapter 4, culture both shapes and is shaped by social structures. Consumers who influence the shaping of the cultural discourse—such as artists, writers, teachers, and professors—should use their influence to educate others about the harm suffered by garment workers, along with the arguments against sweat labor. Others can join groups whose mission is to shape the conceptual and normative debate on the issue of sweatshops. For instance, college students can join United Students Against Sweatshops or found a local chapter.[24]

The next two areas of social life, social punishments and disruptive bodily practices, also concern organized collective actions. Although these areas of social life do shape socially endorsed beliefs, they do so obliquely by making it more difficult for corporate leaders to unjustly harm others. Organized boycotts, unlike individual ones, are often effective social punishments designed to harm the profitability of companies that allow or perpetrate employee abuse. And though boycotts may begin to shape a cultural consensus regarding corporations and their labor practices, the boycott's immediate goal is to punish the corporation and its leaders. Such punishments often spur corporate leaders to institute changes in corporate practice. For example, César Chávez organized boycotts that culminated in improved labor conditions for grape workers in 1970. Academic institutions around the globe boycotted South African institutions from the 1960s to the 1990s, which contributed to the dismantling of the apartheid system in South Africa in the 1990s.

Disruptive bodily practices also have causally contributed to the transformation of social structures. The civil rights movement employed disruptive bodily practices in its struggle for the rights of African Americans. The movement began with just such a practice, Rosa Parks's refusal to move to the back of a bus in Montgomery in 1955. Later, four college students from North Carolina started the lunch counter sit-in movement, which eventually swept through the South in the early 1960s.

More recently, Miguel de la Torre has suggested an ethics *para joder*—an ethics that "screws with" the current power structures.[25] This ethics "constantly disrupts the established norm, shouts from the mountaintop what is supposed to be silent, and audaciously refuses to stay in his or her assigned place."[26] Although my approach is more sanguine regarding structural change than de la Torre's, I agree with his argument for social disruption. His ethics *para joder* maps somewhat with Christian Smith's notion of disruptive bodily practices. De la Torre offers examples of activists chaining themselves to the wheels of vehicles transporting undocumented people to their trials and clergy members verbally disrupting deportation court proceedings.[27] Such practices not only "screw with" social structures; they also have the capacity to transform them.

Again, we find that a structural ethical analysis produces different moral outputs than manualist principles would suggest. Manualist principles often produce binary outputs. From this perspective, buying sweat-made clothing is either licit or illicit cooperation with evil. By using the structures of virtue and vice to guide the analysis, one produces richer, more complex normative claims about what is forbidden and what is good, better, and best. Here we are beyond culpability, and moving toward character.

GENERAL INSIGHTS EMERGING FROM STRUCTURAL ETHICAL ANALYSES

From the above analyses, we can glean additional insights regarding the output power of structural virtue and vice. This two-sentence statement provides a summary: "The structures of virtue and vice do not replace, but rather complement, traditional accounts of the virtuous life by enabling a more insightful moral response to this moral world. These concepts reveal the need for persons to engage with and not retreat from a structurally vicious society through the practice of the virtue of solidarity." Let us now turn to, and unpack, the various parts of this statement.

"Structures of Virtue and Vice Complement Traditional Accounts of Virtue..."

First, the structures of virtue and vice do not subtract from, compete with, or replace traditional understandings of virtue. It suggests a both/and solution to structural vice, not an either/or approach. As I noted above, Professor Doe should still live in his micro-apartment, ride his bike to work, and forgo meat. However, he should not mistake these virtuous practices as solutions to the climate crisis. These practices embody his commitment to the environment, enabling him to build a fraternal relationship with the created world. These are genuinely loving actions, even if they fall short of effecting structural change. They demonstrate active benevolence for the good of creation, and they also have the capacity to, in Pope Francis's words, "call forth a goodness which, albeit unseen, inevitably tends to spread."[28] However, if his love is to be effective and, in Aquinas's words, capable of "producing a good effect," these practices will need to be joined by other practices that can change the social mechanisms that despoil the Earth. In short, Doe should live a morally integrated life in which all his actions promote the ecological good. Doe should strive to always "stay in character" by respecting the value of the created world in all that he does. Notice that the answer is not to focus exclusively on structural transformation. Virtue ethics views the moral life as a whole, in which all of a person's actions contribute to, or subtract from, her relations with God, self, neighbor, and creation.

The virtuous life is more rigorous, not less, when one understands how social structures cause the suffering of others. As shown in the discussion above, a life of solidarity with garment workers is more complicated than an individual boycott of sweat-made clothing or "buycotting."[29] With such knowledge, the virtuous person should contribute to the areas of social life that in turn contribute to structural transformations. This requires the consumer to engage with the issue in ways that go beyond their purchasing habits.

". . . by Responding to This Moral World . . ."

Any account of the virtuous life should be a response to *this moral world* and not some abstract moral universe. Only then can Christian ethicists answer the call of Christine Gudorf, who urges the guild to draw on the social sciences in order to effectively combat the sin that emanates from social structures.[30] How does one live a life of charity, mercy, and solidarity, given that affronts to human dignity are embedded in global institutions and organizations? How does one live a life of eco-justice when the carbon floor in the United States is four times the global average? As the Doe case suggests, withdrawal from the carbon economy is imprudent in *this moral world*, given what we know about the structural causes of the ecological crisis. Our moral response must reflect this understanding.

"... through the Practice of Solidarity"

Throughout the book, I have argued that Christians should love all those persons with whom they share a relation, not merely those with whom they share a relationship. Such love requires that the agent see the distant other as a transcendently valuable person who is loved by God. Further, the virtuous person will promote the good of the distant other when possible. Finally, though a true and real friendship with distant others is not possible as long as they remain distant, the virtuous agent cultivates the conditions for and remains open to friendship. This is the affective union that, according to Aquinas, necessarily precedes the real union of persons who love each other.[31]

I have argued that an active and effective love of workers who sew our garments transpires through engagement in the areas of social life that can transform the structures that harm the well-being of garment workers into structures that promote their well-being. In a highly structured world, the virtuous life involves social engagement for the sake of the common good and is not a life of retreat to preserve an imagined and unreal notion of private moral purity.

This chapter has emphasized that the call to transform oppressive social structures is a call to membership. Isolated individual action is inadequate for structural change. Walking away from structural vice is like walking away from Omelas—the evil remains unchanged. The virtuous citizen of Omelas would organize others in a bid to free the child from his unjust prison sentence. Although each individual—in Omelas and in reality—is helpless to change the situation alone, structural change can happen through the work of social organizations.

One of the habits of the virtuous individual is, then, to walk *toward* institutions and organizations that are capable of reshaping the areas of social life from which structures emerge. This is the work of the virtue of solidarity, which both John Paul and Francis have identified as the remedy to structural moral problems. John Paul argues that the "'structures of sin' are only conquered ... by a diametrically opposed attitude," solidarity.[32] Similarly, Francis argues that practices of solidarity "open the way to other structural transformations."[33] Solidarity, then, can be defined as virtuous membership in organizations that promote the common good.

Solidarity is a paradigmatic virtue for our age because it is a virtue that can be practiced only with others, for the sake of the common good. As I noted above, John Paul II's *Sollicitudo rei socialis* emphasizes this point. There, he describes solidarity as a virtue that required "interdependence" and "togetherness" in order to be practiced. He calls collaboration "the act proper to solidarity among individuals and nations."[34] Writing on this encyclical, Donal Dorr emphasizes that solidarity is about "sharing a life with a group of persons."[35] In a relation of solidarity, there is cooperation between the agents. Importantly, here persons suffering from social marginalization are not passive recipients but are active agents of their liberation with the accompaniment of others. This shared life, cooperation, and accompaniment need not be interpersonal. The virtue of solidarity can be practiced at a distance.

In this way, solidarity promotes both dimensions of the common good identified by David Hollenbach—the common good "fulfills needs that individuals cannot fulfill on their own and simultaneously realizes noninstrumental values that can only be attained in our life together."[36] First, the virtue of solidarity has as a goal a society where all have easy and ready access to its goods. This is the instrumental and material dimension of the common good. Here, the practice of solidarity promotes human goods—such as adequate food, housing, and education—that provide for basic human well-being. However, as David Cloutier argues, "The common good is primarily about relationships and is only secondarily 'materialistic.'"[37] To be in solidarity is to have a common moral cause with others, which people can only realize together. Solidarity facilitates friendship among the persons who are "in solidarity." The practice of solidarity is not merely an instrumental virtue capable of producing good effects but also contains an intrinsic component: the good of being in relation with others.

Solidarity is a virtue whose time has come. Given that structures are significant causal factors in the suffering of so many people, virtuous agents will need to cultivate and practice solidarity. Just as mercy is the proximate expression of charity for those individuals who suffer, solidarity is the proximate expression of charity for communities that suffer. Solidarity reveals itself as a more refined account of Benedict XVI's "institutional path of charity."[38]

There is, however, an obstacle to this solution. As Robert Bellah and colleagues in *Habits of the Heart* and Robert Putnam in *Bowling Alone* have exposed, contemporary American culture is membership-averse.[39] The past half century has seen an individualist culture develop in the United States and much of the Global North. Rates of membership in social organizations reflect this cultural belief. Although Putnam showed a precipitous drop in membership from the 1960s to 1994, recent research suggests that the trend has continued.[40] "Active membership" has also declined, replaced by a less intense "checkbook" membership. The latter form consists of monetary donations but does not engage in face-to-face interactions. In short, the quantity and quality of membership remain in decline. The same is true of social trust, which is "unequivocally declining."[41] Thus, the very modalities capable of contributing to structural transformation are in retreat.

Catholic Institutions as "Islands of Solidarity"

One of the arguments of this book is that if people of goodwill are to practice the virtues and contribute to the global common good, they will need structural support. That is, they will need organizations that facilitate collective action for the sake of, for instance, combating climate change or transforming the working conditions within garment factories. As Putnam's "bowling alone" problem worsens in the twenty-first century, it appears that fewer people will contribute to structural change. These facts present the Catholic Church with an opportunity to advance its mission in a meaningful manner. The Church's mission, along with its already-established organizational structure, require and enable it to play a vital role in structural change. Thus, just as Pope Francis urged Catholic institutions to become "islands of mercy" during the Jubilee Year of Mercy, these same entities should now become "islands of solidarity." Paul VI makes a similar appeal in *Octogesima adveniens*, where he explicitly calls on all Catholic organizations to become more engaged in the transformation of social structures: "It is in this regard too that Christian organizations, under their different forms, have a responsibility for collective action. Without putting themselves in the place of the institutions of civil society, they have to express, in their own way and rising above their particular nature, the concrete demands of the Christian faith for a just, and consequently necessary, transformation of society."[42]

Kevin Ahern has highlighted the capacity of Christian social movements and organizations to fulfill the call of Paul VI. Ahern argues that the Young Christian Workers movement, the Jesuit Volunteer Corps, and the Plowshares movement are "structures of grace." In these and other organizations, one finds the "gratuitous presence of God that manifests itself in movements of people fighting against sin and oppression."[43] These organizations are precisely the kinds of formative communities that the laity need to cultivate virtue and promote the global common good.

All Catholic organizations, such as hospitals and universities, have a responsibility to contribute to structural change. These already-existing organizational structures are optimally positioned to support the creation of and maintenance of suborganizations dedicated to transforming structural vices. Consider the Church's recent emphasis on combating global warming, forcefully articulated in Francis's encyclical *Laudato si'*. The encyclical received global attention when Francis promulgated it in the spring of 2015.

It inspired Catholics and non-Catholics alike in its acknowledgment of the human causes of global warming as well as the variety of solutions proffered by Francis. Francis not only invited individuals to habituate eco-friendly practices but also urged those committed to ecological justice to institutionalize their activity: "Social problems must be addressed by community networks and not simply by the sum of individual good deeds."[44]

To this end, on May 17, 2020, Pope Francis and the Dicastery for Promoting Integral Human Development announced "The *Laudato si'* Action Platform," which aims to transform Church structures that harm our common home.[45] This document outlines a seven-year plan to implement *Laudato si'* in Catholic families, schools, dioceses, universities, hospitals, businesses, and religious orders. Each year, the dicastery will invite these Catholic groups and organizations to publicly commit to implement structural changes that are aimed at promoting "total sustainability." Annual awards will be given to the family, school, diocese, and the like that exemplify the care for creation. Here, Pope Francis and the leadership of the dicastery are exercising their social positions, which empower them to enable or constrain the actions of other position-holders in their institution, the Catholic Church. "The *Laudato si'* Action Platform" endeavors to create a "*Laudato si'*–inspired network" among Catholic institutions that will ultimately transform the Church's structures and culture. Here, Francis's moral invitation to address the ecological problem through "community networks" is met with structural solutions within Catholic organizations. By endorsing and enforcing norms, prescribing practices, and spotlighting exemplars, the Church is attempting to create "structures of solidarity" vis-à-vis a groaning creation.[46]

"The *Laudato si'* Action Platform" provides a structural moral solution to a structural moral problem. It is a solution that enables Catholic organizations and their members to promote the well-being of all God's creatures. In this way, the Church is in effect emulating Saint Benedict's monastery by making it easier to be good and more difficult to be bad. Moreover, just as Benedict created the monk–abbot relation to help the former grow in virtue, "The *Laudato si'* Action Platform" will create a web of relations between social positions that will enable the Church and its members to cultivate virtue and contribute to the global common good.

VIRTUE-IN-REALITY

This study has offered a portrait of virtue-in-reality. Virtue-in-reality is opposed to an Aristotelian-inspired idealized portrait of virtue. In the

Aristotelian framework, the virtues are acquired by persons who enjoy a high degree of moral freedom. Aristotle famously developed his account of the virtues for the Athenian gentleman but not for women or men of lower classes. For Aristotle, the Athenian gentleman confronted few significant external constraints on his acquisition of the virtues. Conversely, I have attempted to show how the interplay of structure and agency can pose both enablements and constraints on the acquisition of the virtues as well as the exercise and cultivation of infused virtues.

In her important book *Burdened Virtues*, Lisa Tessman has argued that Aristotle's account of the virtues "usually takes for granted that the background conditions for virtue are being met: luck has been sufficiently good, material needs have been fulfilled, enough leisure time has been available, no great adversity is presenting itself."[47] Contra Aristotle, Tessman develops an approach for those suffering from significant social oppression: African Americans, women, and persons suffering from poverty in the Global South. Although my account applies to these groups of people, it also applies to persons who enjoy some social advantage: university professors in the United States, the CEOs of multinational corporations, and middle-class consumers in the Global North. As the Professor Doe case shows, even the privileged and powerful are constrained. However, because the powerful have an increased capacity to resist vicious structures, they also have a proportional obligation. Along these lines, Luke 12:48 can be translated using critical realist categories: for whom much is enabled, much is expected.

One advantage of a virtue approach to sociostructural issues is that the virtues offer moral agents an account of moral gradations. As suggested above, there is a meaningful distinction between minimal, ordinary, exemplary acts of virtue.[48] For example, imagine a person is discerning her options for her five-mile commute to work. The minimally ecologically just person would purchase a car with a relatively high miles-per-gallon quotient. Although less convenient and comfortable, commuting via public transportation would be more ecologically friendly and thus a more eco-just choice. Finally, carbon-free commuting, by bike or on foot, would be an act of exemplary ecological virtue.

There will be times when the virtuous person must act in a particular manner, as when she encounters a person dying of dehydration or starvation. The merciful person will never fail to give drink and food to such a person. However, the exemplary mercy of Saint Teresa of Calcutta is not possible for all Christians, given the competing goods and social constraints that most Christians face. Saint Teresa devoted her life to works of mercy, which is not a requirement for living a merciful life. Thus, custodians, for example, can live a life of mercy without devoting their entire lives to such practices. There are many ways in which a person can practice mercy, given the constraints of her time, resources, and other relationships.

Although the person of high moral character will strive for exemplary action, this will not always (or often) be possible. There are two reasons for this. First, one cannot, for example, simultaneously organize against sweatshops, exploited farmworkers, and the carbon energy industry. There are natural constraints of time and energy and the social constraints presented by structures and relationships. Julie Hanlon Rubio puts it this way: "Because I am only one finite human being, I cannot be responsible for everything all at once."[49] Rubio realizes that certain relations compete for an agent's moral attention. Professor Doe's desire to have a low carbon footprint competes with the good of his profession. A married couple with young children and a tight budget experiences the competing goods of, on one hand, respecting worker dignity by buying fair trade clothing for their growing children and, on the other hand, financial responsibility for the sake of their family. In such situations, we would do well to remember that Aquinas maintained that "no one is moved to the impossible."[50]

Second, this study has argued that people often encounter severe social punishments for acting in exemplary ways. Consider the case of Berta Cáceres, who was an advocate for the indigenous population of Honduras as well as an environmental activist. She won the Goldman Environmental Prize in 2015 for leading a movement that successfully blocked the construction of a dam that would have devastated the landscape and the lives of the indigenous population around the Río Blanco. Unsurprisingly, because of her advocacy work, Cáceres, her mother, and her children all received threats of death and of sexual violence.[51] She was assassinated in 2016 in what some have called an extrajudicial killing organized by Honduran military intelligence officers and carried out by soldiers who trained at the Western Hemisphere Institute for Security Cooperation.[52]

Although Cáceres is certainly worthy of emulation, what if she capitulated to the threats? What kind of a person would she have become if she had receded from public life? Would such a person still possess the virtue of ecological justice? I contend that such a person would remain a person of ecological justice. As Kenneth Himes has argued, heroic action to combat social evil is not an obligation: "A person ought not be required to sacrifice friendship, family, or life to oppose the accepted custom of a group."[53] Heroism and a willingness to sacrifice oneself for the good of others are to be lauded but must not be normative for a life of virtue.[54] Although a person's virtue may be weakened through such a change in behavior, this change would be justified by an appeal to her love of self and family. In a broken world, at times moral goods will conflict with each other.

Virtue-in-reality involves maintaining and navigating the moral tensions that arise when there is competition among various relations. It is precisely this tension that Aquinas recognizes in his account of charity in the *Summa theologiae*. In question 31, article 3, of the *Secunda secundae*, he wrestles with the multiple relations that draw an agent's moral attention. He imagines a scenario where an agent is forced to choose between serving the ordinary needs of one's father and the dire needs of a stranger. He responds,

> Now one man's connection with another may be measured in reference to the various matters in which men are engaged together (thus the intercourse of kinsmen is in natural matters, that of fellow-citizens is in civic matters, that of the faithful is in spiritual matters, and so forth): and various benefits should be conferred in various ways according to these various connections, because we ought in preference to bestow on each one such benefits as pertain to the matter in which, speaking simply, he is most closely connected with us.[55]

In short, the order of love should guide the moral priorities of the virtuous person.[56] It is right and proper to begin by doing good to those most closely connected to us and subsequently to those with whom we have a more distant relation. Such general guidance fails, however, when a relationally distant neighbor is in desperate need: "And yet this may vary according to the various requirements of time, place, or matter in hand: because in certain cases one ought, for instance, to succor a stranger, in extreme necessity, rather than one's own father, if he is not in such urgent need."[57]

In such cases, the loving person should attend first to the extreme needs of the distant neighbor before the nonemergent needs of those closely connected to her. Aquinas's thinking on this issue continues later in the same article, where he notes this:

> For it must be understood that, other things being equal, one ought to succor those rather who are most closely connected with us. And if of two, one be more closely connected, and the other in greater want, it is not possible to decide, by any general rule, which of them we ought to help rather than the other, since there are various degrees of want

as well as of connection: and the matter requires the judgment of a prudent man.

Aquinas acknowledges that tension exists between one's ability to practice the virtue of charity toward close and distant relations. Importantly, he does not provide a codified solution to resolve this tension. This reminds us of his oft-cited claim that "as we descend further into detail, ... the greater number of ways in which the principle may fail."[58] Instead, he argues that the tension should be maintained in principle, and only finally resolved through the exercise of prudential reasoning, which is possible with its close attention to circumstances.

This single article from the *Summa theologiae* has much to teach us regarding how to live virtuously in a complex and highly structured world. Indeed, in making any given moral decision, we must decide between serving our children or, as Aquinas put it, "a stranger in extreme necessity." The virtuous person will maintain moral tension by striving to love as many of her relations as well as she possibly can, given the constraints of time, energy, and social structures.

Because we participate in and benefit from so many vicious structures, no one person will be capable of actively and effectively loving all those persons with whom she shares a distant relation. Again, a single person cannot meaningfully contribute to transforming the many vicious structures of the early twenty-first century. We would do well, then, to recall the words of Saint Paul VI in *Octogesima adveniens*. There, he argues that Christians were responsible for contributing to structural transformations: "Thus, amid the diversity of situations, functions, and organizations each one must determine, in his conscience, the actions which he is called to share in."[59] Each Christian is called, in her own manner, to contribute to the transformation of at least one of the aspects of our shared social life that ignores the dignity and harms the well-being of the poor and vulnerable.

CONCLUSION

The preceding pages propose a less inspirational but more realistic and analytical ethics. Inspiration will follow and will need to be grounded in an understanding of the interplay of social reality and human agency. This book moves away from the pious and the sermonic and toward a true understanding of how the social world shapes moral character and human outcomes, for good and for ill. Only then can we fulfill the task of Christian ethics—to provide an account of how to live the Gospel of Jesus Christ today. Only then can we live out the *content* of the Gospel message, which is nothing short of affectively and effectively loving God and God's beloved.

NOTES

1. Magner, *History of Medicine*, 93, 202–8.
2. Magner, 206.
3. This is a paraphrase of Goulet's critique of John Paul II's *Sollicitudo rei socialis*. See Goulet, "Search," 130.
4. Francis, "Address to the Participants of the Second World Meeting." There, he said, "We desire change enriched by the collaboration of governments, popular movements and other social forces. This too we know. But it is not so easy to define the content of change—in other words, a social program which can embody this project of fraternity and justice which we are seeking. It is not easy to define it. So don't expect a recipe from this Pope. Neither the Pope nor the Church have a monopoly on the interpretation of social reality or the proposal of solutions to contemporary issues. I dare say that no recipe exists. History is made by each generation as it follows in the footsteps of those preceding it, as it seeks its own path and respects the values which God has placed in the human heart."
5. Louden, "On Some Vices," 229.
6. Elder-Vass makes this point in *Reality*, 124.
7. As argued in chapter 6, this is not to claim that the entire structure is vicious. It is only to claim that it contains a vicious aspect. Much like persons have character strengths and weaknesses, so too do social structures.
8. Aquinas, *Summa theologiae*, I-II, 18.2 ad 3.
9. Fischer et al., "Paleoclimate Constraints."
10. Smith, *What Is a Person?* 369–76.
11. Francis, *Laudato si'*, 53, 114.
12. McKibben, "Question."
13. McKibben.
14. McKibben.
15. Swinford, "Limits of Using TSR."
16. Lafley, "What Only the CEO Can Do."
17. Kenney, "Should a CEO's Bonus Be Based on Financial Performance Alone?"
18. Bangladeshi Institute of Labor Studies, "In Quest of Minimum Wage Amount."
19. Porpora, "Who Is Responsible?" 13.
20. Finn's book, *Consumer Ethics in a Global Economy*, takes a different position on this issue. Finn has argued that consumers causally exacerbate the unjust effects that garment workers suffer. See especially chapter 7.
21. Francis, "World Day of Peace Message," 2016.
22. Aquinas, *Summa theologiae*, II-II, 35.2. See also Jones and Kelly, "Sloth"; there, they present an updated account of the vice of sloth.

23. Melina, *Epiphany*, 12.
24. See its website, https://usas.org/.
25. De la Torre, *Embracing Hopelessness*, 150.
26. De la Torre.
27. De la Torre, 153.
28. Francis, *Laudato si'*, 212.
29. "Buycotting" is the practice of buying from companies that align with one's moral values.
30. Gudorf, "Admonishing Sinners," 14–22.
31. Aquinas, *Summa theologiae*, I-II, 26.2. See Melina, *Epiphany*, chap. 1.
32. John Paul II, *Sollicitudo rei socialis*, 38.
33. Francis, *Evangelii gaudium*, 189.
34. John Paul II, *Sollicitudo rei socialis*, 39.
35. Dorr, "Solidarity," 152.
36. Hollenbach, *Common Good*, 83.
37. Cloutier, "What Can Social Science Teach," 176.
38. Benedict XVI, *Caritas*, 7.
39. Bellah et al., *Habits*.
40. Painter and Paxton, "Checkbooks."
41. Painter and Paxton, 409.
42. Paul VI, *Octogesima adveniens*, 51.
43. Ahern, *Structures*, 142.
44. Francis, *Laudato si'*, 219.
45. Dicastery for Promoting Integral Human Development, *"Laudato si'."*
46. *The Compendium of Social Doctrine* noted that the structures of sin "must be purified and transformed into *structures of solidarity*" (emphasis in the original). Pontifical Council for Justice and Peace, *Compendium*, 193.
47. Tessman, *Burdened Virtues*, 159.
48. Swanton, "Definition," 317.
49. Rubio, *Hope*, 47.
50. Aquinas, *Summa theologiae*, I-II, 13.5.
51. Lakhani, "Honduras Dam Project."
52. Lakhani, "Berta Cáceres Court Papers." In 2002 the Army School of the Americas (SOA) was renamed WHINSEC. Both the SOA and WHINSEC have been criticized for training military personnel around the globe in tactics that undercut the democratic process, stifle the agency of the poor and marginalized, and murder innocent people. A graduate of the SOA killed Saint Óscar Romero of San Salvador.
53. Himes, "Social Sin," 205.
54. Bernard Brady has argued that "there is a noticeable lack of heroism in [Augustine's and Aquinas's] discussions of love." See his Brady, "Love," 171.
55. Aquinas, *Summa theologiae*, II-II, 31.3.
56. Pope, *Evolution*.
57. Aquinas, *Summa theologiae*, II-II, 31.3.
58. Aquinas, I-II, 94.4.
59. Paul VI, *Octogesima adveniens*, 49.

BIBLIOGRAPHY

Adams, Robert. *A Theory of Virtue: Excellence in Being for the Good*. New York: Oxford University Press, 2006.
Ahern, Kevin. *Structures of Grace: Catholic Organizations Serving the Global Common Good*. Maryknoll, NY: Orbis Books, 2015.
Alpert, Geoffrey P., Edward H. Byers, Bradley A. Campbell, and Justin Nix. "A Bird's Eye View of Civilians Killed by Police in 2015: Further Evidence of Implicit Bias." *American Society of Criminology* 16, no. 1 (2017): 309–40.
Annas, Julia. "Applying Virtue to Ethics." *Journal of Applied Philosophy* 32, no. 1 (2015): 1–14.
———. *Intelligent Virtue*. New York: Oxford University Press, 2011.
———. "Learning Virtue Rules: The Issue of Thick Concepts." In *Developing the Virtues: Integrating Perspectives*, edited by Julia Annas, Darcia Narvaez, and Nancy E. Snow, 224–34. New York: Oxford University Press, 2016.
Anscombe, Elizabeth. "Modern Moral Philosophy." *Philosophy* 33, no. 124 (1958): 1–19.
Anthony, Augustine. "Human Dignity from the Beginning of Life: German and Indian Moral Theological Perspectives in an Attempt at Dialogue with Hinduism." PhD diss., Regensburg University, 2014. https://epub.uni-regensburg.de/30660/1/Dissertation-ANTHONY.pdf.
Aquinas, Thomas. *Disputed Questions on Virtue*. Translated by Ralph McInerny. South Bend, IN: St. Augustine's Press, 1999.
———. *Summa Theologica*. Allen, TX: Christian Classics, 1981.
Archdiocese of Boston. "Guidelines for Parish Pro-Life Committees." No date. www.bostoncatholic.org/pro-life-office/guidelines-parish-pro-life-committees.
Archer, Margaret. *Culture and Agency: The Place of Culture in Social Theory*. New York: Cambridge University Press, 1996.
———. "Structural Conditioning and Personal Reflexivity." In *Distant Markets, Distant Harms: Economic Complicity and Christian Ethics*, edited by Daniel Finn, 25–53. New York: Oxford University Press, 2014.
———. *Structure, Agency, and the Internal Conversation*. New York: Cambridge University Press, 2003.
Archer, Margaret, and Dave Elder-Vass. "Cultural System or Norm Circles? An Exchange." *European Journal* 15, no. 1 (2012): 93–115.
Aristotle. *Nicomachean Ethics*. In *Basic Works of Aristotle*, edited by Richard McKeon, 935–1126. New York: Random House, 2001.
Ashley, Benedict M., Jean DeBlois, and Kevin O'Rourke. *Health Care Ethics: A Catholic Theological Analysis*. 5th ed. Washington, DC: Georgetown University Press, 2006.
Augustine. *Confessions*. Translated by Henry Chadwick. New York: Oxford University Press, 1991.

Austin, Nicholas. *Aquinas on Virtue: A Causal Reading*. Washington, DC: Georgetown University Press, 2017.
———. "Normative Virtue Theory in Theological Ethics." *Religions* 8 (2017).
Austriaco, Nicanor Pier Giorgio. *Biomedicine and Beatitude: An Introduction to Catholic Bioethics*. Washington, DC: Catholic University of America Press, 2011.
Bangladeshi Institute of Labor Studies. "In Quest of Minimum Wage Amount of the RMG Workers in Bangladesh." *Labour* 16 (2013): 45–47.
Barrera, Albino. *Market Complicity and Christian Ethics*. New York: Cambridge University Press, 2011.
Baum, Gregory. "Structures of Sin." In *The Logic of Solidarity: Commentaries on Pope John Paul II's Encyclical On Social Concern*, edited by Gregory Baum and Robert Ellsberg, 110–26. Maryknoll, NY: Orbis Books, 1989.
Beauchamp, Tom L., and James F. Childress. *The Principles of Biomedical Ethics*. 7th ed. New York: Oxford University Press, 2013.
Bellah, Robert, Richard Madsen, William M. Sullivan, Ann Swidler, and Steven M. Tipton. *Habits of the Heart: Individualism and Commitment in American Life*. Berkeley: University of California Press, 1985.
Benedict XVI. "Benediction to Participants of Italian Catholic Action." Vatican website, October 11, 2012. http://w2.vatican.va/content/benedict-xvi/en/speeches/2012/october/documents/hf_ben-xvi_spe_20121011_fiaccolata.html.
———. *Caritas in veritate*. Vatican website, June 29, 2009. www.vatican.va/content/benedict-xvi/en/encyclicals/documents/hf_ben-xvi_enc_20090629_caritas-in-veritate.html.
———. *Dignitas personae*. Vatican website, December 8, 2009. www.vatican.va/roman_curia/congregations/cfaith/documents/rc_con_cfaith_doc_20081208_dignitas-personae_en.html.
———. *Spe salvi*. Vatican website, November 30, 2007. http://w2.vatican.va/content/benedict-xvi/en/encyclicals/documents/hf_ben-xvi_enc_20071130_spe-salvi.html.
———. "United Nations Address of His Holiness Benedict XVI." Vatican website, April 18, 2008. http://w2.vatican.va/content/benedict-xvi/en/speeches/2008/april/documents/hf_ben-xvi_spe_20080418_un-visit.html.
———. "World Day of Peace Message, 2013." Vatican website, December 8, 2012. http://w2.vatican.va/content/benedict-xvi/en/messages/peace/documents/hf_ben-xvi_mes_20121208_xlvi-world-day-peace.html.
Bennett, Mark W., and Victoria C. Plaut. "Looking Criminal and the Presumption of Dangerousness: Afrocentric Facial Features, Skin Tone, and Criminal Justice." *UC Davis Law Review* 31, no. 3 (2018): 745–803.
Bentham, Jeremy. *An Introduction to the Principles of Morals and Legislation*. 1789. www.earlymoderntexts.com/assets/pdfs/bentham1780.pdf.
Berger, Peter. *The Sacred Canopy: Elements of a Sociological Theory of Religion*. Garden City, NY: Doubleday, 1967.
Berger, Peter, and Thomas Luckmann. *The Social Construction of Reality: A Treatise in the Sociology of Knowledge*. New York: Doubleday, 1967.
Beyer, Gerald. "Advocating Worker Justice: A Catholic Ethicist's Toolkit." *Journal of Religious Ethics* 45, no. 2 (2017): 226–50.
———. *Recovering Solidarity: Lessons from Poland's Unfinished Revolution*. Notre Dame, IN: Notre Dame University Press, 2010.

Bhaskar, Roy. *The Possibility of Naturalism: A Philosophical Critique of the Contemporary Human Sciences*. Atlantic Highlands, NJ: Humanities Press, 1979.

Black, Donald. "Dreams of Pure Sociology." *Sociological Theory* 18, no. 3 (2000): 343–67.

Blanco, Adrian, Joe Fox, Wesley Lowery, Jennifer Jenkins, and Julie Tate. "What We've Learned about Police Shootings 5 Years after Ferguson." *Washington Post*, August 9, 2019. www.washingtonpost.com/nation/2019/08/09/what-weve-learned-about-police-shootings-years-after-ferguson/?arc404=true.

Blumgart, Jake. "Sweatshops Still Make Your Clothes." *Salon*, March 21, 2013. www.salon.com/2013/03/21/sweatshops_still_make_your_clothes/.

Boff, Clodovis, and Leonardo Boff. *Introducing Liberation Theology*. Maryknoll, NY: Orbis Books, 2000.

Bourdieu, Pierre. *Distinction: A Social Critique of the Judgment of Taste*. Translated by Richard Nice. Cambridge, MA: Harvard University Press, 1984.

Brackley, Dean, and Thomas Schubeck. "Moral Theology in Latin America." *Theological Studies* 63, no. 1 (2002): 123–60.

Brady, Bernard. "Love and Recent Developments in Moral Theology." *Journal of Moral Theology* 1, no. 2 (2012): 147–76.

Bunge, Mario. "Clarifying Some Misunderstandings about Social Systems and Their Mechanics." *Philosophy of the Social Sciences* 34, no. 3 (2004): 371–81.

Bushlack, Thomas J. "Shadows of Divine Virtue: St. John of the Cross, Implicit Memory, and the Transformation Theory of Infused Cardinal Virtue." *Theological Studies* 81, no. 1 (2020): 88–110.

Cahill, Lisa Sowle. "Reframing Catholic Ethics: Is the Person an Integral and Adequate Starting Point?" *Religions* 8 (2017).

Calhoun, John C. "The Positive Good of Slavery." In *Slavery in the United States: A Social, Political, and Historical Encyclopedia*. Vol. 1. Edited by Junius P. Rodriguez. Denver: ABC-CLIO, 2007.

Campbell, Andy. "Florida Cops Fired over Racist Texts, KKK Video." *Huffington Post*, March 22, 2015. www.huffingtonpost.com/2015/03/22/cops-fired-racist-video_n_6918652.html.

Caño, Antonio, and Pablo Ordaz. "El peligro en tiempos de crisis es buscar un salvador que nos devuelva la identidad y nos defienda con muros." *El País*, January 22, 2017. https://elpais.com/internacional/2017/01/21/actualidad/1485022162_846725.html.

Carroll, Anthony J. "Church and Culture: Protestant and Catholic Modernities." *New Blackfriars* 90, no. 1026 (2009): 163–77.

Casagrande, Michael. "What Nick Saban Said about 'Hateful' Alabama Defense, Jalen Hurts after LSU Win," *AL.com*, November 6, 2016. www.al.com/alabamafootball/index.ssf/2016/11/what_nick_saban_said_about_hat.html.

Catechism of the Catholic Church. Vatican website. www.vatican.va/archive/ENG0015/_INDEX.HTM.

Cates, Diana Fritz. *Choosing to Feel: Virtue, Friendship, and Compassion for Friends*. Notre Dame, IN: University of Notre Dame Press, 1997.

Cavanaugh, William. *Field Hospital: The Church's Engagement with a Wounded World*. Grand Rapids: Wm. B. Eerdmans, 2016.

———. "The Future of Political Theology." In *Witnessing: Prophecy, Politics, and Wisdom*, edited by Maria Clara Bingemeire and Peter Casarella, 86–98. Maryknoll, NY: Orbis Books, 2014.

———. *Migrations of the Holy: God, State, and the Political Meaning of the Church.* Grand Rapids: Wm. B. Eerdmans, 2011.
———. *The Theopolitical Imagination.* London: T&T Clark, 2002.
Clark, Meghan. *The Vision of Catholic Social Thought. The Virtue of Solidarity and the Praxis of Human Rights.* Minneapolis: Fortress Press, 2014.
Clark, Michael. "Ohio Teacher Loses Job for Racist Remark." *USA Today*, April 18, 2014. www.usatoday.com/story/news/nation/2014/04/18/teacher-racism-fired/7876581/.
Clark, Patrick. "The Case for an Exemplarist Approach to Virtue in the Catholic Tradition." *Journal of Moral Theology* 3, no. 1 (2014): 54–82.
———. "The Particularity of Sanctity: Why Paradigms of Exemplarity Matter for Christian Virtue Ethics," *Journal of the Society of Christian Ethics* 39, no. 1 (2019): 111–27.
Clarke, Norris. "Person, Being, and St. Thomas," *Communio* 19 (1992): 601–18.
Clayton, Philip. "Conceptual Foundations of Emergence Theory." In *The Re-emergence of Emergence: The Emergentist Hypothesis from Science to Religion*, edited by Philip Clayton and Paul Davies, 1–34. New York: Oxford University Press, 2006.
Cloutier, David. "Cavanaugh and Grimes on Structural Evils of Violence and Race: Overcoming Conflicts in Contemporary Social Ethics." *Journal of the Society of Christian Ethics* 37, no. 2 (2017): 59–78.
———. *The Vice of Luxury: Economic Excess in a Consumer Age.* Washington, DC: Georgetown University Press, 2015.
———. "What Can Social Science Teach Catholic Social Thought about the Common Good?" In *Empirical Foundations of the Common Good: What Theology Can Learn from Social Science*, edited by Daniel K. Finn, 170–207. New York: Oxford University Press, 2017.
Cloutier, David, and William C. Mattison III. "The Resurgence of Virtue in Recent Moral Theology." *Journal of Moral Theology* 3, no. 1 (2014): 228–59.
Coburn, John. *Personalism and Scholasticism.* Milwaukee: Marquette University Press, 2005.
Congregation for the Doctrine of the Faith. *Compendium of Social Doctrine of the Church.* Vatican website, May 26, 2006. www.vatican.va/roman_curia/pontifical_councils/justpeace/documents/rc_pc_justpeace_doc_20060526_compendio-dott-soc_en.html.
———. "Instruction on Certain Aspects of the 'Theology of Liberation.'" Vatican website, August 6, 1984. www.vatican.va/roman_curia/congregations/cfaith/documents/rc_con_cfaith_doc_19840806_theology-liberation_en.html.
———. "Instruction on Christian Freedom and Liberation." Vatican website, March 22, 1986. www.vatican.va/roman_curia/congregations/cfaith/documents/rc_con_cfaith_doc_19860322_freedom-liberation_en.html.
Cox, James. "Insurance Companies Issued Policies on Slaves." *USA Today*, February 21, 2002. http://usatoday30.usatoday.com/money/general/2002/02/21/slave-insurance-policies.htm.
Curran, Charles. *The Catholic Moral Tradition Today: A Synthesis.* Washington, DC: Georgetown University Press, 1999.
———. *Catholic Social Teaching and Pope Benedict XVI.* Washington, DC: Georgetown University Press, 2014.
———. *The Development of Moral Theology: Five Strands.* Washington, DC: Georgetown University Press, 2013.
———. *The Moral Theology of Pope John Paul II.* Washington, DC: Georgetown University Press, 2005.

———. "Obituary for Bernard Haring." *National Catholic Reporter*, July 17, 1998. http://natcath.org/NCR_Online/archives2/1998c/071798/071898h.htm.

———. "The Risks of Theology: Enda McDonough and Vatican II." *The Furrow* 57, nos. 7–8 (2006): 410–23.

Dalton, Frederick John. *The Moral Vision of César Chávez*. Maryknoll, NY: Orbis Books, 2003.

Daly, Daniel J. "Confronting the 'Normative Abyss': The Challenges and Resources in Catholic Ethics for the Global Age." In *Decentering Discussions on Religion and State: Emerging Narratives, Challenging Perspectives*, edited by Sargon George Donabed and Autumn Quezada-Grant, 157–76. New York: Lexington Books, 2015.

———. "The Relationship of Virtues and Norms in the *Summa theologiae*." *Heythrop Journal* 51, no. 2 (2010): 214–29.

———. "Structures of Virtue and Vice." *New Blackfriars* 92, no. 1039 (2011): 341–57.

Davis, Edward, and Frank Hartmann. "Police Unions Must Police Their Members." *Boston Globe*, June 4, 2020. www.bostonglobe.com/2020/06/04/opinion/police-unions-must-police-their-members/.

Davis, Henry. *Moral and Pastoral Theology*, vol. 1, 4th edition. London: Sheed and Ward, 1945.

de la Torre, Miguel. *Embracing Hopelessness*. Minneapolis: Fortress Press, 2017.

Derrida, Jacques. *Of Grammatology*. Baltimore: Johns Hopkins University Press, 1976.

DiAngelo, Robin. *White Fragility*. Boston: Beacon Press, 2018.

Di Bussolo, Alessandro. "Pope at Mass: 'Indifference Is Opposed to Love.'" *Vatican News*, January 8, 2019. www.vaticannews.va/en/pope-francis/mass-casa-santa-marta/2019-01/pope-francis-mass-indifference-opposed-to-love.html.

Dicastery for Promoting Integral Human Development. "*Laudato si'*: Special Anniversary Year." May 17, 2020. www.humandevelopment.va/content/dam/sviluppoumano/documenti/LAUDATO%20SI'%20Special%20Anniversary%20Year%20Plans.pdf.

Donati, Pierpaolo. "The Morality of Action: Reflexivity, and the Relational Subject." In *Distant Markets, Distant Harms: Economic Complicity and Christian Ethics*, edited by Daniel K. Finn, 54–79. New York: Oxford University Press, 2014.

Dorr, Donal. *Option for the Poor: A Hundred Years of Catholic Social Teaching*. Maryknoll, NY: Orbis Books, 2012.

———. "Solidarity and Human Development." In *The Logic of Solidarity: Commentaries on Pope John Paul II's Encyclical on Social Concern*, edited by Gregory Baum and Robert Ellsberg, 143–54. Maryknoll, NY: Orbis Books, 1989.

Driver, Julia. *Uneasy Virtue*. New York: Cambridge University Press, 2001.

Dussel, Enrique. "Theology of Liberation and Marxism." In *Mysterium liberationis: Fundamental Concepts of Liberation Theology*, edited by Ignacio Ellacuria and Jon Sobrino, 85–102. Maryknoll, NY: Orbis Books, 1993.

Einstein, Elizabeth L. *The Printing Press as an Agent of Change*. Cambridge: Cambridge University Press, 1979.

Elder-Vass, Dave. *The Causal Power of Social Structures*. New York: Cambridge University Press, 2010.

———. *The Reality of Social Construction*. New York: Cambridge University Press, 2012.

Enger, Mark. "Toward the Rights of the Poor." *Journal of Religious Ethics* 28, no. 3 (2000): 339–65.

Falk, Richard. *Law in an Emerging Global Village*. Ardsley, NY: Transnational Publishers, 1998.

Finn, Daniel K. *Consumer Ethics in a Global Economy*. Washington, DC: Georgetown University Press, 2019.

———. "What Is a Sinful Social Structure?" *Theological Studies* 77, no. 1 (2016): 136–64.

Fischer, Hubertus, Katrin J. Meissner, Alan C. Mix, Nerilie J. Abram, et al. "Paleoclimate Constraints on the Impact of 2 °C Anthropogenic Warming and Beyond." *Nature Geoscience* 11 (2018): 174–85. www.nature.com/articles/s41561-018-0146-0.

Flood, Anthony T. *The Metaphysical Foundations of Love: Aquinas on Participation, Unity, and Union.* Washington, DC: Catholic University of America Press, 2018.

Francis. "Address of the Holy Father on Nuclear Weapons." Vatican website, November 24, 2019. www.vatican.va/content/francesco/en/messages/pont-messages/2019/documents/papa-francesco_20191124_messaggio-arminucleari-nagasaki.html.

———. "Address to Participants in the International Seminar on the Pope's Proposal Made in *Evangelii gaudium*, 'Towards a More Inclusive Economy.'" Vatican website, July 12, 2014. http://w2.vatican.va/content/francesco/en/speeches/2014/july/documents/papa-francesco_20140712_seminario-economia.html.

———. "Address to the Participants of the Second World Meeting of Popular Movements." Vatican website, July 9, 2015. www.vatican.va/content/francesco/en/speeches/2015/july/documents/papa-francesco_20150709_bolivia-movimenti-popolari.html.

———. *Amoris laetitia.* Vatican website, March 19, 2016. https://w2.vatican.va/content/dam/francesco/pdf/apost_exhortations/documents/papa-francesco_esortazione-ap_20160319_amoris-laetitia_en.pdf.

———. *Evangelii gaudium.* Vatican website, November 24, 2013. http://w2.vatican.va/content/francesco/en/apost_exhortations/documents/papa-francesco_esortazione-ap_20131124_evangelii-gaudium.html.

———. *Gaudete et exsultate.* Vatican website, March 19, 2019. www.vatican.va/content/francesco/en/apost_exhortations/documents/papa-francesco_esortazione-ap_20180319_gaudete-et-exsultate.html.

———. "General Audience." Vatican website, October 12, 2016. http://w2.vatican.va/content/francesco/en/audiences/2016/documents/papa-francesco_20161012_udienza-generale.pdf.

———. "Homily." Vatican website, March 12, 2015. http://w2.vatican.va/content/francesco/en/homilies/2015/documents/papa-francesco_20150313_omelia-liturgia-penitenziale.html.

———. "Homily." Vatican website, December 12, 2015. http://w2.vatican.va/content/francesco/en/homilies/2015/documents/papa-francesco_20151212_omelia-guadalupe.html.

———. *Laudato si'.* Vatican website, May 24, 2015. http://w2.vatican.va/content/francesco/en/encyclicals/documents/papa-francesco_20150524_enciclica-laudato-si.html.

———. *Lumen fidei.* Vatican website, July 29, 2013. http://w2.vatican.va/content/francesco/en/encyclicals/documents/papa-francesco_20130629_enciclica-lumen-fidei.html.

———. *Misericordiae vultus.* Vatican website, April 11, 2015. https://w2.vatican.va/content/francesco/en/apost_letters/documents/papa-francesco_bolla_20150411_misericordiae-vultus.html.

———. "*Urbi et orbi.*" Vatican website, December 25, 2019. www.vatican.va/content/francesco/en/messages/urbi/documents/papa-francesco_20191225_urbi-et-orbi-natale.html.

———. "World Day of Peace, 2014." Vatican website, December 8, 2013. http://w2.vatican.va/content/francesco/en/messages/peace/documents/papa-francesco_20131208_messaggio-xlvii-giornata-mondiale-pace-2014.html.

———. "World Day of Peace, 2015. Vatican website, December 8, 2014. http://w2.vatican.va/content/francesco/en/messages/peace/documents/papa-francesco_20141208_messaggio-xlviii-giornata-mondiale-pace-2015.html.

———. "World Day of Peace Message, 2016." Vatican website, December 8, 2015. http://w2.vatican.va/content/francesco/en/messages/peace/documents/papa-francesco_20151208_messaggio-xlix-giornata-mondiale-pace-2016.html.
———. "World Day of Peace Message, 2020." Vatican website, December 8, 2019. http://w2.vatican.va/content/francesco/en/messages/peace/documents/papa-francesco_20191208_messaggio-53giornatamondiale-pace2020.html.
———. "World Day of Prayer for Peace, Assisi." Vatican website, September 20, 2016. http://w2.vatican.va/content/francesco/en/speeches/2016/september/documents/papa-francesco_20160920_assisi-preghiera-pace.html.
———. "World Food Day 2013 Address." Vatican website, October 16, 2013. http://w2.vatican.va/content/francesco/en/messages/food/documents/papa-francesco_20131016_messaggio-giornata-alimentazione.html.
Frankena, William K. *Ethics*. 2nd ed. Englewood Cliffs, NJ: Prentice Hall, 1973.
Friedersdorf, Colin. "How Police Unions and Arbitrators Keep Abusive Cops on the Street." *The Atlantic*, December 2, 2014.
Gallagher, John A. *Time Past, Time Future: An Historical Study of Catholic Moral Theology*. New York: Paulist Press, 1990.
Gallup. "US Acceptance of Gay/Lesbian Relations Is the New Normal." May 14, 2012. www.gallup.com/poll/154634/Acceptance-Gay-Lesbian-Relations-New-Normal.aspx.
Giddens, Anthony. *The Constitution of Society: Outline of the Theory of Structuration*. Berkeley: University of California Press, 1984.
Gilson, Etienne. *The Christian Philosophy of St. Thomas Aquinas*. Notre Dame, IN: University of Notre Dame Press, 1956.
Gitlin, Martin. *One Hundred Greatest American Athletes*. New York: Rowman & Littlefield, 2018.
Goff, Philip A., Jennifer L. Eberhardt, Melissa J. Williams, and Matthew C. Jackson. "Not Yet Human: Implicit Knowledge, Historical Dehumanization, and Contemporary Consequences." *Journal of Personality and Social Psychology* 94, no. 2 (2008): 292–306.
Goulet, Denis. "The Search for Authentic Development." In *The Logic of Solidarity: Commentary on Pope John Paul II's Encyclical "On Social Concern,"* edited by Gregory Baum and Robert Ellsberg, 127–42. Maryknoll, NY: Orbis Books, 1990.
Gowri, Aditi. "When Responsibility Can't Do It." *Journal of Business Ethics* 54, no. 1 (2004): 33–50.
Grimes, Katie Walker. "Breaking the Body of Christ." *Political Theology* 18, no. 1 (2017): 1–22.
———. "But Do the Lord Care? Tupac Shakur as Theologian of the Crucified People." *Political Theology* 14, no. 4 (2015): 326–52.
———. "Butler Interprets Aquinas." *Journal of Religious Ethics* 42, no. 2 (2014): 187–215.
———. *Christ Divided: Antiblackness as Corporate Vice*. Minneapolis: Fortress Press, 2017.
———. "Racialized Humility: The White Supremacist Sainthood of Peter Claver." *Horizons* 42, no. 2 (2015): 295–316.
Gudorf, Christine E. "Admonishing Sinners: Owning Structural Sin." In *Rethinking the Spiritual Works of Mercy*, edited by Francis A Eigo, 1–29. Philadelphia: Villanova University Press, 1994.
Gutiérrez, Gustavo. "The Option for the Poor Arises from Faith in Christ." *Theological Studies* 70, no. 2 (2009): 317–26.
———. *A Theology of Liberation: History, Politics, and Salvation*. Translated and edited by Sister Caridad Inda and John Eagleson. Maryknoll, NY: Orbis Books, 2004.

Gutowski, Timothy, Amanda Taplett, Anna Allen, Amy Banzaert, et al. "Environmental Life Style Analysis (ELSA)." Presentation at IEEE International Symposium on Electronics and the Environment, San Francisco, May 19–20, 2008. http://web.mit.edu/ebm/www /Publications/ELSA%20IEEE%202008.pdf.
Haring, Bernhard. *Law of Christ*. Translated by Edwin Kaiser. Paramus, NJ: Newman Press. 1966.
Harris, Sam. *Free Will*. New York: Free Press, 2012.
Hauerwas, Stanley. *A Community of Character: Toward a Constructive Christian Social Ethic*. Notre Dame, IN: University of Notre Dame Press, 1981.
Herdt, Jennifer. *Putting on Virtue: The Legacy of the Splendid Vices*. Chicago: University of Chicago Press, 2008.
Heyer, Kristin. "Social Sin and Immigration: Good Fences Make Bad Neighbors." *Theological Studies* 71 (2010): 410–36.
Himes, Kenneth. "The Formation of Conscience." In *Ethics and Spirituality: Readings in Moral Theology No. 17*, edited by Charles E. Curran and Lisa A. Fullam, 162–82. New York: Paulist Press, 2014.
———. "Social Sin and the Role of the Individual." *Annual of the Society of Christian Ethics* 6 (1986): 183–219.
Hirschfeld, Mary Ann. "How a Thomistic Moral Framework Can Take Social Causality Seriously." In *Distant Markets, Distant Harms: Economic Complicity and Christian Ethics*, edited by Daniel K. Finn, 146–72. New York: Oxford University Press, 2014.
Hogan, Linda. "Toward a Personalist Theology of Conscience." In *An Irish Reader in Moral Theology: The Legacy of the Last 50 Years: Volume 1*. Edited by Enda McDonough and Vincent McNamara. Dublin: Columbia Press, 2009.
Hollenbach, David. "Commentary on *Gaudium et spes*." In *Modern Catholic Social Teaching: Commentaries and Interpretations*, edited by Kenneth Himes, 262–91. Washington, DC: Georgetown University Press, 2005.
———. *The Common Good and Christian Ethics*. New York: Cambridge University Press, 2002.
Hunter, James Davison. *To Change the World: The Irony, Tragedy, and Possibility of Christianity in the Late Modern World*. New York: Oxford University Press, 2010.
Hursthouse, Rosiland. *On Virtue Ethics*. Oxford: Oxford University Press, 1999.
Isasi-Díaz, Ada María. "Spirituality and the Common Good." In *Ethics and Spirituality: Readings in Moral Theology, No. 17*, edited by Charles E. Curran and Lisa A. Fullam, 249–57. New York: Paulist Press, 2014.
John XXIII. *Mater et magistra*. Vatican website, May 15, 1961. www.vatican.va/content/john -xxiii/en/encyclicals/documents/hf_j-xxiii_enc_15051961_mater.html.
———. "Opening Address of Vatican II." Vatican website, October 11, 1962. https://w2 .vatican.va/content/john-xxiii/en/speeches/1962.index.html.
John Paul II. *Centesimus annus*. Vatican website, January 5, 1991. www.vatican.va/content /john-paul-ii/en/encyclicals/documents/hf_jp-ii_enc_01051991_centesimus-annus .html.
———. *Evangelium vitae*. Vatican website, March 25, 1995. www.vatican.va/holy_father/john _paul_ii/encyclicals/documents/hf_jp-ii_enc_25031995_evangelium-vitae_en.html.
———. *Fides et ratio*. Vatican website, September 14, 1998. http://w2.vatican.va/content/john -paul-ii/en/encyclicals/documents/hf_jp-ii_enc_14091998_fides-et-ratio.html.
———. *Reconciliatio et paenetentia*. Vatican website, February 12, 1984. www.vatican.va/content /john-paul-ii/en/apost_exhortations/documents/hf_jp-ii_exh_02121984_reconciliatio -et-paenitentia.html.

———. *Sollicitudo rei socialis*. Vatican website, December 30, 1987. www.vatican.va/content/john-paul-ii/en/encyclicals/documents/hf_jp-ii_enc_30121987_sollicitudo-rei-socialis.html.

———. *Theology of the Body: Human Love in the Divine* Plan. Boston: Pauline Books, 1997.

———. *Veritatis splendor*. Vatican website, June 8, 1993. http://w2.vatican.va/content/john-paul-ii/en/encyclicals/documents/hf_jp-ii_enc_06081993_veritatis-splendor.html.

Johnson, M. Alex. "Nurturing a Community in the Online World: Gay Men and Women Embrace Internet as an Equalizer and a Bridge." NBCNEWS.com, February 8, 2006. http://www.nbcnews.com/id/11046534/ns/technology_and_science-tech_and_gadgets/t/nurturing-community-online-world/.

Jone, Heribert. *Moral Theology*. Westminster, MD: Newman Press, 1962.

Jones, Christopher D., and Conor M. Kelly. "Sloth: America's Ironic Structural Vice." *Journal of the Society of Christian Ethics* 37, no. 2 (2017): 117–34.

Jonsen, Albert R., and Stephen Toulmin. *The Abuse of Casuistry*. Berkeley: University of California Press, 1988.

Jordan, Mark. *Teaching Bodies: Moral Formation in the Summa of Thomas Aquinas*. New York: Fordham University Press, 2017.

Justin Martyr. *Dialogue with Trypho*. New Advent website. www.newadvent.org/fathers/0128.htm.

Kallenberg, Brad J. "The Master Argument of MacIntyre's 'After Virtue.'" In *Virtue: Readings in Moral Theology, No. 16*, edited by Charles E. Curran and Lisa A. Fullam, 21–50. Mahwah, NJ: Paulist Press, 2011.

Kasper, Walter. *Pope Francis' Revolution of Tenderness and Love*. Translated by William Madges. New York: Paulist Press, 2015.

Kaveny, M. Cathleen. "Appropriation of Evil: Cooperation's Mirror Image." *Theological Studies* 61, no. 2 (2000): 280–313.

———. *Law's Virtues: Fostering Autonomy and Solidarity in American Society*. Washington, DC: Georgetown University Press, 2012.

———. "Pope Francis and Catholic Healthcare Ethics." *Theological Studies* 80, no. 1 (2019): 186–201.

Keenan, James F. *A History of Catholic Moral Theology in the Twentieth Century: From Confessing Sins to Liberating Consciences*. New York: Continuum, 2010.

———. "Moral Discernment in History." *Theological Studies* 79, no. 3 (2018): 668–79.

———. "Notes on Moral Theology: Fundamental Moral Theology at the Beginning of the Twenty-First Century." *Theological Studies* 67, no. 1 (2006): 99–119.

———. "Proposing Cardinal Virtues." *Theological Studies* 56, no. 4 (1995): 704–29.

———. "Vatican II and Theological Ethics." *Theological Studies* 74, no. 1 (2013): 162–90.

Kelly, Gerald. *Medico-Moral Problems*. Saint Louis: Catholic Hospital Association, 1958.

Kelly, Gerald, and John Ford. *Contemporary Moral Theology*. Vol. 1. Westminster, MD: Newman Press, 1962.

Kenney, Graham. "Should a CEO's Bonus Be Based on Financial Performance Alone?" *Harvard Business Review*, May 2017. https://hbr.org/2017/05/should-a-ceos-bonus-be-based-on-financial-performance-alone.

Kim, Andrew. "Progress in the Good: A Defense of the Thomistic Unity Thesis." *Journal of Moral Theology* 3, no. 1 (2014): 147–74.

King, Anthony. "The Odd Couple: Archer and Giddens and British Social Theory." *British Journal of Sociology* 61, no. 1 (2010): 253–60.

Kludt, Tom. "Univision Host Fired for First Lady Comment Says White House Complained." CNN Business, March 12, 2015. http://money.cnn.com/2015/03/12/media/univision-fires-rodner-figueroa-michelle-obama/index.html.
Kochuthara, Shaji George. "Dowry as a Socio-Structural Sin." In *Feminist Catholic Theological Ethics: Conversations in the World Church*, edited by Linda Hogan and A. E. Orobator, 108–22. Maryknoll, NY: Orbis Books, 2014.
Kotva, Joseph J., Jr. *The Christian Case for Virtue Ethics*. Washington, DC: Georgetown University Press, 1996.
Lafley, A. G. "What Only the CEO Can Do." *Harvard Business Review*, May 2009. https://hbr.org/2009/05/what-only-the-ceo-can-do.
Lakhani, Nina. "Berta Cáceres Court Papers Show Murder Suspects' Links to US-Trained Elite Troops." theguardian.com, February 28, 2017. www.theguardian.com/world/2017/feb/28/berta-caceres-honduras-military-intelligence-us-trained-special-forces.
———. "Honduras Dam Project Shadowed by Violence." AlJazeera.com, December 24, 2013. www.aljazeera.com/indepth/features/2013/12/honduras-dam-project-shadowed-violence-201312211490337166.html.
Landon, Michael. "The Social Presuppositions of Early Liberation Theology." *Restoration Quarterly* 47 (2005): 13–32.
Latin American Bishops Conference. *The Church in the Present-Day Transformation of Latin America in Light of the Council: Conclusions*. Bogotá: General Secretariat of CELAM, 1970.
———. *Evangelization in Latin America's Present and Future: Final Document of the Third General Conference of the Latin American Episcopate in Puebla and Beyond*. Edited by John Eagleston and Philip Scharper. Translated by John Drury. Maryknoll, NY: Orbis Books, 1979.
Le Guin, Ursula K. "The Ones Who Walk Away from Omelas." In *The Unreal and the Real: Selected Stories of Ursula K. Le Guin*. Vol. 2. London: Orion, 2014.
Leo XIII. *Rerum novarum*. Vatican website, May 15, 1891. www.vatican.va/content/leo-xiii/en/encyclicals/documents/hf_l-xiii_enc_15051891_rerum-novarum.html.
Lonergan, Bernard. *Method in Theology*. New York: Herder & Herder, 1972.
Louden, Robert. "On Some Vices of Virtue Ethics." *American Philosophical Quarterly* 21, no. 3 (1984): 227–36.
MacIntyre, Alasdair. *After Virtue: A Study in Moral Theory*. 2nd ed. Notre Dame, IN: University of Notre Dame Press, 1984.
———. "Plain Persons and Moral Philosophy: Rules, Virtues and Goods." *American Catholic Philosophical Quarterly* 66, no. 1 (1992): 3–19.
———. "Social Structures and Their Threats to Moral Agency." *Philosophy* 74, no. 3 (1999): 311–29.
Magner, Lois. *A History of Medicine*. New York: Dekker, 1992.
Magundayao, Janina Angeli M. "Dispositions and Skills: An Argument for Virtue Ethics Against Situationism." *Kritike* 7, no. 1 (2013): 96–114.
Mariani, Mike. "The New Generation of Self-Created Utopias." *New York Times Style Magazine*, January 16, 2020. www.nytimes.com/2020/01/16/t-magazine/intentional-communities.html.
Martins, Alexandre. *The Cry of the Poor: Liberation Ethics and Justice in Health Care*. Lanham, MD: Lexington Books, 2020.
Massaro, Thomas. *Mercy in Action: The Social Teachings of Pope Francis*. New York: Rowman & Littlefield, 2018.
Massingale, Brian. *Racial Justice and the Catholic Church*. Maryknoll, NY: Orbis Books, 2010.

Matthaei, Julie. "The Sexual Division of Labor, Sexuality, and Lesbian/Gay Liberation: Towards a Marxist-Feminist Analysis of Sexuality in U.S. Capitalism." In *Queer Economics: A Reader*. Edited by Joyce Jacobsen and Adam Zeller. New York: Routledge, 2008.
McCarthy, Justin. "Americans' Views on Homosexuality Remain Split." Gallup, May 28, 2014. www.gallup.com/poll/170753/americans-views-origins-homosexuality-remain-split.aspx.
McKibben, Bill. "The Question I Get Asked the Most." *EcoWatch*, October 14, 2016. www.ecowatch.com/bill-mckibben-climate-change-2041759425.html.
Melina, Livio. *The Epiphany of Love: Toward a Theological Understanding of Christian Action*. Grand Rapids: Wm. B. Eerdmans, 2010.
Miller, Christian B., and Angela Knobel. "Some Foundational Questions in Philosophy about Character." In *Character: New Directions in Philosophy, Psychology, and Theology*, edited by Christian B. Miller, R. Michael Furr, Angela Knobel, and William Fleeson, 19–40. New York: Oxford University Press, 2015.
Moore, G. E. *Principia Ethica*. Cambridge: Cambridge University Press, 1903.
Morrill, Bruce. "Sacramental Liturgy as Negotiation of Power, Human and Divine." *Liturgy + Power: Annual Volume of the College Theology Society* 62 (2016): 3–21.
Murray, John Courtney. "The Problem of Religious Freedom." *Theological Studies* 25, no. 4 (1964): 503–75.
New York City Police Department. *Patrol Guide*. www1.nyc.gov/assets/nypd/downloads/pdf/public_information/public-pguide1.pdf.
New York State Office for the Prevention of Domestic Violence. "What Is 'Mandatory Arrest' for Domestic Violence?" www.opdv.ny.gov/help/fss/part22.html#:~:text=New%20York%20State%20has%20%E2%80%9CMandatory,of%20their%20family%20or%20household.&text=Mandatory%20arrest%20does%20not%20necessarily%20mean%20immediate%20arrest.
Niebuhr, H. Richard. *Christ and Culture*. 50th anniversary edition. San Francisco: Harper, 2001.
O'Keefe, Mark. *What Are They Saying about Social Sin?* New York: Paulist Press, 1990.
O'Meara, Thomas. "Community as Primal Reality." *Theological Studies* 78, no. 2 (2017): 435–46.
Oppel, Richard A., and Lazaro Gamio. "Minneapolis Police Use Force against Black People at 7 Times the Rate of White People." *New York Times*, June 3, 2020. www.nytimes.com/interactive/2020/06/03/us/minneapolis-police-use-of-force.html?action=click&module=Spotlight&pgtype=Homepage.
Painter, Matthew A., II, and Pamela Paxton. "Checkbooks in the Heartland: Change in Time in Voluntary Association Memberships." *Sociological Forum* 29, no. 2 (2014): 408–28.
Paul VI. *Octogesima adveniens*. Vatican website, May 14, 1971. http://w2.vatican.va/content/paul-vi/en/apost_letters/documents/hf_p-vi_apl_19710514_octogesima-adveniens.html.
———. *Populorum progressio*. Vatican website, March 26, 1967. www.vatican.va/content/paul-vi/en/encyclicals/documents/hf_p-vi_enc_26031967_populorum.html.
———. "Speech at the Final Public Session of the Second Vatican Ecumenical Council." Vatican website, December 7, 1965. https://w2.vatican.va/content/paul-vi/en/speeches/1965/documents/hf_p-vi_spe_19651207_epilogo-concilio.html.
Petrella, Ivan. *The Future of Liberation Theology: An Argument and a Manifesto*. New York: Routledge, 2004.
Petrusek, Matthew. "The Relevance of Karl Rahner's View of Human Dignity for the Catholic Social Thought Tradition." *Philosophy and Theology* 27, no. 2 (2015): 513–38.

Pettegree, Andrew. *Brand Luther: 1517, Printing, and the Making of the Reformation.* New York: Penguin, 2015.

Pfeil, Margaret. "Magisterial Use of the Language of Social Sin." *Louvain Studies* 27, no. 2 (2002): 132–52.

Pinckaers, Servais. *The Sources of Christian Ethics.* Washington, DC: Catholic University of America Press, 1995.

Pius XI. *Quadragesimo anno.* Vatican website, May 15, 1931. http://w2.vatican.va/content/pius-xi/en/encyclicals/documents/hf_p-xi_enc_19310515_quadragesimo-anno.html.

Police Benevolent Association of the City of New York. "PBA President: The Facts Are Clear, Exonerate Pantaleo." June 6, 2019. www.nycpba.org/press-releases/2019/lynch-exonerate-pantaleo/.

Pontifical Council for Justice and Peace. *Compendium of Social Doctrine.* 2006. www.vatican.va/roman_curia/pontifical_councils/justpeace/documents/rc_pc_justpeace_doc_20060526_compendio-dott-soc_en.html.

Pope, Stephen J. *The Evolution and the Ordering of Love.* Washington, DC: Georgetown University Press, 1994.

———. "Overview of the Ethics of Thomas Aquinas." In *The Ethics of Aquinas*, edited by Stephen Pope, 30–56. Washington, DC: Georgetown University Press, 2002.

Porpora, Douglas V. "Four Concepts of Social Structure." In *Critical Realism: Essential Readings*, edited by Margaret Archer, Roy Bhaskar, Andrew Collier, Tony Lawson, and Alan Norrie, 339–55. New York: Routledge, 1998.

———. "Who Is Responsible? Critical Realism, Market Harms, and Collective Responsibility." In *Distant Markets, Distant Harms: Economic Complicity and Christian Ethics*, edited by Daniel Finn, 3–24. New York: Oxford University Press, 2014.

Porter, Jean. "Moral Virtues, Charity, and Grace: Why the Infused and Acquired Virtues Cannot Co-exist." *Journal of Moral Theology* 8, no. 2 (2019): 40–66.

———. "Virtue Ethics in the Medieval Period." In *The Cambridge Companion to Virtue Ethics*, edited by Daniel C. Russel, 70–91. New York: Cambridge University Press, 2013.

———. "Virtue and Sin: The Connection of the Virtues and the Case of the Flawed Saint." *Journal of Religion* 75, no. 4 (1995): 521–39.

Powell, Benjamin. *Out of Poverty: Sweatshops in the Global Economy.* New York: Cambridge University Press, 2014.

Ragazzi, Maurizio. "The Concept of Social Sin in Its Thomistic Roots." *Journal of Markets and Morality* 7, no. 2 (2004): 363–408.

Ratzinger, Josef. "Concerning the Notion of Person in Theology." *Communio* 17, no. 3 (1990): 439–54.

Regan, Ethna. *Theology and the Boundary Discourse of Human Rights.* Washington, DC: Georgetown University Press, 2010.

Reichberg, Gregory. "The Intellectual Virtues." In *The Ethics of Aquinas*, edited by Stephen J. Pope, 131–50. Washington, DC: Georgetown University Press, 2002.

Romero, Óscar. *Voice of the Voiceless: The Four Pastoral Letters and Other Statements.* Translated by Michael J. Walsh. Maryknoll, NY: Orbis Books, 1985.

Ross, Robert J. *Slaves to Fashion.* Ann Arbor: University of Michigan Press, 2004.

Rothchild, Jonathan, and Mathew Petrusek, eds. *Dignity and Conflict: Contemporary Interfaith Dialogue.* Notre Dame, IN: University of Notre Dame Press, 2020.

Rubio, Julie Hanlon. "Cooperation with Evil: The Moral Duty of Resistance." *Theological Studies* 78, no. 1 (2017): 96–120.

———. *Hope for Common Ground: Mediating the Personal and the Political in a Divided Church*. Washington, DC: Georgetown University Press, 2016.

———. "Moral Cooperation with Evil and Social Ethics." *Journal of the Society of Christian Ethics* 31, no. 1 (2011): 103–22.

Salzman, Todd, and Michael Lawler. "Method and Catholic Theological Ethics in the Twenty-First Century." *Theological Studies* 74, no. 4 (2013): 903–33.

———. *Virtue and Theological Ethics: Toward a Renewed Ethical Method*. Maryknoll, NY: Orbis Books, 2018.

Sanders, A. R., E. R. Martin, G. W. Beecham, S. Guo, et al. "Genome-Wide Scan Demonstrates Significant Linkage for Male Sexual Orientation." *Psychological Medicine* 45, no. 7 (2015): 1379–88. doi:10.1017/S0033291714002451.

Saslow, Eli. "Against His Better Judgment." *Washington Post*, June 6, 2015. www.washingtonpost.com/sf/national/2015/06/06/against-his-better-judgment/.

Scannone, Juan Carlos. "Pope Francis and the Theology of the People." *Theological Studies* 77, no. 1 (2016): 118–35.

Schilbrack, Kevin. "Embodied Critical Realism." *Journal of Religious Ethics* 42, no. 1 (2014): 167–79.

Searle, John. *The Construction of Social Reality*. New York: Free Press, 1995.

Second Vatican Council. *Dei verbum*. Vatican website, November 18, 1965. www.vatican.va/archive/hist_councils/ii_vatican_council/documents/vat-ii_const_19651118_dei-verbum_en.html.

———. *Gaudium et spes*. Vatican website, December 7, 1965. www.vatican.va/archive/hist_councils/ii_vatican_council/documents/vat-ii_const_19651207_gaudium-et-spes_en.html.

———. *Lumen gentium*. Vatican website, November 21, 1964. www.vatican.va/archive/hist_councils/ii_vatican_council/documents/vat-ii_const_19641121_lumen-gentium_en.html.

Segundo, Juan Luis. "Human Rights, Evangelization, and Ideology." In *Signs of the Times: Theological Reflections*, edited by Alfred T. Hennelly and translated by Robert R. Barr, 53–66. New York: Orbis Books, 1993.

Selling, Joseph A. *Reframing Catholic Ethics*. New York: Oxford University Press, 2016.

Shin, Wonchul, and Elizabeth M. Bounds. "Treating Moral Harm as Social Harm: Toward a Restorative Ethics of Christian Responsibility." *Journal of the Society of Christian Ethics* 37, no. 2 (2017): 153–69.

Singer, Peter. "Famine, Affluence, and Morality." *Philosophy of Public Affairs* 1, no. 3 (1972): 229–43.

Slater, Thomas. *Cases of Conscience*. New York: Benzinger, 1911.

Slote, Michael. *Morals from Motives*. New York: Oxford University Press, 2001.

Smith, Brad W. "Structural and Organizational Predictors of Homicide by Police." *Policing: An International Journal of Police Strategies and Management* 27, no. 4 (2004): 539–57.

Smith, Christian. *What Is a Person? Rethinking Humanity, Social Life, and the Moral Good from the Person Up*. Chicago: University of Chicago Press, 2010.

Snow, Nancy. "Models of Virtue." In *The Routledge Companion to Virtue Ethics*, edited by Lorrain Besser and Michael Slote, 359–74. New York: Routledge, 2015.

Spardaro, Antonio. "A Big Heart Open to God: The Exclusive Interview with Pope Francis." *America*, September 30, 2013. http://www.americamagazine.org/print/156341.

Spinello, Richard. "The Enduring Relevance of Karol Wojtyla's Philosophy." *Logos* 17, no. 3 (2014): 16–46.

Spohn, William. *Go and Do Likewise: Jesus and Ethics*. New York: Continuum, 2000.
———. "The Return of Virtue Ethics." *Theological Studies* 53, no. 1 (1992): 60–75.
Stichter, Matt. "Virtue as a Skill." In *The Oxford Handbook of Virtue*, edited by Nancy E. Snow, 57–84. New York: Oxford University Press, 2018.
Swanton, Christine. "The Definition of Virtue Ethics." In *The Cambridge Companion to Virtue Ethics*, edited by Daniel C. Russell, 315–38. New York: Cambridge University Press, 2013.
Swinford, David N. "The Limits of Using TSR as an Incentive Measure." Paper presented at Harvard Law School Forum on Corporate Governance and Financial Regulation, October 13, 2015. https://corpgov.law.harvard.edu/2015/10/13/the-limits-of-using-tsr-as-an-incentive-measure/.
Synod of Bishops. *Justicia in mundo*. In *Catholic Social Thought: The Documentary Heritage*, 3rd ed., edited by David J. O'Brien and Thomas A. Shannon, 304–18. Maryknoll, NY: Orbis Books, 2016.
Taylor, Charles. *Sources of the Self: The Making of the Modern Identity*. New York: Cambridge University Press, 1989.
Tessman, Lisa. *Burdened Virtues*. New York: Oxford University Press, 2005.
Thomas, Jo. "Anita Hill Plans to Leave Teaching Post in Oklahoma." *New York Times*, May 13, 1996. www.nytimes.com/1996/11/13/us/anita-hill-plans-to-leave-teaching-post-in-oklahoma.html.
Traina, Cristina. "'This Is the Year': Narratives of Structural Evil." *Journal of the Society of Christian Ethics* 37, no. 2 (2017): 3–20.
Turri, John, Mark Alfano, and John Grecco. "Virtue Epistemology." *The Stanford Encyclopedia of Philosophy*, summer 2018 edition. Edited by Edward N. Zalta. https://plato.stanford.edu/archives/sum2018/entries/epistemology-virtue/.
US Conference of Catholic Bishops. *Economic Justice for All*. November 1, 1986. www.usccb.org/upload/economic_justice_for_all.pdf.
———. *The Ethical and Religious Directives for Catholic Health Care Services*. 6th ed. June 2018. www.usccb.org/about/doctrine/ethical-and-religious-directives/upload/ethical-religious-directives-catholic-health-service-sixth-edition-2016-06.pdf.
Vidal, Marciano. "Structural Sin: A New Category in Moral Theology?" In *History and Conscience: Studies in Honor of Fr. Sean O'Riordan, CSsR*, edited by Raphael Gallagher and Brendan McConvery, 181–98. New York: Gill & Macmillan, 1989.
Vogt, Christopher. "Virtue: Personal Formation and Social Transformation." *Theological Studies* 77, no. 1 (2016): 181–96.
Waddell, Paul. *Friendship and the Moral Life*. Notre Dame, IN: University of Notre Dame Press, 1990.
———. *The Primacy of Love: An Introduction to the Ethics of Thomas Aquinas*. New York: Paulist Press, 1992.
Ward, Kate. "Jesuit and Feminist Hospitality: Pope Francis' Virtue Response to Inequality." *Religions* 8, no. 4 (2017).
Weaver, Darlene Fozard. "Christian Anthropology and Health Care." *Health Care Ethics USA*, Fall 2018, 1–6.
Wilkins, Jeremy. "Grace and Growth: Aquinas, Lonergan, and the Problematic of Habitual Grace." *Theological Studies* 72, no. 4 (2011): 723–49.
Wojtyla, Karol. *The Acting Person*, translated by Anna-Teresa Tymieniecka. Boston: D. Reidel, 1979.

Wolterstorff, Nicholas. *Reason within the Bounds of Religion*. 2nd ed. Grand Rapids: Wm. B. Eerdmans, 1984.
Young, Iris Marion. "Responsibility and Global Justice: A Social Connection Model." *Social Philosophy and Policy* 23, no. 1 (2006): 102–30.
Zagzebski, Linda Trinkaus. "Exemplarism and Admiration." In *Character: New Directions from Philosophy, Psychology, and Theology*, edited by Christian Miller, R. Michael Furr, Angela Knobel, and William Fleeson, 251–70. New York: Oxford University Press, 2015.
———. *Exemplarist Moral Theory*. New York: Oxford University Press, 2017.
———. "Exemplarist Virtue Theory." *Metaphilosophy* 41, nos. 1–2 (2010): 41–57.
Zenor, John. "No. 1 Alabama's Defense Embracing That 'Hateful' Mentality." *Daily Herald*, November 7, 2016. www.dailyherald.com/article/20161107/sports/311079822.

INDEX

Abercrombie and Fitch, 13
abortion, 28, 31, 53, 186
Adams, Robert, 139, 141, 159n68
Affordable Care Act, 186
aggregated agency, 18
Ahern, Kevin, 212
Amoris laetitia, 109
Annas, Julia, 136, 138, 139
Anscombe, Elizabeth, 125
Anthony, Augustine, 105
antiblackness supremacy, 52, 183
appropriation of evil, principle of, 18, 19
Aquinas, Thomas: on acquired virtue, 37; on affective union, 132; on charity, 130, 131; on circumstances, 28; on common good, 133; on consequences of action, 135; on dignity, 105; on faith and reason, 66–68; on habit, 107, 137, 138; on infused virtue, 137; on mercy, 108, 113, 114; on natural law, 131; and sixteenth century ethics, 25; and theocentrism, 98, 130; and virtue ethics, 98, 100; and virtue theory, 123, 124, 126–28, 130
archaism, 29
Archer, Margaret: critique of Giddens, 72; on culture, 81–84; definition of social structure, 75; on emergence, 77, 91; on internal conversation, 90, 91, 93; and prudential reasoning, 176–78; on structure and agency, 89–91, 176–78, 180
Aristotle: and burdened virtue, 214; on friendship, 157n14; on virtue, 127, 128, 130, 136, 139
Augustine of Hippo, 141, 219n54
Austin, Nicolas: on grace and virtue, 142, 143, 159n87, 159n89; on virtue ethics, 124, 157n2

baptism, 36, 142
bargain hunting, 174, 187
Barrera, Albino, 13–16, 18, 20, 188
Baum, Gregory, 39, 48, 186
Beauchamp, Tom, 24
Bellah, Robert, 211
Benedict of Nursia, Saint, 175, 176, 190, 213
Benedict XVI (pope): on charity, 107, 131, 190, 211; on dignity, 105, 106; and personalism, 103; and social change, 70, 71; and structures of sin, 43, 44, 57n52; and theology in ethics, 99–101
Bennett, Mark, 166, 167, 173, 191
Bentham, Jeremy, 69
Berger-Luckmann approach, 49, 50, 54, 58n84, 58n86
Beyer, Gerald: on principle of cooperation, 19, 20, 29, 31n15, 65, 156, 180; on social structures, 51
Bhaskar, Roy: on methodological individualism, 69; on position-practice system, 76, 79, 176; on relation vs. interaction, 74; on reproduction of social structure, 84
Black, Donald, 69
"black dangerousness," 184
Black Lives Matter, 190
bloodletting, 195
bodily performance, 173
bodily practice: and acquisition of virtue, 147; disruptive, 86, 88, 190, 201, 207, 208; and social structure, 75, 86, 187
Boff, Clodovis, 36, 45, 53
Boff, Leonardo, 36, 45, 53
Bounds, Elizabeth, 51, 52
Bourdieu, Pierre, 51, 52, 54
"bowling alone" problem, 211, 212
boycott, 206, 207, 209

237

Brady, Bernard, 132, 219n54
burdened virtues, 214
Butkus, Dick, 175
"buycott," 209, 219n29

Cáceres, Berta, 215
Cahill, Lisa Sowle, 48
Calhoun, John, 163, 191n2
cardinal virtues, 124, 128, 129, 158n45
Caritas in veritate, 99, 100, 107, 189
casuistry, 24–26, 168
Catechism of the Catholic Church, 20, 21, 57n41, 106, 189
Cavanaugh, William, 51, 59n96
Centessimus annus, 41, 100, 102
charity: Aquinas on, 130, 157n14, 158n40; defined, 131, 134; growth of, 142–44, 163; Pope Benedict XVI on, 100, 107; Pope Francis on, 109, 112, 113, 115, 118n81, 160n103; Pope Pius XI on, 99; and prudence, 143, 144, 197, 216, 217; and social structures, 36, 190; and solidarity, 211; Vatican II on, 99
Chávez, César, 154, 207
The Children's Place: and collapse at Rana Plaza, 12, 13, 15, 18, 21; and structural moral character, 164; and structures of vice, 203, 205
Childress, James, 24
Christ and Culture, 12
Cicero, 165
circumstances: and action, 140, 151, 155; and casuistry, 24–26; and infused virtue, 143, 144; and internal conversation, 177; and Pope John Paul II, 191n5; and prudence, 200, 217; structures as, 18, 165–68; and Thomas Aquinas, 28, 191n5; and virtue, 125, 135, 136, 138
Clark, Patrick, 153, 154
Clarke, Norris, 103
Cloutier, David: on the common good, 133, 211; on social structures, 51, 52, 54, 59n96; on theology and ethics, 100; on virtue, 48, 107, 189
Coburn, John, 117n29
common good: in Catholic social teaching, 34; instrumental vs. intrinsic, 133, 211;

social justice and, 19, 189; solidarity and, 41, 114, 115, 172, 210; structures and, 169, 170, 182, 188, 190, 212; structures of sin and, 39, 40; virtue and, 112, 134
"common view" of social change, 64, 70. *See also* Bhaskar, Roy: on methodological individualism
complicity in structural evil, 12, 19
confession, 27, 32n54. *See also* penance
conscience: individual, 42, 44, 50; of society, 42
consumerism, 46, 11, 112
control beliefs: and Catholicism, 66–69; and critical realism, 73, 74, 92; defined, 55, 65, 66
conversion: communal, 111; inadequacy of personal, 38, 47; priority of personal, 36, 46; relation to structural transformation, 35, 36, 57n33
cooperation in evil, principle of: critique of use of, 12, 18, 20, 125, 196, 197, 208; defined, 16, 17, 30n13, 31n15; and social/structural sin, 17–19
counsel, 155, 177
COVID-19, 135, 152
critical race theory, 4, 5
critical realism: and Christian ethics, 51–54; on culture, 64, 81–83; embodied, 73, 94n45; on emergence, 77, 78; on organizations vs. institutions, 80, 81; on social structure, 61, 75, 76; on transformation of structures, 84–87
"cross-cutting" social positions, 180
culpability, moral: defined, 20, 21; and social structures, 22, 23, 164, 185, 204, 205, 208; and virtue and vice, 29
cultural system (Archer), 81–83
culture: in critical realism, 81–83; defined, 64; and liberation theology, 103; of life and death, 42, 43; and moral values, 37, 46; and structural transformation, 207, 211; in theological ethics, 2. *See also* indifference, culture of

Davis, Henry, 30n13
decision procedures in ethics, 155, 160n130
de La Torre, Miguel, 208

de Lubac, Henri, 103
Derrida, Jacques, 69
determinism: historical, 40; neurological, 55, 72, 73; sociological/structural, 38, 72, 73
de Vitoria, Francisco, 25
dialectical explanation of poverty, 36, 45
DiAngelo, Robin, 192n23
Dignitas personae, 100, 105
dignity: as central moral value, 34, 100; defined, 105, 106, 118n59, 118n68; inherent, 69, 106; normative, 106, 164, 172; and personalism, 102; and structures of virtue and vice, 168, 169, 180, 182, 185, 186, 215; and virtue, 134, 135
discernment, moral: and ethical theory, 154, 155; and virtues, 109, 155, 196, 197, 200
disposition: and action, 138; habit and, 136–39; and *habitus*, 51; and practices, 147; and social structures, 79
dispositive causality, 159n87. *See also* infused virtue
Donati, Pierpaolo, 51, 69, 75
Dorr, Donal, 41, 211
double effect, principle of: applied to sweatshop labor, 14; critique of use of, 14–16, 20, 125, 188, 196, 197; defined, 14, 30n6; emergence of, 25, 26;
downward causation, 78, 83
Driver, Julia, 135, 136
Dussel, Enrique, 36, 37, 53
duty to rescue, 166

Elder-Vass, Dave: on culture, 81–83; on definitions of social structure, 1; on human action, 91–92; on normative social institutions vs. organizations, 80–81, 160, 183; on norm circles, 79; on resisting influence of social structures, 176; on structure-agency problem, 63; on structure and human action, 167, 168, 192n36
Elfers, Jane, 203–5
emergence: and gay marriage, 87–89; of habits, 139–42; of structures of virtue and vice, 186–88; and transformation of structures, 84–89; and virtuous action, 207

emergentist theory of action, 91–92, 137, 140
emergentist theory of virtue, 139–41, 180–81
Enger, Mark, 23, 32n38
The Ethical and Religious Directives, 31n15
ethics *para joder*, 208
ethnography, 4, 5
Eucharist, 36, 142
Evangelii gaudium, 44–46
Evangelium vitae, 42, 45, 107
evangelization, 57n33
exemplarism, 152–56
exemplars: and action guidance, 125, 144; and Laudato si' Action Platform, 213; in *Rule of St. Benedict*, 175, 176; and social positions, 198, 199; and vice, 175; and virtue formation, 145, 150–56, 163
explanatory capacity: and control beliefs, 65; defined, 24, 32n42; ethical methods lacking, 25, 27, 28, 156, 32n54; and structures of virtue and vice, 196; and virtue ethics, 124, 163
externalization, 50, 58n84

faith: as infused virtue, 107, 126, 134, 142; and love, 108, 112; and reason, 25, 66–68; and theological vision, 101
Falk, Richard, 28
fasting, 27
fideism, 68
Finn, Daniel, 2, 7n7, 52–54, 218n20
fixism, 29
Flood, Anthony, 131
Floyd, George, 183, 185
Ford, Christine Blasey, 96n102
fortitude, 128
Francis (pope): and dignity, 106; on indifference to suffering, 111, 112, 206; and personalism 103–5; and theocentrism, 100, 101; on unjust social structures and institutions, 44–47, 54, 71, 210, 212, 213; and virtue ethics, 108–16
Francis of Assisi, 152, 153
Frankena, William, 149, 151
free will, 20, 65, 130, 143
friendship: and affective union, 210; Aristotle on, 157n14; and charity, 126,

friendship (*continued*)
  130–33; as context for moral development, 127; and Eucharist, 142; love and, 113; and moral manuals, 27; and sin, 36; and social structures, 169, 174–76, 179; and solidarity, 211

Galileo, 68
Gap, 13
Garner, Eric, 184, 185, 192n43
Garrigou-Lagrange, Réginald, 102
Gaudete et exsultate, 108, 111, 119n113
Gaudium et spes: and Catholic ethics, 24, 34, 99; on dignity, 105; on faith and reason, 67; and liberation theology, 35; and personalism, 102
Gera, Lucio, 103
Giddens, Anthony, 71, 72, 91, 94n35
Gilleman, Gerard, 99
Gilson, Etienne, 94n15
global warming: cause of, 2; and Christian ethics, 27, 53; as emergent reality, 187; as overdetermined, 200; transformation of, 201, 202, 212, 213
good(s), moral: and moral deliberation, 177, 178; and the natural law, 131, 204; and norms, 148–50; and practices, 146; and relationality, 129–33; and social positions, 180; and solidarity, 211; and structures of virtue and vice, 190, 202, 204, 206; supernatural vs. natural, 137; and virtue ethics 157n2
Good Samaritan, 145, 155
Goulet, Denis, 41, 218n3
grace: and free will, 143, 159n89; and infused virtue, 126, 131, 142, 143, 148; and sin, 56n12
Grimes, Katie, 51, 52, 59n96
Grotius, Hugo, 28
Gudorf, Christine, 32n54, 48, 49, 54, 209
Gutierrez, Gustavo: on charity, 131, 169; on poverty, 45; on social sciences, 36, 53; on unjust situations, 36

habit: and dispositions, 136–39; emergence of, 139–42, 180; growth of infused, 142, 143; in Pope Francis, 109–12, 115; and structures of virtue and vice, 168, 172, 179, 210; virtue as a, 133, 134
habitus (Bourdieu), 51, 52
Haring, Bernhard, 23, 27, 99
Harris, Sam, 65
Hauerwas, Stanley, 127, 130
Hegelian idealism, 64
Herdt, Jennifer, 127
heroism, moral, 215, 219n54
Heyer, Kristin, 50, 54, 58n86
Hill, Anita, 86
Himes, Kenneth, 21, 49, 153, 215
Hogan, Linda, 107, 116
Hollenbach, David, 99, 133, 211
holistic social theory, 71–73, 89
homophobia, 174
Honduras, 215
Hope for Common Ground, 31n20
human development, integral, 44
human flourishing, 34, 134
human projects, 84, 90
human rights, 22, 23, 32n38, 37
humility, 175, 176
Hunter, James, 64, 70
Hursthouse, Rosiland, 154, 155, 157n2, 160n130

image of God, 106, 116
indifference: culture of, 112, 206; and mercy, 113, 114; and solidarity, 114, 115
inequality, 45, 108
infused virtue: and action, 126, 159n89; charity as, 131, 134; cultivation of, 142–44, 163; defined, 134, 137; and free will; and human consent, 142; and initial infusion of grace, 142; and the sacraments, 142; transformation theory of, 158n45
Instruction on Certain Aspects of the "Theology of Liberation," 53, 58n86
Instruction on Christian Freedom and Liberation, 40
internal conversation: defined, 90, 91, 93; and prudential reasoning, 176–78
internalization, 50, 58n84
internet, 81, 86, 88
Isasi-Díaz, Ada María, 50, 55

Jarvie, Ian, 69
Jesuit Volunteer Corps, 212
Jesus Christ: and Christian ethics, 24, 30, 31n31, 218; as exemplar, 153, 154; and faith, 68, 101, and poverty, 43, 131
John XXIII (pope), 113, 193n52
John Paul II (pope): on circumstances, 165, 191n5; on dignity, 105, 106; on faith and reason, 67, 68; on personalism, 98, 102; use of philosophy in ethics, 99, 100; on solidarity, 114, 115, 206, 210, 211; on structures of sin, 39–43, 45, 47, 53, 154; and virtue, 107, 153
Jone, Heribert, 26, 27
Jones, Christopher, 218n22
Jonsen, Albert, 24–26, 32n44
Jordan, Mark, 142, 151, 158n40, 193n55
justice: acquisition of, 143, 149; and charity, 99, 100, 190; contributive, 99, 193n52; and distant others, 17, 129; ecological, 46, 152, 153, 213, 215; education and, 36, 113; Keenan on, 128; social, 34, 169, 189, 193n52
Justicia in mundo, 36
Justin Martyr, 66

Kasper, Walter, 103
Kavanaugh, Brett, 96n102
Kaveny, Cathleen, 18, 19, 31n24, 31n26, 70, 111
Keenan, James: on cardinal virtues, 127–29; on *Caritas in veritate*, 100; on principle of double effect, 25, 26; on purpose of moral theology, 23
Kelly, Conor, 218n22
Kelly, Gerald, 30n6, 32n31
King, Jr., Martin Luther, 152, 169
Knobel, Angela, 32n42
Kochuthara, Shaji George, 50

Landon, Michael, 63
Latin American Bishops Conference (CELAM), 35–38, 41, 43
Laudato si': on institutions, 44, 46, 47, 110, 201, 213; on theological anthropology, 104, 106; on universal fraternity, 101; and virtue ethics, 109, 212, 213

Laudato si' Action Platform, 213
Lawler, Michael, 106, 107
Le Guin, Ursula, 11
Leo XIII (pope), 34, 46
Letter to the Romans, 66
liability, moral, 5, 6, 21, 22, 29
liberation theology: and attention to the poor, 4; on human rights, 22, 23, 32n38; and Magisterium, 38–40, 53; and Pope Francis, 103; on unjust social structures, 35–38, 53, 63
Lonergan, Bernard, 136, 160n129
Louden, Robert, 154
Louis, Pierre Charles Alexandre, 195
love: and charity, 112, 113; defined, 131, 135; faith and, 108; God's, 100, 101, 106, 148, 218; and the human good, 129–34; and mercy, 114, 119n113; order of 216, 217; in *Rule of St. Benedict*, 175, 176; and social/structural sin, 39; as union, 132, 133; and virtue, 134. *See also* charity
Lumen fidei, 101, 104
Lumen gentium, 34
lunch counter sit-in movement, 86, 207
Luther, Martin, 86

MacIntyre, Alasdair: on practices, 146; and virtue formation, 127, 144–46, 149; virtue and social role, 130, 178
Magundayao, Janina Angeli M., 158n63
manualism: critique of, 26, 27, 29, 32n54, 55; and moral norms, 107
Market Complicity and Christian Ethics, 13–16
Maritain, Jacques, 102
marriage, 84, 87, 88
Martins, Alexandre, 4
Marx, Karl, 37, 53
Marxist analysis, 36, 38, 45, 48, 53
Massaro, Thomas, 103
Massingale, Brian, 192n23
Mattison, William, 48, 107
McKibben, Bill, 201, 202
Medellín Conference, 35–37, 46
medical ethics, 188, 195, 202
Melina, Livio, 132, 206
mercy: Aquinas on, 118n2, 119n113; charity and, 211; cultivation of, 172,

mercy (continued)
  190; islands of, 212; Pope Francis on, 108, 113–16, 119n113, 119n125; works of, 147, 149
method, ethical: in casuistry, 24–26; and double effect, 16, 26, 188; in moral manuals, 26; and social structures, 20, 188; in virtue ethics, 98, 116, 126, 155, 157n2, 157n19
#MeToo, 86
Miller, Christian, 32n42
Montgomery bus boycott, 207
Moore, G. E., 158n48
moral manuals, 26, 27, 32n54, 55, 98, 107
Morrill, Bruce, 173, 181
Murray, John Courtney, 29
Mutors, example of the, 135, 136

narrative, virtue and, 127, 144, 145, 155
natural law theory, 98, 99, 107, 131
New Orleans Saints, 175
Newton, Isaac, 26
New York City Police Department, 184, 185, 192n42, 192n43
New York Life, 164
Niebuhr, H. Richard, 2
Nixon, Richard, 166
normative social institutions, 80, 162, 163, 182–87
norm circles, 78–83, 186
norms: in social structures, 175–78, 182–87, 193n46; virtue and, 107, 144, 145, 148–51

objectification, 50, 58n84
obstetrics and gynecology, 186
O'Keefe, Mark, 49, 50, 54, 92
O'Meara, Thomas, 118n55
The Ones Who Walk Away from Omelas, 11, 12, 202, 210
Optatam totius, 99
organizations, 80, 81, 182–86, 189, 190, 209–13
output power: defined, 24, 32n42, 196; and moral manuals, 27; and structure-agency problem, 55; and structures of virtue and vice, 202, 208; and virtue ethics, 27

Pantaleo, Daniel, 184, 192n43
Paris Climate Accords, 202
Parks, Rosa, 86, 207
Patagonia, 205
Paul VI (pope), 99, 131, 212, 217
penance, 26, 31n31, 36, 142
person: defined, 68, 69, 102–5; and dignity, 105, 106; and the human good, 129–33; in personalism, 101–6; and virtue, 107, 108, 126
personalism: defined, 68, 69, 101–5; and relationality, 128, 129; and virtue, 107
Petrusek, Matthew, 118n59
Pfeil, Margaret, 34
Pius XI (pope), 98, 99
Plowshares movement, 212
police unions, 184, 185
Pope, Stephen, 134
Popper, Karl, 82
popular movements, 218n4
Porpora, Douglas, 74, 77, 81, 84
Porter, Jean, 134, 158n45, 191n16
position-practice system, 76, 79, 176
Powell, Benjamin, 30n8
practice: defined, 146; and solidarity, 210, 211; and structures of virtue and vice, 172–80, 184–86, 198–201; and virtue formation, 110, 115, 144, 144–48
prAna, 205
prayer, 148
preferential option for the poor, 4, 38, 131, 182, 187
printing press, 86, 88
prudence: defined, 128, 177; and infused virtue, 134, 135, 144; and norms, 150, 151
Puebla Conference, 37–39
Putnam, Robert, 211, 212

Quadragesimo anno, 98

"racial threat," 192n46. *See also* "black dangerousness"
racism: as cultural, 83; defined, 192n23; as structural/institutional, 42, 51; as a vice, 174, 185
Ragazzi, Maurizio, 56n5

Rana Plaza Collapse: cause of, 12, 13, 15; and Christian ethics, 27, 55, 129, 164; and structural ethical analysis, 146, 202–8
Rana, Sohel, 12–13, 164, 165, 202–3
rational choice theory, 70
Ratzinger, Josef, 102, 103
Reconciliatio et paenetentia, 39–42
reflexivity, 90, 91, 177
relation: vs. interaction, 74, 75; and the moral good, 130, 131; and personhood, 68, 69, 102–5, 128; vs. relationship, 128–29; structures as, 74–76; and structures of virtue and vice, 168–70; and virtue, 134
relativism, moral, 46
responsibility, moral: in church teaching, 20, 29, 39, 40; and corporations, 12; vs. culpability and liability, 21–22; environmental, 109, 150; individual, 17, 49, 51, 70, 72, 103, 204, 205; shared, 51; and social structures, 36, 49, 72
Robert's Rules of Order, 183
Romero, Oscar, 56n30, 219n52
routine, 136–38
Rubio, Julie Hanlon: on distant others, 17, 21, 129; on moral responsibility, 215; on principle of cooperation, 16–20, 30n13, 31n15, 31n20
Rule of St. Benedict, 175, 176

Saban, Nick, 175
sacraments, 36, 142, 146–48, 173
Saint Anselm College, 96n114
Salzman, Todd, 106, 107
Schilbrack, Kevin, 73, 94n45
Searle, John, 73
Segundo, Juan Luis, 22, 23, 36, 37
Selling, Joseph, 58n75
sexism, 51, 174
Shin, Wonchul, 51, 52
sin: and charity, 144; original, 1, 57n41; personal, 20, 26, 27, 31n31, 67; social; social/structures of, 1, 34–45, 48–54
Singer, Peter, 160n131
situationist critique of virtue, 158n63
Slater, Thomas, 20, 26, 27, 31n31

slavery: as a "positive good," 163, 191n2; as a social structure, 85, 86, 163, 164; as a vicious structure, 164, 168
Slote, Michael, 127, 135
sloth, 206, 218n22
social construction of reality, 49, 58n84
social justice: and Catholic ethics, 34; and common good, 169, 193n52; defined, 189
social sin: Himes on, 21, 49; O'Keefe on, 49; Pope John Paul II on, 39, 40; and principle of cooperation, 17–19; and Vatican II, 34
social structure: Christian ethics and, 1–6, 11–22, 27–30, 33–56; critical realist definition of, 74–81; holistic definition of, 71–73; individualist definition of 69–71; relation to culture, 81–83; reproduction and transformation of, 84–87
solidarity: as antidote to structural sin, 38, 41; César Chávez as exemplar of, 154; defined, 41, 206; Pope Francis on, 112, 114–16, 119n125; and social/structural sin, 35, 219n46; structures of virtue and vice, 206, 208–13
Sollicitudo rei socialis: critique of, 41; on solidarity, 41, 210; on structures of sin, 40, 48, and theology, 99; and virtue, 107, 210
South Africa, international boycott of, 207
Spohn, William, 107, 123, 127
stored decisions, 91, 92, 140
structural character, 169, 182–86, 188, 189
structural ethical analysis, 29, 196, 202, 208
structural reproduction, 72, 83, 84–87
structuration theory, 71–73, 91
structure-agency problem: church teaching and, 48; critical realism and, 4, 52, 63; defined, 2, 54; and theological ethics, 5, 29, 33, 49, 53–56, 92
structures of grace, 212
structures of sin: 1, 2, 19, 34–56, 210, 219n46
structures of virtue and vice: and Christian ethics, 188–91, 195–96; defined, 168–70; influence on personal moral character, 170–82; influence on social outcomes, 181–86; and social justice, 189; and virtue ethics, 213–17

Summa theologiae: on charity, 144, 160n103, 193n55, 216, 217; on faith and reason, 66, 93n9; on the moral act, 177, 191n5; and sixteenth century, 25; on theology, 98
Swanton, Christine, 157n2
sweatshop labor, 12–16, 19–23, 164, 202–8

Target, 13
Taylor, Charles, 29, 65
temperance, 110, 113, 118n81, 128, 141, 142, 176
Ten Commandments, 149, 150
tenure, academic: relation to adjunct faculty, 19; as a social structure, 89, 90, 92, 171, 198, 199
Teresa of Calcutta, 214
Tessman, Lisa, 214
theocentrism, 6, 98–101, 188
theological virtues, 107, 109, 134
Thomas, Clarence, 86
Tillman, Fritz, 99
Toulmin, Stephen, 24–26, 32n44
tradition, 144, 145
Traina, Christina, 52
trait consequentialism, 134–36, 158n48

United Farm Workers, 154
United Students Against Sweatshops, 207
Universal Declaration of Human Rights, 22
utilitarianism, 46, 126, 157n2

Veritatis splendor, 107, 153, 165, 191n5
Vermeersch, Arthur, 31n31
Vidal, Marciano, 56n5
violence: against Black persons by police, 183–86; institutionalized, 37, 52, 56n30

virtue: as action guiding, 154–56; acquired, 142, 143, 158n40, 163; defined, 133–36; and exemplars, 151–54; habit and, 136–39; infused, 134, 142–44, 158n40, 163; "-in-reality," 213–17; and norms, 148–51; and practices, 146–48
virtue ethics: critique of, 126, 127, 154; defined, 126; and exemplarism, 153, 154; method of, 155, 156, 157n2; and Pope Benedict XVI, 107, 108; and Pope Francis, 108–15; strengths of, 124–26
virtue theory: consequentialist vs. nonconsequentialist, 134–36; defined, 126; personalist, 127–34; and skill analogy, 136
Vogt, Christopher, 127, 144
v-rules, 154–55, 160n130

Waddell, Paul, 127, 144
Ward, Kate, 108
war on Drugs, 166
Weaver, Darlene Fozard, 106
Weller, Mark, 166, 167, 173
Western Hemisphere Institute for Security Cooperation (WHISC), 215, 219n52
white supremacy, 183
Wilkins, Jeremy, 136
Wojytwa, Karol, 102
Wolterstorff, Nicolas, 65
works of mercy: as antidote to indifference to suffering, 113, 114; and charity, 119n113, 190; as practices, 147, 148

Young Christian Workers, 212
Young, Iris Marion, 21, 50, 51, 54

Zagzebski, Linda, 123, 127, 152, 153, 156

ABOUT THE AUTHOR

Daniel J. Daly is an associate professor of moral theology at Boston College's School of Theology and Ministry. He has served as a clinical medical ethicist at Catholic and secular hospitals, and is a member of the Theologian/Ethicist Committee for the Catholic Health Association. He has published articles and book chapters on a variety of topics in theological ethics, including virtue ethics, the ethics of social structures, and medical ethics. This is his first book.

www.ingramcontent.com/pod-product-compliance
Lightning Source LLC
Chambersburg PA
CBHW021351300426
44114CB00012B/1184